A

N
S

The 1984
Olympic Scientific
Congress
Proceedings
Volume 8

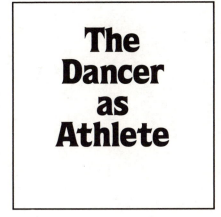

The
Dancer
as
Athlete

Series Editors:

Jan Broekhoff, PhD
Michael J. Ellis, PhD
Dan G. Tripps, PhD

University of Oregon
Eugene, Oregon

The 1984
Olympic Scientific
Congress
Proceedings
Volume 8

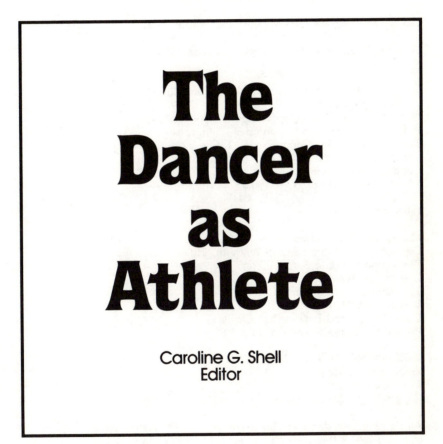

The Dancer as Athlete

Caroline G. Shell
Editor

Human Kinetics Publishers, Inc.
Champaign, Illinois

Library of Congress Cataloging-in-Publication Data

Olympic Scientific Congress (1984 : Eugene, Or.)
    The dancer as athlete.

    (1984 Olympic Scientific Congress proceedings ; v. 8)
    Bibliography: p.
    1. Dancing—Physiological aspects—Congresses.
2. Dancing—Accidents and injuries—Congresses.
3. Sports medicine—Congresses.   I. Shell, Caroline G.,
Congress (1984 : Eugene, Or.).   1984 Olympic Scientific
Congress proceedings ; v. 8.
GV565.O46   1984 vol. 8   796 s   85-18119
[RC122O.D35]   [612'.044]
ISBN 0-87322-016-1

Managing Editor: Susan Wilmoth, PhD
Developmental Editor: Susan Wilmoth, PhD
Production Director: Sara Chilton
Copyeditor: Jean Berry
Typesetter: Yvonne Winsor
Text Layout: Denise Mueller
Cover Design and Layout: Jack Davis
Printed By: Braun-Brumfield, Inc.

ISBN: 0-87322-006-4   (10 Volume Set)
ISBN: 0-87322-016-1

Copyright © 1986 by Human Kinetics Publishers, Inc.

Printed in the United States of America

10 9 8 7 6 5 4 3 2 1

Human Kinetics Publishers, Inc.
Box 5076, Champaign, IL 61820

Contents

Series Acknowledgments

The Congress organizers realize that an event as large and complex as the 1984 Olympic Scientific Congress could not have come to fruition without the help of literally hundreds of organizations and individuals. Under the patronage of UNESCO, the Congress united in sponsorship and cooperation no fewer than 64 national and international associations and organizations. Some 50 representatives of associations helped with the organization of the scientific and associative programs by coordinating individual sessions. The cities of Eugene and Springfield yielded more than 400 volunteers who donated their time to make certain that the multitude of Congress functions would progress without major mishaps. To all these organizations and individuals, the organizers express their gratitude.

A special word of thanks must also be directed to the major sponsors of the Congress: the International Council of Sport Science and Physical Education (ICSSPE), the United States Olympic Committee (USOC), the International Council on Health, Physical Education and Recreation (ICHPER), and the American Alliance for Health, Physical Education, Recreation and Dance (AAPHERD). Last but not least, the organizers wish to acknowledge the invaluable assistance of the International Olympic Committee (IOC) and its president, Honorable Juan Antonio Samaranch. President Samaranch made Congress history by his official opening address in Eugene on July 19, 1984. The IOC durther helped the Congress with a generous donation toward the publication of the Congress papers. Without this donation it would have been impossible to make the proceedings available in this form.

Finally, the series editors wish to express their thanks to the volume editors who selected and edited the papers from each program of the Congress. Special thanks go to Caroline G. Shell of The University of Oregon for her work on this volume.

Jan Broekhoff,
Michael J. Ellis, and
Dan G. Tripps

Series Editors

Series Preface

The Dancer as Athlete contains selected proceedings from this interdisciplinary program of the 1984 Olympic Scientific Congress, which was held at the University of Oregon in Eugene, Oregon, preceding the Olympic Games in Los Angeles. The Congress was organized by the College of Human Development and the cities of Eugene and Springfield. This was the first time in the history of the Congress that the event was organized by a group of private individuals, unaided by a federal government. The fact that the Congress was attended by more than 2,200 participants from more than 100 different nations is but one indication of its success.

The Congress program focused on the theme of Sport, Health, and Well-Being and was organized in three parts. The mornings of the eight-day event were devoted to disciplinary sessions, which brought together specialists in various subdisciplines of sport science such as sport medicine, biomechanics, sport psychology, sport sociology, and sport philosophy. For the first time in the Congress' history, these disciplinary sessions were sponsored by the national and international organizations representing the various subdisciplines. In the afternoons, the emphasis shifted toward interdisciplinary themes in which scholars and researchers from the subdisciplines attempted to contribute to crossdisciplinary understanding. In addition, three evenings were devoted to keynote addresses and presentations, broadly related to the theme of Sport, Health, and Well-Being.

In addition to the scientific programs, the Congress also featured a number of associative programs with topics determined by their sponsoring organizations. Well over 1,200 papers were presented in the various sessions of the Congress at large. It stands to reason, therefore, that publishing the proceedings of the event presented a major problem to the organizers. It was decided to limit proceedings initially to interdisciplinary sessions which drew substantial interest from Congress participants and attracted a critical number of high-quality presentations. Human Kinetics Publishers, Inc. of Champaign, Illinois, was selected to produce these preceedings. After considerable deliberation, the following interdisciplinary themes were selected for publication: Competitive Sport for Children and Youths; Human Genetics and Sport; Sport and Aging; Sport and Disabled Individuals; Sport and Elite Performers; Sport, Health, and Nutrition; and Sport and Politics. The 10-volume set published by Human Kinetics Publishers is rounded out by the disciplinary proceedings of Kinanthropometry, Sport Pedagogy, and the associative program on the Scientific Aspects of Dance.

Jan Broekhoff,
Michael J. Ellis, and
Dan G. Tripps

Series Editors

Preface

This collection of articles represents the proceedings of an international dance symposium held in association with the Olympic Scientific Congress in Eugene, Oregon, July 19-26, 1984. The 7-day event attracted dancers, dance teachers and choreographers, physicians, therapists, scientists, and physical educators, all of whom sought to question and learn, to partake and reciprocate.

The Olympic Scientific Congress is primarily concerned with sports medicine. Because dance medicine and related dance research are now sufficiently matured to benefit from an increased interchange of ideas with sports medicine practitioners and researchers, the symposium was planned to initiate such an interface, hence its theme, "The Dancer as Athlete—Similarities and Differences." The two objectives were (a) to compare medical and health problems seen in dance medicine with those seen in athletic medicine, and (b) to assess the present state of the art of dance medicine and science and to predict the future state of the art through research in the field. The event marked the first time, to our knowledge, that the discipline of dance was fully discussed and presented in the same arena as all other disciplines that address efficient motor performance.

Research in orthopaedics and medicine for dance-related problems has stimulated great interest in dance science during the past decade and is on the verge of tremendous acceleration. Sports medicine practitioners are taking greater interest in dancers' injuries and environment. Nutritionists and exercise physiologists are researching the level of wellness and fitness of the dancing athlete. Biomechanists are eager to help unravel the mysteries underlying great technical achievements of outstanding performers in order to facilitate sound training practices. Scientific evidence is beginning to add validity to the theories behind long-established modalities in movement repatterning, or body therapies. As in sports medicine, all of this research has ultimately contributed to injury prevention. Dancers, teachers, and choreographers are developing intelligent pedagogical practices for longer careers. A new, intelligent dance population is interested in aspects of dance beyond the traditional ones of performance and choreography. The presentations during the dance symposium suggested specific areas in which to work.

Almost all of the presentations addressed comparisons between dancers and athletes. This was the first objective of the symposium. The comparisons revealed differences in (a) facilities and equipment or clothing suitable for safe and lifelong participation, (b) prevention as well as immediate care of injuries, (c) causes of ankle, knee, and back pain, (d) stretching techniques, (e) endurance capacity and leg strength, and (f) nutritional habits. In general, the research indicates that dancers as a group are slower than athletes to integrate the latest findings into their daily, professional lives; athletes appear eager to apply the latest information to their training regimen to enhance their performance.

The scope of subject matter covered during the symposium suggests that dance medicine and science are healthy and growing. Barely 15 years ago the literature contained only sparse references to medical or biomechanical research on dancers. Today the literature is pregnant with research in virtually every scientific aspect of movement science that applies to dance. Dance may well be the new frontier for significant study.

This collection includes all of the symposium presentations that were available at the time of printing and that had not been previously published. Although a few editorial changes have been made, the articles are generally reproduced here in their original form.

Caroline G. Shell
Editor

The 1984
Olympic Scientific
Congress
Proceedings
Volume 8

The Dancer as Athlete

PART I

*Musculoskeletal Considerations:
The Classical Dancer
Versus the Athlete*

Hardly a dance teacher today, young or old, does not know the names of Celia Sparger and Raoul Gelabert. Their works were the earliest and most accessible publications in dance science and have enjoyed both international acclaim and loyal readership. For two decades Sparger's name alone was synonymous with the study of ballet and anatomy. Her *Anatomy and Ballet* (1949) was followed a decade later by Gelabert's articles and eventually his book *Anatomy for the Dancer* (1964).

A dividend of their work has been the inquiry into dancers' injuries by physicians, movement scientists, and well-informed artist-teachers. A glance through bibliographic resources reveals a surge of interest in the 1970s. Much of the literature concerns the work of physicians who have treated dancers (e.g., Arnheim, 1975; Dunn, 1974; Featherstone, 1970; Hamilton, 1978-1979; Vincent, 1978, 1979). A wealth of articles also appear in periodicals such as *The Physician and Sports Medicine*, *Foot and Ankle*, *Medical World News*, *Clinical Orthopaedics*, and *American Journal of Physical Medicine*. However, research into dancers' injuries is not limited to the medical community. Dancers and dance teachers today are contributing substantially to the growing body of knowledge (Alter, 1983; Hessel, 1978; Lawson, 1973; Paskevska, 1981). Furthermore, movement scientists who are interested in the peculiarities of dance, dancers, and dance-related injuries have found a venue for communicating with dancers through the recently initiated newsletters, *Kinesiology for Dance* (1977-) and *Dance Medicine/Health Newsletter* (1983-).

Most of the research in dance science has been in the area of musculoskeletal problems of dancers. In his survey of the research, Washington summarizes the developmental history of dance medicine, emphasizing the kinship with sports medicine. Dancers, like athletes, seem to suffer from musculoskeletal-related injuries more often than from physiologic or psychological ones.

Musculoskeletal injuries can be caused by dancers' forcing their bodies to comply with an ideal standard rather than working within their own structural limits or they can be caused by any number of overuse practices that result in musculoskeletal breakdown in spite of dancers' consciousness of structural limits. The balance of the articles in Part I address different body parts and different types of injuries.

Hardaker, Erickson, and Myers, in their discussion of the pathogenesis of dance injury, lay a foundation for future clinical and basic science investigations into injury management and prevention. They stress the dangers of repeated impact loading of the lower extremities on a hard unyielding surface. Whereas athletes wear protective footwear for shock absorption, dancers wear flimsy slippers or no slippers at all, and this contributes to potential stress on the body's shock absorber and lever systems. When either of these systems fails, the body is susceptible to injury. Dancers' most vulnerable areas are the back and the lower extremities.

Hardaker further describes, in his second article, the specific types of injuries to the foot and ankle that can be experienced by both dancers and athletes. Specifically, these injuries manifest themselves as impingement syndromes in and around the ankle, tendinitis, and stress fractures. Unlike the athlete, the dancer cannot easily alter choreography, footwear, or the performing surface in order to accommodate an injury. Usually dancers must refrain from dancing in order to allow healing to occur; however, getting them to do so is difficult. One solution may be alternate exercise activities similar to modified training programs prescribed by the athletic trainer or physical therapist for recuperating athletes.

Kravitz offers practical solutions for the recuperating dancer that show concern for the dancer's longevity as a performer as well as simplicity of use. These range from tried-and-true "towel set" isotonic exercises for the feet and ankles to taping techniques similar to those used by athletic trainers. His article represents yet another attempt by a knowledgeable medical practitioner, since Arnheim's breakthrough publication in 1975, to render therapeutic techniques accessible to the dancer—almost a decade of effort, and still the medical profession has not given up on us!

Available data on dancers' injuries vary regarding the frequency of foot and ankle injuries and knee injuries. The literature indicates that knee complaints are more frequent in dancers than are foot and ankle complaints. Perhaps dancers hesitate to seek medical care for injuries to the feet simply because they consider these as manageable nuisances. On the other hand, the knee is surrounded by a certain mystique because of the media attention given to the knee surgeries of celebrated athletic and dance personalities in recent years. Thus, because of simple fear or common sense, dancers will generally not hesitate to report a knee complaint. The ultimate benefit has been an increased understanding of dancers' knee complaints and disseminating of resultant information in the medical literature.

Clippinger-Robertson, perhaps the first kinesiologist to generate adequate quantitative data on patellofemoral complaints in dancers, concludes that the incidence of knee pain in dancers is similar to or greater than it is in the serious distance runner. Furthermore, she substantiates a high incidence of chondromalacia patella in dancers and relates this specific knee problem to the plié in dance training. Teitz, in her article, shares specific treatments of dancers' knee injuries based on orthopaedic practices at her institution. As with all injuries, appropriate immediate care may prevent the need for surgical treatment.

What has become apparent in the last decade is the similarity of injuries between athletes and dancers. Impact loading and overuse syndromes eventually cause or reveal a musculoskeletal weakness, usually in the lower extremities of both dancers and athletes. However, dancers are also susceptible to lower back injuries, which are not quite so common in athletes, who generally are not required to lift each other or to arch the back frequently. While these injuries are often caused by repeated impact loading on the lower extremities, many pains and injuries in the dancer are ultimately traceable to dysfunction or derangement of the lower back or pelvis. In his article, Bachrach contends that the disposition of the iliopsoas—whether dysfunctional or tight from lack of stretching—is key to the function of the lower back and pelvis. This has long been the thesis of movement scientists and dance pedagogues and was substantiated in the early research writings of Todd and Sweigard.

Micheli provides information on specific types of back injuries among dancers. While he concurs that many back disorders in young dancers are associated with the hyperlordotic posturing described by Bachrach, he also describes symptoms of injuries caused by the dance technique itself. His discussion on spondylolysis in dancers ("the incidence. . .among dancers perhaps equals that of gymnasts") is particularly enlightening for teachers.

As these articles on musculoskeletal considerations indicate, the dancer and dance teacher today have options that were not readily available or acceptable to the dance community 20 years ago. There is no longer any excuse for sacrificing sound anatomical practices to aesthetic quality and athletic strength. To take full advantage of the options will require, however, greater coordination and cooperation between dancer, teacher, therapist, and physician than has previously existed.

References

Alter, J. (1983). *Surviving exercise*. Boston: Houghton Mifflin.

Arnheim, D.D. (1975). *Dance injuries: Their prevention and care*. St. Louis: Mosby.

Dunn, B. (1974). *Therapy for dancers*. London: Heinemann Health Books.

Featherstone, D.F. (1970). *Dancing without danger*. Cranbury, NJ: A.S. Barnes.

Hamilton, W.G. (1978-1979). Ballet and your body: An orthopedist's view. Parts I through XII. *Dance Magazine*.

Hessel, S. (1978). *The articulate body*. New York: Saint Martin's Press.

Lawson, J. (1973). *The teaching of classical ballet: Common faults in young dancers and their training*. London: Adam and Chas. Black.

Lawson, J. (1975). *Teaching young dancers muscular coordination in classical ballet*. New York: Theatre Arts Books.

Paskevska, A. (1981). *Both sides of the mirror: The science and art of ballet*. Brooklyn: Dance Horizons.

Sweigard, L.E. (1949). Psychomotor function as correlated with body mechanics and posture. *Trans. New York Academy of Science, 2,* 243-248.

Sweigard, L.E. (1961). The dancer's posture. *Impulse,* pp. 38-43.

Sweigard, L.E. (1965). Better dancing through better body balance. *Journal of Health, Physical Education and Recreation, 36,* 22-23, 56.

Sweigard, L.E. (1974). *Human movement potential: Its ideokinetic facilitation.* New York: Dodd, Mead.

Todd, M.E. (1920). Principles of posture. *Boston Medical and Surgical Journal,* **182,** 645.

Todd, M.E. (1929). *The balancing of forces in the human being: Its application to postural patterns.* New York: Published privately.

Todd, M.E. (1968). *The thinking body.* Brooklyn: Dance Horizons.

Vincent, L.M. (1978). *The dancer's book of health.* Kansas City: Sheed Andrews and McMeel.

Vincent, L.M. (1979). *Competing with the sylph.* Kansas City: Sheed Andrews and McMeel.

1

The Emergence of Sports Medicine and Dance Medicine as an Important Field of Study

Ernest L. Washington
INTERNATIONAL CENTER FOR DANCE ORTHOPEDICS AND DANCE THERAPY
LOS ANGELES, CALIFORNIA, USA

The medical and health aspects of any activity, including dance medicine and sports medicine, are as old as the activity itself. The participants in the first Olympic Games in ancient Greece undoubtedly recognized the importance of preparing themselves for games by eating a proper diet to ensure sufficient energy and strength to perform the activity at the time of competition. They also practiced the activity many times before actual competition to sharpen skills and strengthen the proper musculature. Furthermore, they performed appropriate warm-up activities immediately preceding the activity to make sure that the muscles were sufficiently warmed up and were receiving an adequate blood supply to participate in the activity effectively. All of these activities represent preventive measures because, without them, the athlete would certainly have encountered particular injuries and illnesses. These activities represent the practice of preventive sports medicine.

Preventive dance medicine may be said to be older than diagnostic or therapeutic dance medicine. For years before the medical community recognized dance medicine as a special area, dancers were aware of the importance of warm-up prior to dance activity and the importance of proper resilience in a floor surface if injuries were to be prevented. At the time of the first Olympiad in ancient Greece, celebrations and entertainments consisted of singing and dancing. Therefore, the practice of dance medicine principles is as old as the practice of athletic or sports medicine.

The information of specific societies for sports medicine and the presentation of special meetings on dance medicine were necessarily preceeded many years by articles and reports in the literature on these subjects. The American College of Sports Medicine, for instance, was incorporated in 1955, but the first articles on athletic medicine were published long before that. Articles on the subject of dance medicine and other health problems in dancers had also appeared in literature many years before the first national dance medicine symposium on the orthopaedic and medical aspects of dance, which was presented in October 1979 and sponsored by the International Center for Dance Orthopaedics and Dance Therapy.

Early workers in both fields encountered initial skepticism regarding the need for considering these two areas as distinct entities within orthopaedic surgery. (Sports medicine is a subdivision of orthopaedic surgery, and many authorities classify dance medicine as a subdivision of sports medicine.) Critics of the early sports medicine workers claimed that musculoskeletal problems and the physiologic parameters of the athlete were no different from those of nonathlete and that injuries occurring to athletes could be treated the same as injuries occurring to nonathletes. Subsequent work and research in the area of sports medicine have shown this to be false.

As one of the early workers and proponents of dance medicine in the early 1970s, I encountered considerable skepticism and sarcasm for even daring to suggest that orthopaedic and medical problems in classical dancers might be different from those encountered in athletics in general or in the general population. Authorities now recognize that the peculiar and particular use of the body in dance does give rise to the following problems that are specific to dance or are seen, to a lesser extent, in other forms of athletics:

1. Specific impingement syndromes about the ankles in classical dancers secondary to the use of the foot and ankle in extreme equinus
2. Definite and specific problems that occur as a result of "turnout" at the hip joint
3. Specific and peculiar stresses applied to the lower extremity as a result of turnout
4. The use of sustained slow flexion of the knees in the turned-out position known as *grand plié* and *demi-plié*
5. The identification of a high incidence of anorexia nervosa, bulimia, and menstrual irregularities in classical dancers indicating that there may be psychological as well as physiological differences between the dancer and the individual engaging in general athletics

The current acceptance of dance medicine and sports medicine as definite and specific areas that demand separate treatment is growing. This is evidenced by the founding in 1972 of the *American Journal of Sports Medicine*, the official publication of the American Orthopaedic Society for Sports Medicine and by the *Physician and Sports Medicine*, also founded in the mid-1970s. The presentation of multiple symposia since 1979 on the medical aspects of dance, the publication of Thomasen's text on diseases and injuries of ballet dancers, the publication of a similar book by Bolshoi Ballet physician Ivan Badnin (1974), the founding of the *Dance Medicine-Health Newsletter* by this author in 1983, and the inclusion of dance medicine, in addition to sports medicine in the activities of the 1984 Olympic Scientific Congress, are all evidence that dance medicine is now accepted as a specific and definite international entity.

References

Badnin, I. (1974). *Orthopaedic problems in classical ballet dancers* (Text). Moscow, Russia: CTO.

Brodelius, A. (1961). Osteoarthritis of the talar joints in footballers and ballet dancers. *Acta Orthopaedica Scandinavica,* **30,** 308.

Burrows, H.J. (1956). Fatigue infarction (incomplete fracture) of middle of tibia in ballet dancers. *Journal of Bone and Joint Surgery,* **38B,** 83.

Gordon, B., et al. (1924). Observations of a group of marathon runners with special reference to the circulation. *Archives of Internal Medicine,* **33,** 425.

Hamilton, W. (1976). *Dancers' tendinitis of the flexor hallucis longus.* Paper presented at the meeting of the American Orthopaedic Society for Sports Medicine.

House, A.J.G. (1972). Orthopaedists aid ballet. *Clinical Orthopaedics,* **89,** 52-53.

Mashkara, K.T. (1960). Dynamics and the symptoms of working hypertrophy of the osseous system in certain physical working ballet dancers. *Archives of Anatomy,* **38,** 93.

Nikolik, V. (1968). The functional changes of tarsal bones of ballet dancers. *Rad. Med. Fak. Zagreb,* **50**(16), 131.

Pressman, L.P. (1935). Neurovascular factor by limitation of muscular reaction in ballet dancers. *Kinesiology of Medicine,* **13,** 43.

Sammarco, G.J., & Miller, E.H. (1979). Partial rupture of the flexor hallucis longus in classical ballet dancers. *Journal of Bone and Joint Surgery,* **61A,** 149-150.

Volkob, V. (1970). Occupational accidents in ballet performers and their prevention. *Orthop Travmatol Protezm,* **31,** 57.

Washington, E.L. (1978). Musculoskeletal injuries in theatrical dancers. *American Journal of Sports Medicine,* **6**(2), 75-98.

Washington, E.L. (1983-). *Dance Medicine-Health Newsletter.* Published quarterly at 9201 Sunset Boulevard, Los Angeles.

Weaver, J. (1923). *Anatomical and Mechanical Lectures on Dance* (John Weaver was an English dance teacher who retained French names for dance movement.)

Wilce, J.W. (1942). The range of the normal heart in athletes. *American Journal of Physiology,* **132,** 757.

2

The Pathogenesis of Dance Injury

William T. Hardaker, Jr. and Lars Erickson
DUKE UNIVERSITY MEDICAL CENTER
DURHAM, NORTH CAROLINA, USA

Martha Myers
DEAN OF THE AMERICAN DANCE FESTIVAL
DURHAM, NORTH CAROLINA, USA

The discussion on the pathogenesis of dance injury is based on clinical observations while examining and treating students and professional participants in the American Dance Festival.* The material is intended to provide an organizational framework on which to develop future clinical and basic science investigations.

Pathomechanics is the study of the origin of injury. It is the discipline in which one attempts to explain how and why a particular injury occurs. A knowledge of pathomechanics is important not only for the management of injuries but also for injury prevention. An understanding of pathomechanics is fundamental to the physician who treats musculoskeletal injury. It provides a basis for precise diagnosis, logical treatment, and accurate prognosis. In essence, it allows the physician to treat a given injury most effectively and most efficiently.

Pathomechanics is also important in injury prevention, not only to prevent recurrence of an injury in a given patient but also to decrease the incidence of such injuries in other dancers. In this regard, pathomechanics is vitally important to all concerned with the dancer's health—the artistic director, the dance teacher, the dance therapist, and the physician.

---

*The American Dance Festival is an international festival of dance held each summer on the campus of Duke University, Durham, N.C. The festival consists of intense workshops for 200 to 250 dance students. Although modern dance is emphasized, all disciplines, including ballet, ethnic, and mixed forms, are included in the curriculum.

Although acute injuries can and do occur in theatrical dancers (Hamilton, 1982), the majority of injuries are chronic in nature. They arise from a single mechanism of injury, that is, the repetitive impact loading of the lower extremities on a hard unyielding surface. Unlike the long-distance runner, who wears a specially designed shoe to absorb shock, the ballet dancer wears only a thin slipper or toe shoe. The modern dancer wears no shoes at all. Therefore, in dance the majority of the forces of repetitive impact loading must be borne by the lower extremities and low back. It is the failure to effectively dissipate these forces which may lead to injury. From an anatomic standpoint, the skeletal muscles are the primary structures responsible for energy dissipation or shock absorption. In this regard, they function as shock absorbers in the lower extremities.

The Shock-Absorber System

The skeletal muscles are the primary shock absorbers of the body. It is these lower extremity muscle groups that must effectively dissipate the forces of repetitive impact loading. If a 150-pound person jumps to the floor from a chair 3 feet in height, with the ankles, hips and knees rigid (allowing no movement), the individual will strike the floor with 450 foot-pounds of force (see Figure 1). Laboratory studies indicate that the femur may fail with fracture

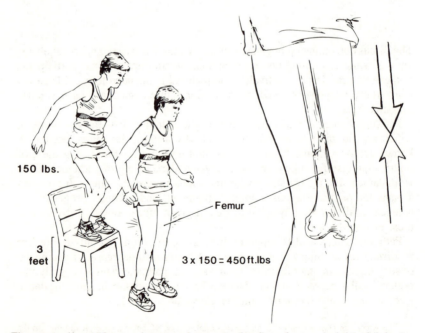

150 lbs.

3
feet

Femur

3 x 150 = 450 ft.lbs

Figure 1. If a 150-pound person jumps to the floor from a height of 3 feet, the force of impact will be 450 foot-pounds of force (3 × 150). Such force, if not properly dissipated, can lead to fracture.

at forces greater than 400 foot-pounds. Such forces occur daily but fractures do not occur because the force is effectively dissipated through the eccentric contraction of muscles controlling the hips, knees, and ankles (see Figure 2). Specifically, it is the eccentric contraction of the quadriceps muscles about the knee and the gastroc-soleus complex about the ankle that prevent collapse of these two joints and thus allow the jumper to effectively absorb the shock and break the fall.

Eccentric contraction is defined as the controlled lengthening of the muscle while under tension and following application of an external force. In many circumstances, skeletal muscles perform primarily by contracting and therefore shortening (see Figure 3). In such concentric contractions, an increase in muscle tension is accompanied by shortening. In isometric contraction, tension is produced with neither shortening nor lengthening. However, in eccentric contraction, tension is still achieved, but with concomitant lengthening.

Eccentric contractions are important not only in jumping from a chair but also in dissipating the repetitive impact forces during a long day of dance class, rehearsal, or performance. Indeed, eccentric contractions are essential to the dynamic stabilization of the body segments by controlling displacement and velocity (see Figure 4). Perhaps this is not more critical than in such activities as gymnastics, diving, and dance where the aesthetic precision of the maneuver is as important as its execution (Teitz, 1983).

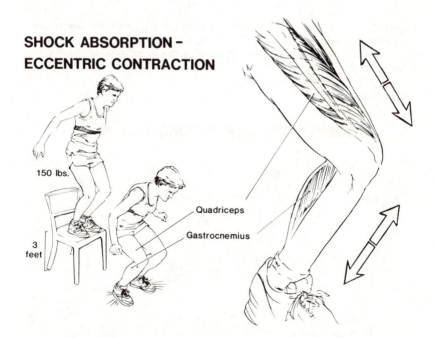

SHOCK ABSORPTION – ECCENTRIC CONTRACTION

150 lbs.

3 feet

Quadriceps

Gastrocnemius

Figure 2. Eccentric contraction of the quadriceps and gastro-soleus muscle groups effectively dissipates the force of impact following a jump from a height.

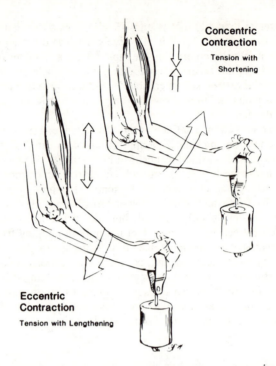

Figure 3. Concentric contraction is characterized by an increase in tension with shortening of the muscle. Eccentric contraction of a muscle group involves the controlled lengthening of the muscle while maintaining tension.

ECCENTRIC CONTRACTIONS IN DANCE

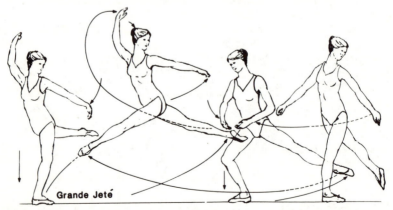

Figure 4. Eccentric contractions are important in dance for dissipating the forces of repetitive impact of the lower extremities on the dance floor.

Skeletal muscles dissipate the forces of repetitive impact through a system of levers—the bones and joints. For the skeletal muscles to effectively function as shock absorbers, there must be a lever system that is performing efficiently and one that is mechanically sound. For the lever system to be effective, therefore, it must be free from anatomic variation that might prevent the muscles from performing effectively.

Failure to effectively absorb or dissipate these forces of repetitive impact leads to stress on (a) the shock-absorber system (skeletal muscles), (b) the lever system (the bones and joints), or (c) a combination of both. When either system is under stress, it is particularly vulnerable to injury. In summary, failure to effectively absorb the forces of repetitive impact loading can be due to factors or problems relating to the shock-absorber system, the lever system, the environment, or any combination of these elements.

Shock-Absorber Failure

Shock-absorber failure can be secondary to weakness, fatigue, or lack of sufficient flexibility. A major cause of shock-absorber failure is inadequate muscle strength in the lower extremities. Some injuries occur more frequently in the beginning dancer, whose particular muscle groups may lack the proper strength to support the strenuous demands of dance. On occasion, weakness in a specific muscle group may lead to injury.

The quadriceps mechanism, which is responsible for extension of the knee joint, consists of three major muscle groups: the rectus femoris, the vastus lateralis, and the vastus medialis. In the normal situation, these muscle forces exert a balanced force and the patella tracks centrally in the intercondylar groove of the femur. However, in some circumstances, particularly in the young developing female athlete or dancer, the vastus medialis may be weak and not effectively counterbalance the force of the vastus lateralis (see Figure 5). In this situation, the patella may mildly sublux and displace laterally within the intercondylar groove (see Figure 6). With time, this leads to irritation of the articular cartilage as well as the peri-articular synovial structures. Eventually the dancer will report retropatellar pain made worse with pliés and jumps. With chronic repeated subluxation, damage to the articular cartilage can occur. The diagnosis is chondromalacia patella, or softening of the undersurface of the articular cartilage of the patella. The clinical problem is patella subluxation, but the mechanism of the injury is shock-absorber failure or, specifically, weakness in the vastus medialis obliquus.

High-performance athletes and professional dancers rarely lack proper muscle conditioning, yet these individuals may also become injured. Injury can occur to elite athletes or dancers if they continue to train past the point of fatigue (Howse, 1972). Injuries can occur within the muscle-tendon unit when fatigued, not unlike those seen in the poorly conditioned athlete or dancer. Fatigued muscles no longer have the strength, power, or endurance to effectively dissipate the forces of repetitive impact loading and to function properly as shock absorbers.

A common injury often relating to fatigue is Achilles tendinitis. The dancer complains of pain in the posterior calf, usually several inches above the ankle. Further history may reveal a recent extended class or rehearsal schedule. The

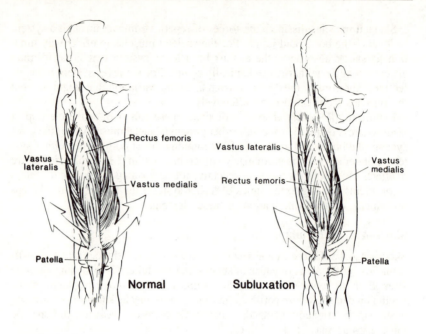

Figure 5. During knee extension the three muscle groups of the quadriceps mechanism exert a balanced force, and the patella tracks centrally in the intercondylar groove. With patellar subluxation, the vastus medialis may be weak and may not effectively balance the forces of the vastus lateralis.

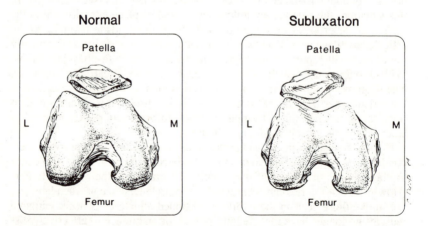

Figure 6. In the normal situation, the muscle forces are balanced and the patella tracks centrally within the intercondylar groove. With subluxation, the patella tracks laterally. With time, this may lead to injury of the articular cartilage on the undersurface of the patella.

symptoms are made worse with jumps and pliés. There is a significant difference in "being up" or "almost all the way up" in relevé, not only in terms of aesthetic line but also in terms of the energy requirements of the gastroc-soleus complex. With fatigue, the dancer may have difficulty maintaining the full plantar flexion required of relevé and the situation compounds itself. The examination is consistent with the inflammation of the Achilles tendon and the surrounding peritendinous structures. The diagnosis is Achilles tendinitis or, more correctly, peritendinitis (Thomasen, 1982), but the underlying problem is shock-absorber failure secondary to fatigue.

Lack of Flexibility

Another cause of shock-absorber failure is lack of sufficient flexibility in the shock-absorber system. Skeletal muscle-tendon units that are contracted, shortened, and stiff can no longer effectively perform eccentric contractions. The repeated use of inflexible muscles often produces muscle soreness contributing to further tightness and inflexibility. Furthermore, a tight muscle group may create an imbalance of forces across a given joint contributing to stress on other structures about that joint.

A flexibility program is the dancer's personal preparation for class or rehearsal. It should consist of both a warm-up and a stretching program. The warm-up can be jogging, brisk walking, or stationary cycling. The goals of warm-up are to increase respiration, heart rate, and especially blood flow to the muscle-tendon units that will perform their necessary role of eccentric contraction during class and rehearsal. Usually a minimum of 10 minutes is required for proper warm-up.

The second component of the flexibility program is the actual stretching exercises and necessarily requires more time. The goals are to slowly lengthen the shock absorber units, more specifically the muscle components of the muscle-tendon unit. The techniques of proprioceptive neuromuscular facilitation (Knott & Voss, 1965) are preferred to static or ballistic forms of stretching. Stretching should be performed slowly and methodically and directed toward all muscle groups about each of the joints of the lower extremities. There should be no bouncing, forcing, or pain associated with the various maneuvers.

The Lever System

Lever-system failure relates to variations in lower extremity anatomy that decrease the mechanical efficiency of the shock-absorber system (see Figure 7). These anatomic variations can have either a direct or an indirect influence on the production of a given injury (see Figure 8). Directly, the skeletal anatomic variations may place abnormal stress on the shock-absorber system by requiring it to perform at an unusual angle, attitude, or position. Alternatively, the anatomic variation may redirect forces to other structures that are unaccustomed or ill-suited to handle stress. For example, ligamentous struc-

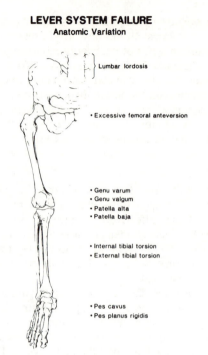

LEVER SYSTEM FAILURE
Anatomic Variation

Lumbar lordosis

• Excessive femoral anteversion

• Genu varum
• Genu valgum
• Patella alta
• Patella baja

• Internal tibial torsion
• External tibial torsion

• Pes cavus
• Pes planus rigidis

Figure 7. Lever-system failure refers to any anatomic variation in the lower extremities that can decrease the mechanical efficiency of the shock-absorber system.

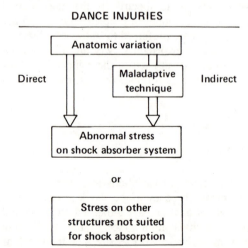

DANCE INJURIES

Anatomic variation

Direct   Maladaptive   Indirect
                technique

Abnormal stress
on shock absorber system

or

Stress on other
structures not suited
for shock absorption

Figure 8. Anatomic variations in the lower extremity can directly or indirectly relate to the production of the injury by placing abnormal stress on the shock-absorber system or diverting stress to other structures not well suited for shock absorption.

tures provide static stability to joints but perform poorly in the role of shock absorption.

Anatomic variations can also indirectly produce abnormal stresses on the shock-absorber system or on other structures. For example, an individual might compensate for a given anatomic variation by the development of a maladaptive, compensatory technique. Although it is the improper technique that produces the injury, the anatomic variation indirectly is responsible for the injury.

As discussed previously, malalignment or tracking problems of the patella can relate to shock-absorber failure, specifically weakness in a component of the vastus medialis muscle. Patellar malalignment and subluxation can also be secondary to lever-system failure. This is well demonstrated in an individual with significant genu valgum, or knock-knees. Normally the tibia has a slight valgus angle with respect to the femur. The pelvis places the hip joints considerably further apart than the knees. In order to stand with the knees and ankles together, some genu valgus must be present in all individuals.

The measurement of valgus alignment is called the Q-angle, the angle formed by a line drawn from the anterior superior iliac spine to the center of the patella and a second line drawn from the tibial tuberosity to the center of the patella (see Figure 9). In males, the normal Q-angle is approximately 8 to 10°. In

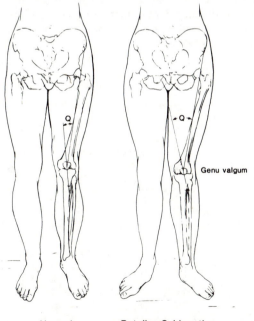

Normal   Patellar Subluxation

Figure 9. The Q-angle is an angle formed by a line drawn from the anterior-superior iliac spine to the center of the patella and a second line drawn from the tibial tuberosity to the center of the patella. Patellar subluxation is often associated with individuals with an excessively large Q-angle and genu valgum.

women, because of the wider pelvis, the Q-angle is approximately 15°. Individuals with knock-knees or excessive Q-angles, can develop a disproportionate mechanical advantage in the vastus lateralis as compared to the vastus medialis. This creates, once again, a basis for patellar malalignment and subsequent tracking problems. Individuals with excessive Q-angles are at greater risk for patellar subluxation and the symptoms of chondromalacia of the patella. The problem is further compounded by the increased lateral stresses placed on the knee by the continued emphasis on external rotation of the leg in dance (Gelabert, 1977; Hamilton, 1977; Miller, Schneider, Bronson, & McLain, 1975; Sammarco, 1982). Such emphasis is seen in the various dance positions and further increases the risk of patellar subluxation.

Anatomic variations can also have indirect influence on an injury, particularly if the dancer develops a maladaptive technique to compensate for such variations. One example of a maladaptive technique that can lead to abnormal stress on other structures is the problem of forced external rotation at the knee in order to achieve a greater turnout in an individual who lacks this rotation at the hip (Gelabert, 1977; Howse, 1972; Miller, Schneider, Bronson, & McLain, 1975; Thomasen, 1982).

The ability to externally rotate the hip is fundamental to all forms of theatrical dance, including ballet, modern, ethnic, and mixed forms. Turnout is especially emphasized in classical ballet, where each of the five basic positions have in common maximum external rotation of the leg (Figure 10). Indeed, all movements begin or end with one of these five basic positions.

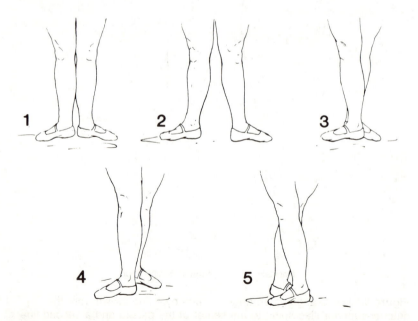

Figure 10. The position of extreme external rotation, although emphasized in the five basic positions in classical ballet, is present in all dance disciplines.

In ideal circumstances, the 90° of turnout is achieved by 60 to 70° external rotation at the hip, with the remaining 20 to 30° of rotation accounted for by the natural outward inclination of the knee and the foot and ankle complex (Figure 11). Five degrees of outward inclination is present at the knee, with the remaining 25° usually present at the ankle. To achieve the desired 90° of turnout, the dancer will theoretically require 60 to 70° of external rotation at the hip joint. In actual circumstance, however, few of even the most distinguished professional dancers have a full 70° of external rotation at the hip. Nevertheless, dancers with "natural turnout" can externally rotate to a considerable degree at the hip and usually have no difficulty achieving the desired 90° of overall turnout without abnormal stress placed elsewhere in the extremity.

Factors that determine the ability to externally rotate at the hip include

1. the angle of femoral anteversion,
2. the orientation of the acetabulum,
3. the elasticity of the anterior hip capsule, specifically the ilio-femoral ligament, and
4. the flexibility of the muscle-tendon units that cross the hip joint (Figure 12).

In the skeletally mature dancer, no alteration in the bony constraints of femoral anteversion and the orientation of the acetabulum can be anticipated (Figures 13 and 14). Flexing or extending the pelvis can vary the orientation of the acetabulum, but such maneuvers often destroy the aesthetic line. The anterior ligaments of the hip capsule are extremely strong and contain little elastic tissue.

THE DANCER'S HIP-TURNOUT

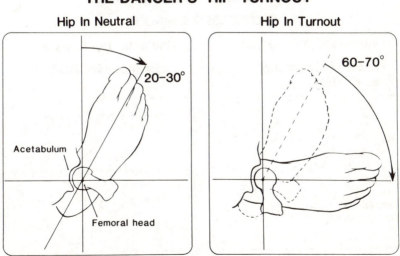

Figure 11. From a theoretical standpoint, the 90° of turnout are achieved by 60 to 70° of external rotation at the hip, with the remaining 20 to 30° of rotation accounted for by the natural outward inclination of the knee and the foot-ankle complex.

THE DANCER'S HIP-TURNOUT

DETERMINANTS OF TURNOUT

- Angle of Anteversion
- Orientation of Acetabulum
- Elasticity of Hip Capsule
- Flexibility of Hip Muscles

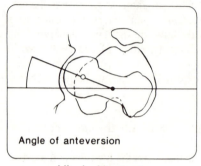

Hip in Neutral

Hip in Turnout

Figure 12. The ability to externally rotate the hip is based on several factors including the angle of femoral anteversion, the orientation of the acetabulum, the elasticity of the anterior hip capsule, and the flexibility of the muscle-tendon units which cross the hip joint.

THE DANCER'S HIP-TURNOUT

DECREASED TURNOUT

- Increased Anteversion
- Anterior Orientation of Acetabulum
- Inelastic Hip Capsule
- Inflexible Hip Muscles

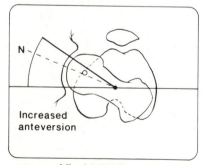

Hip in Neutral

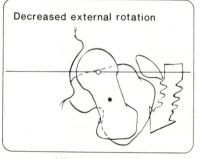

Hip in Turnout

Figure 13. Decreased turnout in the dancer can be secondary to increased femoral anteversion, an anterior oriented acetabulum, or inelasticity of the hip capsule as well as inflexibility of the hip muscles.

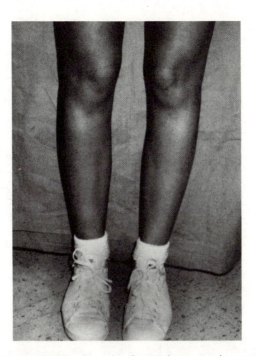

Figure 14. Individuals with excessive femoral anteversion can present clinically with "squinting patellae." The feet will be oriented straight ahead but the patellae will be oriented inward, suggesting the increased femoral anteversion.

These ligaments are extremely resistant to even the most vigorous stretching program.

Dancers who have a poor turnout at the hip may "cheat" by attempting to achieve greater external rotation either at the knee or at the foot and ankle (Hamilton, 1977; Sammarco, 1982). When this forced external rotation occurs at the knee, the dancer attempts to excessively rotate the tibia beneath the femoral condyles (Figure 15). This maneuver creates unusually severe stresses on the medial structures of the knee—particularly the medial retinaculum, the tibial collateral ligament, and the medial meniscus. The meniscus is a fibrocartilaginous structure that acts as a shock absorber and stabilizer of the knee. Abnormal forces, such as forced external rotation, can cause the meniscus to become trapped beneath the femoral condyle and the tibial plateau (see Figure 16). In this position, the meniscus may become torn in its midsubstance. The dancer complains of pain, tenderness, and swelling along the medial joint line. The diagnosis is a tear of the medial meniscus. The clinical problem is the maladaptive technique of forced external rotation at the knee placing abnormal stress on the meniscus. The underlying basic mechanism, however, is anatomic variation or lever system failure secondary to excessive femoral anteversion.

Rolling-in is another example of indirect lever-system failure or a maladaptive technique diverting stress to other structures that are poorly suited for

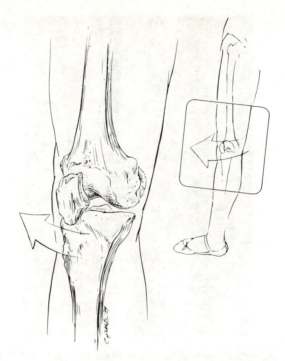

Figure 15. Dancers with a poor natural turnout may attempt to achieve greater external rotation by forced external rotation at the knee.

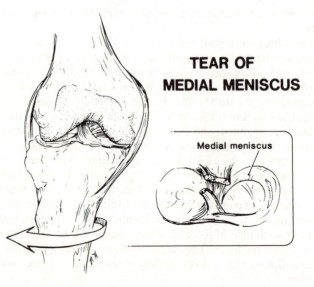

TEAR OF
MEDIAL MENISCUS

Medial meniscus

Figure 16. Forced external rotation of the tibial plateau beneath the femoral condyles can cause injury to medial meniscus.

DECOMPENSATORY MECHANISMS
TO ACHIEVE TURNOUT

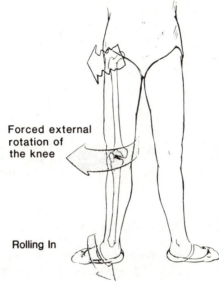

Forced external
rotation of
the knee

Rolling In

Figure 17. Rolling-in and forced external rotation of the knee are examples of maladaptive techniques that divert stress to structures poorly suited for energy absorption.

energy absorption (see Figure 17). Rolling-in is a technique to achieve greater external rotation of the extremity in a dancer who lacks natural turnout at the hip (Howse, 1972). The maneuver involves hyper-pronation of the foot with gripping of the floor by the first three toes and forcing the forefoot outward. The heel is deviated into valgus allowing the medial longitudinal arch to roll-in to a position of excessive pronation. If the forefoot and midfoot are pronated to extreme in relevé, the condition is called sickling-out. The consequence of the forced pronation of rolling-in or sickling is excessive strain on the structures of the medial foot (Ambre & Nilsson, 1978; Hamilton, 1977; Howse, 1983; Sammarco, 1982). This leads to a variety of acute and chronic conditions involving the forefoot, the midfoot, and the hindfoot (see Figure 18).

Hallux valgus is an acquired condition in dancers which often relates to repetitive activities which stress the medial structures of the forefoot (Sammarco, 1982). Repeated loading of these structures, particularly in dancers who roll-in, can create this deformity. The diagnosis will be hallux valgus but the clinical problem is the maladaptive technique of rolling-in. The underlying problem remains, however, the anatomic variation of excessive femoral anteversion.

The relationship of significant anatomic variation to the production of dance injuries suggests a possible self-selective process that, through attrition, removes the less well-adaptive body from dance. The physical demands of dance

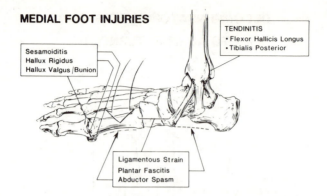

MEDIAL FOOT INJURIES

Sesamoiditis
Hallux Rigidus
Hallux Valgus /Bunion

TENDINITIS
• Flexor Hallicis Longus
• Tibialis Posterior

Ligamentous Strain
Plantar Fascitis
Abductor Spasm

Figure 18. The forced pronation associated with rolling-in places excessive strain on the structures of the medial foot, leading to a variety of acute and chronic conditions involving the forefoot, the midfoot, and the hindfoot.

are well recognized (Hamilton, 1978; Kirkendall & Calabrese, 1983; Micheli, Gillespie, & Walafzek, 1984; Nicholas, 1976; Rovere, Webb, Gristina, & Vogel, 1983; Teitz, 1983; Thomasen, 1982). The dancer, similar to the elite athlete, represents the top of a broad-based field of competitive students (McLain, 1983), who because of significant anatomic variation may have been selected from dance because of inability to perform without repeated injury. Indeed, there may be operative in training for the dance a "Darwinism" that requires the successful student to be free from significant anatomic variation (see Figure 19).

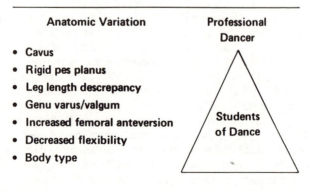

DARWINISM OF DANCE

Anatomic Variation	Professional Dancer
• Cavus	
• Rigid pes planus	
• Leg length descrepancy	
• Genu varus/valgum	
• Increased femoral anteversion	Students of Dance
• Decreased flexibility	
• Body type	

Figure 19. There may be operative a Darwinism of dance representing a self-selective process where dancers with significant anatomic variation are selected from dance because of their inability to perform without repeated injury.

Table 1. Dance injuries shoe comparison

Runner's shoe	Ballet shoe
Soft rubber	Hard rubber
Open mesh nylon	Satin
Sorbothane	Leather
Spenco	Burlap
Plastozote	Wheat paste
	Cardboard

Environmental Factors

Environmental factors can contribute significantly to both lever-system failure and shock-absorber failure. Environmental factors relating to dance injuries include primarily problems of footwear and the dance surface.

In the long-distance and marathon runner, like the dancer, a primary mechanism of injury is the cyclic loading of the lower extremities on a hard unyielding surface, in this case, the roadway. Over the last decade, major advances have been made in the design and construction of running shoes through the use of high-technology materials. These new materials have improved the shock-absorbing characteristics, reduced friction, enhanced stability, and thereby reduced the frequency of injury. Such materials as Sorbathane, Spenco, and Plastozote are incorporated in running shoes to promote two major goals: stability and shock absorption (Table 1).

In contrast, the emphasis of classical dance footwear is on style and tradition. Traditional dance disciplines employ shoes that have undergone little or no modification for generations despite the vastly improved materials available. Indeed, the major construction materials of the ballet toe shoe are burlap, wheat paste, satin, cardboard, hard rubber, and leather (Bentley, 1984; Thomasen, 1982). With this construction, the dancer's feet receive essentially no protection from external forces. The clinical and radiographic examination of dancers' feet corroborates the result of such chronic energy absorption (Sammarco & Miller, 1982).

The dance surface is another environmental factor which can contribute to injury (Seals, 1983; Washington, 1978). The ideal dance floor should absorb some of the impact energy and also return some energy to the dancer. Likewise, a delicate balance of friction and resiliency is necessary to prevent injury. All too often, young dancers are required to perform on surfaces that are hard, unyielding, or unpredictable in the degree of energy return or friction.

Summary

This discussion on the pathogenesis of dance injuries is based on clinical observations. These observations suggest potential mechanisms responsible for injury in dancers. Further investigation in the clinical and basic science laboratory will be necessary to corroborate and confirm these impressions. Such research is now underway in several centers associated with dance companies and dance students. Research programs are investigating the biomechanics of performance, using computerized force-plate analysis, muscle testing, and high-speed videotape analysis. Other research is directed toward muscle physiology, specifically analysis of muscle fiber types, as well as the macro- and ultra-structure of injury in dancers and athletes. Additional investigations are reviewing the fundamental concepts of stretching and their relationship to injury and injury prevention. Still other projects are studying the various environmental factors with a special emphasis on shoe design, dance floor construction, and the influence of room temperature on injury production and prevention.

One of the most important aspects of studying the pathomechanics of dance injuries is applying this knowledge to injury prevention. All members of the dance medicine team must be alert to and concerned with all aspects of injury prevention. This team includes the artistic director, the dance teacher, the dance therapist, and the company physician.

The artistic director can assist in injury prevention by allowing sufficient rest in the rehearsal and tour schedule to prevent fatigue among company members. This individual should insist on proper floor surface and stage temperature for rehearsal and performance. In addition, the artistic director can appreciate the physical limitations of a particular dancer in terms of the choreographic requirements for a given part. The dance teacher can insist that proper strengthening and conditioning be present before the young dancer attempts difficult maneuvers. Again, emphasis should be placed on proper technique. The teacher and the therapist together must instill in the young dancer the principles of proper warm-up and stretching and emphasize their role in injury prevention.

Physicians must, in their treatment of dancers, be sensitive to the unique demands of dance. They must be aware that the basic problems and mechanisms of dance injury are frequently far removed from the injury site, and often the diagnosis does not immediately suggest the underlying mechanism for the injury. The treatment protocol must, therefore, consider the diagnosis, the contributing factors, and the pathomechanics of the injury itself.

References

Ambre, T., & Nilsson, B.E. (1978). Degenerative changes in the first metatarsophalangeal joint of ballet dancers. *Acta Orthopaedica Scandinavica, 49*, 317.

Bentley, T. (1984). The toe shoe makes its pointe. *Smithsonian, 15*, 88.

Gelabert, R. (1977). Turning out. *Dance Magazine, 86*.

Hamilton, W.G. (1977). Tendinitis about the ankle joint in classical ballet dancers. *American Journal of Sports Medicine, 5*, 84.

Hamilton, W.G. (1978, February-June). Ballet and your body: An orthopaedist's view. *Dance Magazine*.

Hamilton, W.G. (1982). Sprained ankles in ballet dancers. *Foot and Ankle, 3*, 99.

Howse, A.J.G. (1972). Orthopaedists aid ballet. *Clinical Orthopaedics and Related Research, 89*, 52.

Howse, A.J.G. (1983). Disorders of the great toe in dancers. *Clinics in Sports Medicine, 2*, 499.

Kirkendall, D., & Calabrese, L.H. (1983). Physiologic aspects of dance. *Clinics in Sports Medicine, 2*, 525.

Knott, M., & Voss, D. (1965). *Proprioceptive neuromuscular facilitation.* New York: Harper and Row.

McLain, D. (1983). Artistic development in the dancer. *Clinics in Sports Medicine, 2*, 563.

Micheli, L.J., Gillespie, W.J., & Walafzek, R.A. (1984). Physiologic profiles of female professional ballerinas. *Clinics in Sports Medicine, 3*, 199.

Miller, E.G., Schneider, H.J., Bronson, J.L., & McLain, D. (1975). A new consideration of athletic injuries. The classical ballet dancer. *Clinical Orthopaedics and Related Research, 111*, 181.

Nicholas, J.A. (1976). Risk factors, sports medicine and the orthopaedic system: An overview. *American Journal of Sports Medicine, 3*, 243.

Rovere, G.D., Webb, L.X., Gristina, A.G., & Vogel, J.N. (1983). Musculoskeletal injuries in theatrical dance students. *American Journal of Sports Medicine, 11*, 195.

Sammarco, G.J. (1982). The foot and ankle in classical ballet and modern dance. In JAHSS, *Disorders of the Foot* (pp. 626-659). Philadelphia: W.B. Saunders.

Sammarco, G.J., & Miller, E.H. (1982). Forefoot conditions in dancers. Parts I and II. *Foot and Ankle, 3*, 85.

Seals, J.G. (1983). A study of dance surfaces. *Clinics in Sports Medicine, 2*, 557.

Teitz, C. (1983). Sports medicine concerns in dance and gymnastics. *Clinics in Sports Medicine, 2*, 571.

Thomasen, E. (1982). *Diseases and injuries of ballet dancers.* Arhus, Denmark: Universitetsforlaget I.

Washington, E.L. (1978). Musculoskeletal injuries in theatrical dancers: Site, frequency and severity. *American Journal of Sports Medicine, 6*, 75.

3

Foot and Ankle Injuries in Dance and Athletics: Similarities and Differences

William T. Hardaker, Jr. and Claude T. Moorman, III
DUKE UNIVERSITY MEDICAL CENTER
DURHAM, NORTH CAROLINA, USA

Theatrical dance is an art form and is to be distinguished from social, ballroom, and aerobic dance. It encompasses the various disciplines of classical ballet, modern dance, ethnic dance, and mixed forms such as Broadway and jazz.

The theatrical dancer is a combination of superior artist and high-performance athlete. Few would argue the incredible grace of the accomplished dancer, but it has been only recently that many have come to appreciate the extraordinary coordination, strength, and endurance that this group of athletes possesses. In an investigation conducted by the Lenox Hill Institute of Sports Medicine in New York City (Nicholas 1976), the performance demands of many highly competitive sports were reviewed. Similar performance demands were also analyzed for the theatrical dancer. When the results were tabulated, the professional dancer compared favorably with high-performance athletes participating in football, basketball, and other competitive sports.

In essence, the professional theatrical dancer must possess the agility and balance of the gymnast, the speed and strength of the football running back, the reaction time and accuracy of the baseball player, and the coordination and jumping ability of the basketball player. Many exercise physiologists and kinesiologists now consider the theatrical dancer to represent the ultimate athlete. Indeed, many professional athletes now attend dance class in the off-season to enhance and improve their overall athletic skills.

Dancers as athletes can and do become injured, and a major site of injury is the foot and ankle (Quirk, 1983; Rovere, Webb, Gristina, & Vogel, 1983). In a recent review of injuries to dancers of the American Dance Festival, 211 injuries were reported over a 2-year period, and in this group 38% involved the foot and ankle. Foot and ankle injuries also are very common in athletics. In contact and collision sports, acute injuries predominate. These injuries are characterized by the sudden absorption of considerable energy by the bony and soft tissue structures (see Figure 1). In contrast, chronic injuries are seen more frequently in endurance sports such as tennis, swimming, and long-distance running.

Although acute injuries do occur to the foot and ankle in theatrical dancers (Hamilton, 1982a), the vast majority of injuries are chronic and relate to a single primary mechanism—the repetitive impact loading of the lower extremities on a hard, unyielding surface. Unlike the runner and the jogger, who wear specially designed shoes to absorb shock, the classical ballet dancer wears nothing but a soft slipper or toe shoe (Bentley, 1984), and modern dancers wear no shoes at all. All of the forces of the repetitive impact loading must therefore be dissipated by the lower extremities and the low back. The failure to effectively dissipate these forces can lead to injuries to the foot and ankle.

Several factors can contribute to this inability to effectively dissipate the forces of repetitive impact loading. Anatomic factors may play an important role in the production of injury. These factors are nothing more than variations of normal anatomy, but when exposed in the extreme environment of cyclic loading, they can lead to injury. Excessive femoral anteversion, genu varus, genu valgum, internal rotation of the tibia, extreme pes valgus, or pes cavus can all contribute to the inability to effectively dissipate forces in the lower extremities. Other contributing factors include training errors such as improper technique, inadequate conditioning, lack of flexibility, or fatigue (Gelabert, 1977; Howse, 1972; Sammarco, 1984).

Figure 1. Acute injuries are more frequently associated with contact and collision sports.

Impingement Syndromes

The extreme dorsiflexion and plantar flexion required by certain ballet positions can lead to talar impingement syndromes involving the anterior and posterior aspect of the ankle joint (Hamilton, 1982b; Howse, 1982; Kleiger, 1982).

The demi-plié is a ballet position that can lead to actual impingement of the anterior lip of the tibia on the talar neck (see Figure 2). The initial symptoms are poorly localized, and the major complaint of the dancer is lack of adequate depth on the plié. This may be interpreted incorrectly as tight heel cords, and some dancers are actually placed on a program of heel-cord stretching by their dance therapist or dance instructor. This only serves to aggravate the situation. With time the symptoms become more and more localized to the anterior aspect of the ankle.

Physical examination reveals tenderness medially between the medial malleolus and the anterior tibial tendon. Laterally, similar tenderness and sometimes mild swelling are located between the lateral malleolus and the extensor digitorum communis. In advanced cases, one can actually palpate small exostoses on the tibia and the talar neck. The symptoms can be reproduced by hyper-dorsiflexion of the foot and ankle complex. The tibial-talar contact can be demonstrated radiographically on lateral x-ray taken with the foot in

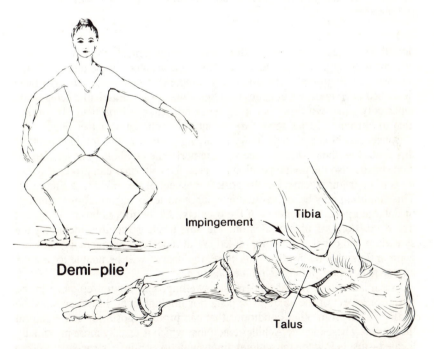

Figure 2. The extreme positions of dorsiflexion required by certain dance positions can lead to actual impingement of the anterior lip of the tibia on the talar neck.

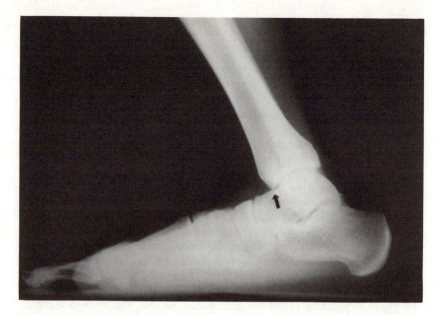

Figure 3. The tibial-talar contact of the anterior impingement syndrome can be demonstrated radiographically on a lateral x-ray taken with the foot in dorsiflexion.

dorsiflexion (see Figure 3). With repeated impingement, the exostoses will become more and more prominent and the natural sulcus in the talar neck will be lost (see Figure 4). The anterior impingement syndrome has also been described in competitive athletics (O'Donoghue, 1957). Baseball catchers who repeatedly squat with the foot in hyper-dorsiflexion are particularly vulnerable to chronic injuries secondary to anterior impingement (see Figure 5).

Dancer's heel is a chronic injury involving posterior talar impingement. In this condition, the position of demi-pointe performed by both male and female dancers and also the pointe position reserved for ballerinas can produce symptoms of talar impingement in the posterior aspect of the ankle (see Figure 6). This condition may be aggravated by a large posterior tubercle, os trigonum, or enlarged posterior process of the oscalcis. As the foot is brought into extreme positions of plantar flexion, the soft tissue structures including the synovium and capsule are compressed. With repeated impingement, they become inflamed and fibrotic. With time, the dancer will be unable to assume an adequate demi-pointe or pointe position.

Examination will reveal tenderness, swelling, and often crepitance in the posterior aspect of the ankle. The posterior impingement, however, must be distinguished from other conditions that can produce posterior ankle pain in the dancer. These include Achilles tendinitis, which is usually more proximally located—just below the musculotendinous junction of the gastroc-soleus complex. Flexor hallucis longus tendinitis is seen medially and peroneal tendinitis is seen laterally in the posterior aspect of the ankle. However, in none of these

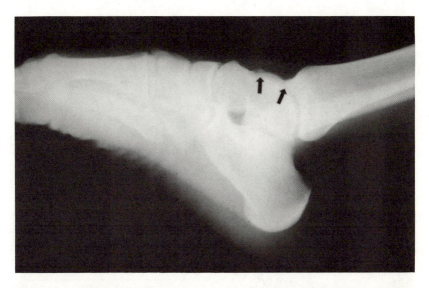

Figure 4. A radiograph of an early case of anterior impingement demonstrates small exostoses on the anterior lip of the tibia and the talar neck.

Figure 5. The anterior impingement syndrome can be seen in competitive athletics requiring extreme positions of dorsiflexion, as demonstrated in this baseball catcher.

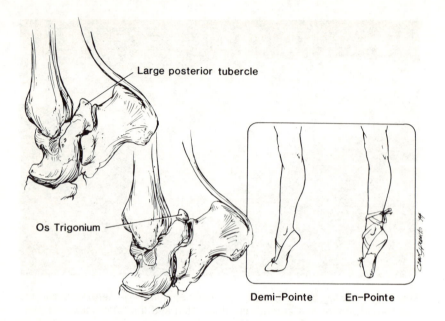

Figure 6. The demi-pointe and pointe are positions of extreme plantar flexion that may lead to posterior impingment, a condition that may be seen in dancers with a large posterior tubercle, os trigonum, or enlarged posterior process of the os calcis.

Figure 7. The posterior impingement syndrome can be seen in sports such as soccer or football (punting) that require repeated stress on the posterior foot-ankle complex.

conditions are the symptoms made worse by plantar flexion of the foot. In posterior impingement, the symptoms can be reproduced clinically by plantar flexion of the foot and are usually improved by traction on the heel. If there is any question concerning the diagnosis, the area can be infiltrated with 1 to 2 cc of 1% xylocaine in order to corroborate the diagnosis. Radiographically, the offending os trigonum, or posterior tubercle, may be demonstrated. Football punters and soccer players (Ecker, Ritter, & Jacobs, 1967; McDougall, 1955) can repeatedly stress the posterior foot-ankle complex and in some cases, develop the characteristic signs and symptoms of posterior impingement (see Figure 7). Unlike dancers, who may be disabled with this condition, these athletes rarely note significant functional disability.

Tendinitis

Any of the tendons that cross the ankle joint can produce symptoms of inflammation and later tendinitis when stressed by repetitive impact loading. In sprinters, the hamstrings are most frequently involved, whereas in distance runners, the Achilles tendon is more frequently injured (Clancy, Niedhart, & Brand, 1976; James, Bates, & Osternig, 1978). A commonly involved tendon in classical ballet is the flexor hallucis longus.

Two conditions can lead to tendinitis. One is an anatomic variation in which the dancer has an abnormally distally placed muscle belly on the flexor hallucis longus tendon (Hamilton, 1982b). In positions of extreme dorsiflexion, the muscle belly can actually impact into the mouth of the fibro-osseous canal of the flexor hallucis longus. This will create symptoms of pain on the posterior medial aspect of the ankle. Examination will usually reveal tenderness and possibly mild swelling in this region. However, the most striking aspect of the physical examination is the functional hallux ridigis that can accompany this problem. As the foot is brought into dorsiflexion, the examiner is often unable to hyper-dorsiflex the great toe because of the impaction of the muscle belly in the flexor tendon sheath.

Other mechanisms probably more frequently responsible for tendinitis of the flexor hallucis longus are *rolling-in* and *sickling* (see Figure 8). Both may represent compensatory mechanisms for decreased turnout at the hip (Gelabert, 1977; Howse, 1972; Sammarco, 1984). Some dancers lack the external rotation at the hip for a satisfactory natural turnout. In order to achieve the desired external rotation of the lower extremity they will "cheat" by excessively externally rotating at either the knee or the ankle joints (Gelabert, 1977; Howse, 1972; Miller, Schneider, Bronson, & McLain, 1975; Quirk, 1983; Thomasen, 1982). When this is done in stance, the foot is rolled into valgus at the hindfoot and the fore- and midfoot are hyperpronated. In some cases, the pronation is so exaggerated that the lateral two metatarsal heads will actually be lifted from the dance floor. If this position of hyperpronation is duplicated in the demi-pointe position it is called sickling.

Dancers who repeatedly roll-in or sickle may develop pain and tenderness in the posterior aspect of the medial malleolus. With continued inflammation, a small nodule can form in the flexor hallucis tendon. An examiner may ob-

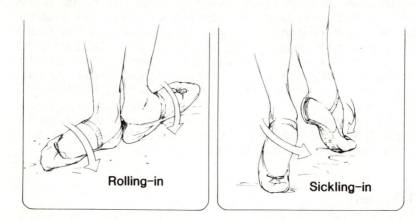

Figure 8. Rolling-in and sickling-out are positions of extreme pronation of the foot assumed by some dancers in order to improve the overall turnout of the extremity.

serve actual triggering of the great toe as it is moved through plantar flexion and dorsiflexion (see Figure 9). In this regard, the condition is similar to triggering of flexor tendons in the hand as fusiform nodules within the tendon substance slide into and out of the pulley mechanism.

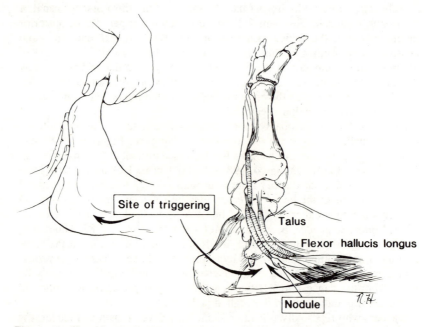

Figure 9. Chronic tendinitis of the flexor hallucis longus may involve triggering of the great toe secondary to a nodule present in the tendon substance.

Stress Fractures

Stress fractures are common foot injuries in dancers and in runners (Burrows, 1956; Drez, Young, Johnston, & Parker, 1980; McBryde, 1976; Miller et al., 1975). They result from repeated submaximal cyclic loading of the foot on a relatively hard surface. The fractures may be subtle, often initially very indistinct radiographically, and probably represent a continuum rather than a single episode of trauma. With repetitive impact, the ability to spontaneously heal the injury gradually is lost and the fracture occurs.

Stress fractures in runners and dancers are seen most frequently in the second and third metatarsals, which are relatively immobile when compared with the first, fourth, and fifth metatarsal rays. In runners the distal diaphysis of the metatarsal neck is most frequently involved (see Figure 10). Dancers will often have a fracture in the proximal metatarsal, a site rarely involved in the long-distance runner (see Figure 11). Gradually increasing pain in the area of the fracture, usually following activity, may be relieved by rest but will recur with the return of exercise. Stress fractures may be difficult to demonstrate on plain films (Burrows, 1956; Prather et al., 1977). Multiple projections as well as serial evaluations may be required. In some cases, a bone scan may be necessary to demonstrate an early lesion (Grahame, Saunders, & Maisey, 1979; Pavlov, Torg, Hersh, & Freiberger, 1981). With time, however, the healing stress fracture can be readily demonstrated on plain film.

The runner, unlike the dancer, has distinct advantages when dealing with stress fractures. The athlete can vary the running surface, the footwear, and the training routine to accommodate the injury while still maintaining some form of participation. The dancer, however, cannot readily manipulate these environmental factors and frequently must withdraw from dance until satisfactory healing has occurred.

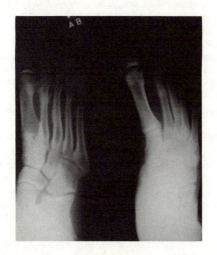

Figure 10. The distal second metatarsal ray is a common site for stress fracture in runners.

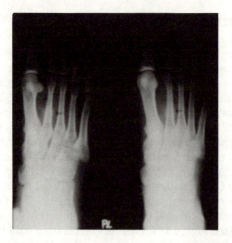

Figure 11. Stress fractures will often be located more proximally within the metatarsal diaphysis in the dancer than in the long-distance runner.

References

Bentley, T. (1984). The heart and sole of a ballerina's art: Her toe shoes. *Smithsonian, 15,* 88.

Burrows, F.J. (1956). Fatigue infraction of middle of tibia in ballet dancers. *Journal of Bone and Joint Surgery, 38B,* 83.

Clancy, W.G., Niedhart, D., & Brand, R.L. (1976). Achilles tendinitis in runners: A report of five cases. *American Journal of Sports Medicine, 4,* 46.

Drez, D., Young, J.C., Johnston, R.D., & Parker, W.D. (1980). Metatarsal stress fractures. *American Journal of Sports Medicine, 8,* 123.

Ecker, M.L., Ritter, M.A., & Jacobs, B.S. (1967). The symptomatic os-trigonum. *Journal of the American Medical Association, 204.*

Gelabert, R. (1977). Turning out. *Dance Magazine, 86.*

Grahame, R., Saunders, A.S., & Maisey, N. (1979). The use of scintigraphy in the diagnosis and management of traumatic foot lesions in ballet dancers. *Rheumatics and Rehabilitation, 18,* 235.

Hamilton, W.G. (1982). Sprained ankles in ballet dancers. *Foot and Ankle, 3,* 99.

Hamilton, W.G. (1982). Stenosing tenosynovitis of the flexor hallucis longus tendon and posterior impingement upon the os-trigonum in ballet dancers. *Foot and Ankle, 3,* 74.

Howse, A.J.G. (1972). Orthopaedists aid ballet. *Clinical Orthopaedics and Related Research, 89,* 52.

Howse, A.J.G. (1982). Posterior block of the ankle joint in dancers. *Foot and Ankle, 3,* 8.

James, S.L., Bates, B.T., & Osternig, L.R. (1978). Injuries to runners. *American Journal of Sports Medicine, 6,* 40.

Kleiger, B. (1982). Anterior tibial talar impingement syndromes in dancers. *Foot and Ankle, 3,* 69.

McBryde, A. (1976). Stress fractures in athletes. *Journal of Sports Medicine, 3,* 212.

McDougall, A. (1955). The os-trigonum. *Journal of Bone and Joint Surgery, 37B,* 257.

Miller, E.H., Schneider, H.J., Bronson, J.L., & McLain, D. (1975). A new consideration of athletic injuries. *Clinical Orthopaedics and Related Research*, **111**, 181.

Nicholas, J.A. (1976). Risk factors, sports medicine and the orthopaedic system: An overview. *American Journal of Sports Medicine*, **3**, 243.

O'Donoghue, D.H. (1957). Impingement exostoses of the talus and tibia. *Journal of Bone and Joint Surgery*, **39A**, 865.

Pavlov, H., Torg, J.S., Hersh, A., & Freiberger, R.H. (1981). The Roentgen examination of runners' injuries. *Radiographics*, **1**, 17.

Prather, J.L., Nusynawitz, M.L., Snowdy, H.A., Hughes, A.D., McCartney, W.H., & Bagg, R.J. (1977). Scintigraphic findings in stress fractures. *Journal of Bone and Joint Surgery*, **59A**, 869.

Quirk, R. (1983). Ballet injuries: The Australian experience. *Clinics in Sports Medicine*, **2**, 507.

Rovere, G.D., Webb, L.X., Gristina, A.G., & Vogel, J.N. (1983). Musculoskeletal injuries in theatrical dance students. *American Journal of Sports Medicine*, **11**, 195.

Sammarco, G.J. (1984). Diagnosis and treatment of dancers. *Clinical Orthopaedics and Related Research*, **187**, 176.

Thomasen, E. (1982). *Diseases and injuries of ballet dancers*. Arhus, Denmark: Universitetsforlaget. I.

4

Biomechanical Implications of Dance Injuries

Steven R. Kravitz, Carla J. Murgia, Stephen Huber, and Karl R. Saltrick
PENNSYLVANIA COLLEGE OF PEDIATRIC MEDICINE
PHILADELPHIA, PENNSYLVANIA, USA

Dance, as an athletic activity, incorporates movement that may be common in this choreographed motion but uncommon to other athletic activity classified as sport. The study of these peculiar motions, their biomechanical implications, and the injuries related to them, as well as the treatment of these injuries, has led to the development of a branch of orthopaedics known as dance medicine. It is an extension of sports medicine utilizing many of the same basic orthopaedic concepts.

An overuse syndrome occurs when a specific body part develops inflammation in response to the physical demands placed upon it. In athletes it is often related to a compensatory mechanism. If one area of the body does not work appropriately, another part must compensate for this. The physical load related to athletic activity often causes the compensating part to become inflamed. The compensating mechanism may be able to handle normal daily activity effectively but added stress often leads to overload and inflammation and pain develops. Thus, where the pain occurs does not necessarily indicate where the only problem is. The painful area may be caused by another body part that is not operating effectively. Examples of lower extremity pain often related to overuse syndromes are metatarsalgia, heel-spur syndrome, tendinitis (of many different tendons and inflammation of their associated musculature), stress fractures, dancer's knee, and a myriad of others.

The authors gratefully acknowledge the assistance of Karen L. Fink, Mark W. Shaffer, and Lorraine L. Varela.

Preventing these pain syndromes is important for two reasons. First, they obviously can affect performance and thus prevent optimal performance from being achieved. Second, many dancers and other athletes will attempt to perform while subject to the pain of overuse syndrome. This leads to guarding, as they attempt to decrease pressure on the painful area. The resultant fatigue often decreases reaction time and makes performers more likely to lose their footing, more accident-prone, and more likely to develop a significant injury elsewhere. As this implies, by controlling appropriate body mechanisms it is possible to decrease the probability of developing the overuse syndrome that may indirectly cause a major injury.

Pronation

Substantial injuries often produce a large amount of *down time*[1] (Subotnick, 1975), regardless of the type of athletic pursuit. Pronation of the foot has been identified as the frequent cause of many common overuse syndromes (Hoerner et al., 1982). Dance literature has described this motion as rolling in at the ankle. Orthopaedic study has shown the phenomenon to be related to motion around the subtalar joint. Calcaneal eversion with associated subtalar joint pronation decreases the amount of obliquity between the calcaneocuboid and talonavicular joint axes (Mann & Inman, 1964). As these axes approach a parallel relationship, the midtarsal joint becomes unlocked and an apparent collapse of the arch is induced. The pronatory mechanism allows for abduction of the forefoot on the rearfoot, often with splaying of the metatarsals as they evert relative to the supporting surface. The first ray becomes hypermobile and dorsiflexes, and the foot loses its medial support as it everts. Pronatory motion induces internal rotation of the lower extremity with the leg segment rotating at a faster speed (2:1) than the thigh (Root, Orien, & Weed, 1977). The patellar tendon is pulled internal to its normal axis of motion. This chain reaction has been shown to produce many overuse syndromes in runners; however, it also can be destructive to dancers.

Pronation can occur secondary to various anatomical factors. Genu varum and tibial varum possibly related to coxa valga, rearfoot varus, and forefoot varus are common causes of excessive pronation. A short leg syndrome, possibly with a related pelvic tilt, is also a pronation producer on the long extremity (Root et al., 1977). However, this type of motion can also occur as a result of athletic activity. In runners, adduction of the lower extremity toward the midline of the body necessitates increased eversion of the foot during the support phase to allow the forefoot an opportunity to attain an attitude parallel to the supporting surface. The varus wedge utilized in some running shoes was an attempt to balance this reactionary angular deviation.

The turnout to attain the five classical dance positions may be an important initiator of excessive pronation if the position cannot be attained solely at the

---

[1]Down time is a period of time during which a dancer or athlete is not able to perform because of an injury.

hip joint. Ideally, the feet should face 180° from each other, heel to heel. To be performed appropriately, the positions should be achieved by the femoral segments externally rotating 90° at the hip joint, to allow for a full 180° relationship at the feet. Many dancers, however, must force the turnout by applying external rotatory force to the knee and foot. The dancer, in a flexed knee (plié) position, can attain an added 10° of tibial external rotation (relative to the femur), approximating the ideal aesthetic foot alignment. As the dancer straightens the knee from plié, this external rotational position between tibia and femur can no longer exist; thus the leg is forced to internally rotate relative to the femur. The stress and shear generated at the knee structures becomes apparent.

The foot, while this occurs, is planted firmly on the supporting surface and is forced to abduct relative to the leg as the tibial segment internally rotates. The calcaneus (heel bone) everts, the subtalar joint pronates, and the arch structure collapses as the midtarsal joint becomes unlocked through the development of a parallel relationship between the axes of calcaneal-cuboid and talar-navicular articulations. As the foot flattens and everts, tissues on the plantar surface are placed under tension, leading to the development of plantar fasciitis (heel spur syndrome). Stress fractures of the metatarsals become more likely because the lesser metatarsals are forced to bear increased weight as the first ray becomes hypermobile and thus no longer supports the medial column of the foot (Irvin & Steven, 1983). Stress fractures of the fibula, which frequently occur approximately 4 in. above the lateral malleolus, are possibly also more likely due to the torque placed through the internally rotating leg (Miller, Schneider, Bronson, & McLain, 1975). The rotation also pulls the patella internally as the leg rotates relative to the thigh, inducing the common chondromalacia of the patella (Insall, 1979) that is called dancer's knee or runner's knee (names specific to activity skill). Shin splints become increasingly likely as musculature attempts to support the unstable skeletal framework of the foot (Haycock, 1980).

Examination

If excessive pronatory motion is present, full biomechanical examination can be extremely helpful in locating the cause. Study of body alignment (shoulders to feet) and gross assessment of motion of various joints (hip to feet), as well as gait analysis, are useful in studying how the foot functions with respect to the rest of the body. The biomechanical examination is used for many types of athletes. Practitioners of various health fields should work together so that when a local pathology is determined outside an area of specialization, appropriate referral is made to ensure the utmost in quality care.

Further analysis of dancer-patients involves observing them in classical ballet positions. The abductory relationship of the feet in the first position is noted and compared to the external rotation measurement of the hip in extended position. External malleolar positioning should also be assessed when attempting to determine if the dancer has forced the turnout beyond that of the hip joint. Calcaneal stance position and the amount of calcaneal eversion present relative to the lower third of the leg is also determined in second, third, and fourth open and fifth positions. Measurement for plié in second position and observance of any sickling in relevé are also useful in grossly determining muscular control and strength (Kravitz, 1984).

Exercise

The measurements and impressions noted during the examination can be used to aid and guide the dancer toward either decreasing turnout or increasing it to osseous limitation through flexibility programs. The goal is to place this motion solely at the hip, thus decreasing stress placed on other body parts. Exercise programs for flexibility as well as strengthening can be helpful to the patient in attaining optimal performance.

Specially, "towel set" isotonic exercises are very helpful (Kravitz, 1984). They utilize the full range of motion of the foot in an adducted inversion direction to abduction eversion direction against resistance. Digital plantar flexion to strengthen intrinsic and extrinsic musculature can also be incorporated as one moves a weighted towel toward oneself by "toe grabbing." A myriad of other exercises can be helpful to all athletes. Each practitioner should have sets of exercises to prescribe for different muscle groups.

For dancers, the authors use a low-weight, high-repetition program. For other athletes, where increased muscle bulk is preferred, a high-weight, low-repetition program may be more desirable. A well-toned muscle (strength and flexibility) is an excellent shock absorber and should help to contain the stress produced through athletic activity and thus reduce risk of injury. More specifically, dance should attempt to develop leg musculature that can assist stabilization in a supinatory direction. The dancer should be guided to make a conscious effort to hold the arch up and thus decrease the tendency to roll in and pronate the foot.

When appropriately developed, the musculature of the tibialis anterior, tibialis posterior, and stabilizers of the first metatarsal, such as the peroneus longus, can aid in resisting pronation and maintaining a viable medial column of support. These muscles, as well as those of the peroneus brevis, are of particular importance in preventing sickling and maintaining a healthy pointe-stance attitude.

Taping

Many taping techniques may be useful to the athlete. Among the most common are several types of plantar rest straps utilizing 1-in. and 1½-in. adhesive tape to support the foot and decrease pronatory motion. Practitioners will often have several strapping techniques that they prefer using. Many are interchangeable for similar conditions. Two points to remember are that (a) the support is effective only as long as the adhesive contact remains intact and (b) prolonged or repeated tape applications with chronicity may lead to skin irritation. Skin adherent applied to the skin surface prior to tape application is an effective means of decreasing the possibility of dermatological sensitivity to tape adhesives.

Other Common Injuries and Overuse Syndromes

The practitioner and the dancer or athlete should be aware of and able to recognize injuries common to his or her specific skills. Many affect the foot and ankle.

Ankle Sprains

One of the most common injuries in all athletic activity is the ankle sprain. The most frequent mechanism is one of inversion with sprain of the lateral ligaments. When the foot is plantar flexed, the talus moves with the foot in a plantar direction, allowing the narrow aspect of its articular surface to enter the ankle joint. This motion occurs frequently as a basketball player jumps for the hoop or as a dancer propels for a jeté. It also occurs in ballet as the dancer elevates to go on toe. When the dancer has achieved pointe stance, the ankle joint is locked and stable. A few degrees short of full plantar flexion, however, as the dancer rises or lowers from pointe, the joint is most unstable and a sprain injury is most likely to occur.

The initial treatment for an injury of this type is described by the pneumonic RICE (rest, ice, compression, and elevation).[2] Through strict adherence the athlete should attempt to decrease swelling and further injury. Medical attention, if necessary, should be sought as soon as possible. The author has used rigid immobilization to treat sprains involving significant damage to at least two of the three lateral ligaments or for avulsion type fracture of the malleolus. An aggressive range-of-motion exercise program should be utilized as soon as possible following the injury. A strengthening program is also important as range of motion returns to the damaged joint. Strengthening musculature that courses the sprained area has been helpful in decreasing the probability of recurrence. Ruptured ligaments heal with fibrous tissue; this is nonelastic and thus has a tendency to be partially ruptured again if tension is applied. A well-planned strengthening program decreases the possibility of reinjury by adding stability to the damaged joint. The "towel set" exercise is an excellent isotonic method of developing muscular strength as well as increased range of motion of the subtalar joint.

Anterior Ankle Strain

Anterior ankle strain occurs in pointe dance as the dancer tends to roll over the anterior aspect of the ankle and foot. This creates a strain at the anterior capsule of the ankle and may be associated with extensor tendinitis. The injury can develop with other athletic activity but, in the authors' experience, is most commonly associated with pointe dance. Treatment through conservative means has been effective. The dancer's technique may have to be modified.

---

[2]*Rest* the part. Apply *ice* to the area for approximately 20 min continuously out of each 40- to 60-min period. Use an elastic wrap or other form of mild *compression*. *Elevate* the part above the level of the heart.

Talar Compression Syndrome

Talar compression syndrome is a pathology preventing the ballet dancer from fully plantar flexing the foot to attain pointe stance. It results from one of three types of bony blockages. A dancer with limited plantar flexion of the foot should seek medical advice. Forced plantar flexion impacts bone upon bone, possibly initiating a proliferative response. The development of more bone would limit the desired motion further. The dancer should attempt to limit ankle plantar flexion to the (bony) end range of motion in order to prevent further osseous development. Physical therapy and oral antiinflammatories may be useful adjunctive methods of treating the acute case. Surgical excision may be required if all conservative methods yield unsatisfactory results. The osseous etiologies are enlarged posterior talar process, os-trigonum, or hypertrophy of the superior posterior aspect of the calcaneus.

Flexor Hallucis Longus Tendinitis

Flexor hallucis longus tendinitis is an inflammation of the long flexor tendon to the great toe, a syndrome that the authors have seen only in dancers. The muscle involved is important in stabilizing the great toe against the supporting surface. A partial rupture of its tendon may lead to a trigger toe, described by Sammarco (1984) as a hypertrophy of the tendon at the posterior talus and beneath the calcaneal sustentaculum tali. It can snap the hallux into an attitude of plantar flexion as the enlarged tendon attempts to slide through its course posteriorly. Crepitus along the course of the tendon can often be palpated as the dancer-patient moves the great toe. Chronic tendinitis can also lead to pseudo hallux rigidus due to stenosis of the tendon near the posterior talus (Hamilton, 1984).

Treatment for a trigger toe has been described as a release of the hypertrophy. Conservative treatment using rest, ice, and antiinflammatories is often effective (for treating the tendinitis) prior to the development of a tendon hypertrophy. Local steroid injection in the area of major tendons should generally be avoided, especially when dealing with the athletic individual. Range-of-motion exercise and ultrasound may be helpful forms of physical therapy. Excessive pronation, gripping the floor, sickling, and other factors of poor technique may have to be addressed. An asymptomatic crepitus along the tendon is common in many dancers, however, and often poses no problems or complaints.

Sesamoiditis

Sesamoiditis, with associated inflammation of the plantar capsule of the first metatarsal phalangeal joint and the conjoined tendon, is a common problem in many athletic individuals. Modern dancers, gymnasts, and other athletes who work with their bare feet are naturally more susceptible to injuring the sesamoid apparatus or fracturing these small bones. Sesamoiditis has been described as a chondromalacia of the cartilage on the undersurface of the small sesamoid bones. A pad of 1/8-in. adhesive felt is an effective regimen of treatment. The use of ice and oral antiinflammatories may also be helpful. Developmental bunion deformity is possible following the surgical excision of a painful tibial sesamoid nonunion.

Cuboid Peroneal Syndrome

Cuboid peroneal syndrome involves pain along the lateral aspect of the foot due to passing of the peroneal tendon through the peroneal groove (Weil, 1983). Symptoms can be similar to that of a fracture of the cuboid bone.

Sinus Tarsi Syndrome

The opening of the sinus tarsi lies anterior and inferior to the lateral ankle malleolus and thus pain in this area must be differentiated from ankle pain. The etiology of sinus tarsi syndrome has been hypothesized to be sprain of the lateral and interosseous talocalcaneal ligaments or a synovitis of the joint. Palpation over the sinus tarsi or forcibly inverting and everting the calcaneus to end range of motion often produces subtalar tenderness. A high index of suspicion of sinus tarsi syndrome should be maintained when a patient relates a history of frequent ankle sprain.

Inflammation within this joint can be the result of acute injury; however, more chronic or recurrent histories may be indicative of excessive pronation. A full biomechanical examination is useful in analyzing related functional abnormalities in the recurrent case. Treatment consisting of plantar (rest) strapping and padding (longitudinal arch) or orthotics is sometimes effective. Local steroid injection may be necessary. Intractible cases may require rigid immobilization in a walking cast. Strengthening and flexibility exercises have proven to be an effective adjunctive treatment program. Though surgical methods (arthrotomy) have been described for cases not responding to conservative care, the first author has not found this necessary.

Mortons Neuroma

Mortons neuroma most commonly affects the third digital nerve to the contiguous sides of the third and fourth toes. Balanced metatarsal padding using adhesive felt is sometimes effective as a conservative treatment regimen. This technique, however, is often not tolerated by pointe dancers and thus not effective. Compression of the metatarsal heads by the toe box may irritate the condition, particularly when dealing with a pointe shoe. Steroid infiltration can be utilized with adjunctive physical therapy (ultrasound). The literature recommends observing a high level of care to protect the metatarsal phalangeal joints from dislocations related to tissue atrophy and to protect from abscess development, when infiltration of cortisone is applied. If persistent, and the neuroma affects the dancer's ability to perform, a surgical excision should be considered.

Summary

Pronation and its biomechanical implications have been discussed. In the opinion of the authors, the mechanism presented is a common etiology for many overuse syndromes and injuries seen in athletic activity. Anatomical malalignment is a common etiology for increased pronatory movement. Pedal pronation beyond that considered normal may also occur as a result of specific types of physical activity even when alignment is within normal limits. Lower extremity adduction toward the body's midline and the subsequent pronation produced has been a well-documented finding secondary to running (Subotnick, 1975).

The authors have presented a comparable pronatory analysis for dance as related to the turnout utilized in classical ballet. A systematic examination has also been presented to analyze pronatory motion in dance as compared to normal walking status. The exam has also been used to interpret the mechanics not only of ballet but also of modern dancers. The degree to which other forms of dance are similar to ballet suggests the value of interpreting biomechanical relationships in the classical dance positions described. Control of this motion through conscious effort and an aggressive exercise program has been shown to be helpful.

An adjunctive use of strapping, padding, or orthotics may be useful in decreasing this motion and thus decreasing the possibility of developing overuse injuries related to the mechanism. Several overuse injuries have been discussed. The athlete or dancer should remember the pneumonic RICE when sustaining an acute injury. To decrease the likelihood of injury, strength and flexibility are probably the most valuable tools athletes can use. A few guidelines for an exercise program are offered.

References

Hamilton, C. (1984). *Traumatic disorders of the ankle*. New York: Springer-Verlag.

Haycock, Christine. (1980). *Sports medicine for the athlete* (p. 171). NJ: Medical Economics.

Hoerner, et al. (1982). *Sports injuries. The unthwarted epidemic* (p. 262). MA: PSG Publishing Co.

Insall, J. (1979). Chondromalacia patellae: Patellar malalignment syndrome. *Orthopedic Clinics of North America, 10*, 117-123.

Irvin, R., & Steven, R. (1983). *Sports medicine prevention, evaluation, management and rehabilitation* (p. 404). Englewood Cliffs, NJ: Prentice Hall.

Kravitz, R. (1984). *Clinics in Podiatry, 1*, 417-430.

Mann, R., & Inman, V.T. (1964). Biomechanics of the midtarsal joint. *Journal of Bone and Joint Surgery, 46A*, 476.

Miller, E.H., Schneider, H.J., Bronson, J.L., & McLain, D. (1975). A new consideration in athletic injuries—the classical ballet dancer. *Clinical Orthopedics, 111*, 181.

Root, M.L., Orien, W.P., & Weed, J.H. (1977). *Normal and abnormal function of the foot*, (Vol. 2, p. 301). CA: Clinical Biomechanics.

Sammarco, J.G. (1984). Treating dancers. *Contemporary Orthopedics*, **8**(4), 22.

Subotnick, S.I. (1975). *Podiatric sports medicine*. Mt. Kisco, NY: Futura Publishing Co.

Weil, L.S. (Lecturer). (1983). Dance medicine (Tape 2, Side 2). Hershey, PA: Pennsylvania Podiatry Association, Hershey Surgical Seminar.

5

Mechanical and Anatomical Factors Relating to the Incidence and Etiology of Patellofemoral Pain in Dancers

Karen S. Clippinger-Robertson, Robert S. Hutton,
Doris I. Miller, and T. Richard Nichols
UNIVERSITY OF WASHINGTON
SEATTLE, WASHINGTON, USA

In the professional experience of the author, the incidence of chondromalacia patella in dance patients has been quite high. Similary, Hamilton (1978), Howse (1972), and Vincent (1978) noted the common occurrence in dancers of knee problems including patellofemoral complaints. However, little quantitative information is available. The intent of this study was to examine the occurrence of this type of injury in dancers as well as possible etiological factors so that better preventative and rehabilitative procedures may be developed.

A brief literature review will be presented on the general description and mechanics of chondromalacia patella. This will be followed by the results of a survey of experienced ballet and modern dancers to assess the incidence of patellofemoral complaints and the dance movements that appear to aggravate the condition. Because of the importance of the plié as a common element of dance vocabulary and also the common report of pain associated with its execution, findings from an anatomical, electromyographical, and cinematographical analysis of the plié will be presented.

The author wishes to thank Pacific Northwest Ballet, Bill Evans Dance Theatre in Seattle, and other dancers who made this study possible.

Chondromalacia Patella—Description and Mechanics

The patella functions to increase the moment arm of the quadriceps femoris (Caillet, 1977; Ficat & Hungerford, 1977; Frankel, 1974), centralizes the divergent pulls of the muscles of the quadriceps femoris complex (Garrick, 1980; Meachim, 1983), and allows for a better distribution of compression stresses on the femur by increasing the surface contact area between the patellar tendon and femur (Caillet, 1977; Frankel & Nordin, 1980). The posterior surface of the patella is covered with hyaline articular cartilage, which further facilitates a reduction of compression stresses on the femur. The viscoelastic properties of this cartilage allow sufficient deformation under load to distribute contact forces over a relatively broad area, allowing great forces to be passed painlessly to the underlying bone (Hungerford & Barry, 1979; Meachim, 1983). In addition, these viscoelastic properties assist with transmission of quadriceps power around an angle during knee flexion with minimal losses due to friction.

In some instances, however, this cartilage can become damaged and undergo degeneration. The early stage of degeneration is characterized by a softening of the cartilage as it begins to imbibe water (Ficat, 1983) and hence this disorder is termed chondromalacia patella. Although chondromalacia patella literally means softened cartilage, it is most frequently diagnosed by its typical history and physical findings (Reider, Marshall, & Warren, 1981). Classical symptoms include nonspecific retropatellar or peripatellar pain, pain with knee flexion, pain going down stairs, weakness, swelling, and pain during or after activity (DeHaven, Dolan, & Mayer, 1979; Ficat & Hungerford, 1977; Garrick, 1980; Henry & Crosland, 1977; James, 1979, 1982; Reider et al., 1981). The most reliable and consistent signs appear to be tenderness with palpation of the patellar facets and a positive patellofemoral compression test performed with 20° of knee flexion (Insall, 1979; Levine & Splain, 1979).

A common theme among classic symptoms and signs is thus patella pain. It has been hypothosized that a biomechanical failure of the articular cartilage results in a functional disruption of load transference to the subchondral bone. This force may surpass the pain threshold of bone (Ficat, 1983; Ficat & Hungerford, 1977; Goodfellow, 1983; Insall, 1979) or result in changes in the bone and bone marrow (Ficat, 1983; Pickett & Radin, 1983) leading to elevated intramedullary pressures and pain. In addition, the products of articular cartilage destruction may act as irritants to the synovium and may also be a factor in the genesis of patellofemoral pain (Ficat, 1983; Ficat & Hungerford, 1973; Meachim, 1983).

Movements of the Patella

To understand the genesis of this cartilage destruction it is useful to examine patellofemoral mechanics. Movements of the patella are controlled by static and dynamic elements of the extensor mechanisms and the angular and torsional alignment of lower extremity segments proximal and distal to the patellofemoral joint (James, 1979). Static stabilizing elements include patellofemoral joint congruency and the various surrounding retinaculum and ligaments. The major dynamic stabilizer is the quadriceps femoris group, with particular importance being given the vastus medialis because of its function in preventing lateral movements of the patella (Bishop, 1977; Paulos, Rusche, Johnson, & Noyes, 1981). The medial angulation of the femur gives rise to the Q angle, which produces the tendency to pull the patella laterally. This Q angle, or quadriceps angle, is defined as the angle between lines connecting the anterior superior iliac spine of the pelvis to the center of the patella and the midpatella to the tibial tubercle (James, 1979). The underlying tendency for lateral movement of the patella that the Q angle produces is often termed the law of valgus and has been implicated in patellar pathomechanics.

Patellar Tracking

Although the valgus tendency is present in everyone, it can be profoundly exaggerated in some individuals for either structural or functional reasons. For example, extensor mechanism laxity results from such factors as patella alta, hypermobile patella, genu recurvatum, weakness of the anterior medial retinaculum, and vastus medialis weakness, which can all contribute to greater lateral excursion of the patella (Larson, 1974; Paulos et al., 1981). Similarly, patellar tracking can be influenced by malalignment of the extremity including genu valgus (Hlavac, 1977; Klein, 1983; Maron, 1978; Subotnick, 1975), femoral anteversion (Paulos et al., 1981), excessive foot pronation (Brody, Roneche, Woodley, & Kryder, 1981; Davies, Wallace, & Malone, 1981; James, 1979; Paulos et al., 1981), and an increased Q angle (Brody, 1979; Insall, Falvo, & Wise, 1976; James, 1982; Reider et al., 1981).

In turn, maltracking has been implicated in chondromalacia patella. The theory is that in many cases chondromalacia is caused by indirect trauma to the cartilage (Insall et al., 1976; Larson, 1974) from altered patellofemoral mechanics that results in abnormal absorption of stresses. Lateral motion of the patella is thought to produce excessive shear forces that, with repeated application, could produce pain (Insall, et al., 1979). One commonly presented scenario is that immobilization or overuse leads to atrophy of the quadriceps femoris muscle complex. This weakness, and particularly that of the vastus medialis, disrupts the delicate balance of the extensor mechanism in favor of the law of valgus (Paulos et al., 1981; Williams, 1974). This disruption of patellofemoral mechanics is further magnified by, or perhaps in some cases initiated by, other etiological factors such as anatomical deficiencies, extensor mechanism laxity, and lower extremity malalignment.

Survey Results

Surveys were given to 156 ballet and 206 modern dancers to ascertain the incidence of patellofemoral complaints in dancers. An attempt was made to gain a representation of the serious versus recreational dancer by selecting participants from summer workshops and the advanced and company classes associated with a professional ballet and a professional modern dance school in the Seattle area (Pacific Northwest Ballet and Bill Evans Dance Theatre in Seattle). The respondents were involved in approximately 3 to 8 hours of dance classes or rehearsals per day. Thus the results of this portion of the survey would not be reflective of the recreational dancer who takes a few classes per week. To exemplify this difference and to act as a comparison, 188 student from aerobic dance classes were also surveyed.

In examining the results of the survey (see Table 1), one can see that 62% of ballet dancers and 68% of modern dancers reported knee pain associated with dance at some time during their career. A general increase in the reported incidence of knee pain with higher levels of dance was also noted. This is not surprising in that the hours and technical demands increase as dance training progresses. The difference in knee pain versus the absence of knee pain by level reached statistical significance for modern dancers ($X^2 = 18.91$, $df = 3$, $p < .01$), but not the ballet dancers ($p < .05$). It was also interesting that a higher incidence of knee pain was reported by professional modern dancers (92%) than by professional ballet dancers (67%). Further studies would be necessary to determine if this difference was reflective of practices employed by these particular companies or of modern and ballet dancers in general.

In an effort to look more specifically at patellofemoral complaints, five questions were included on the survey that reflected five of the classical symptoms of chondromalacia previously listed. For the purposes of this study, a response of three or more classic symptoms of chondromalacia was considered indicative of the presence of patellofemoral complaints. From examining the diagnoses that were given on the surveys, this cutoff seemed to provide a good compromise for minimizing the counting of respondents with diagnoses other than patellofemoral complaints while also minimizing loss of repondents with diagnosed chondromalacia patella.

Including both modern and ballet dancers, 38% of 362 dancers reported having three or more of these classic symptoms of chondromalacia patella (see Table 1). However, although this response should reflect the incidence of patellofemoral complaints quite well, because 48% of ballet and 53% of modern dancers did not consult a physician and so did not list a diagnosis, it was impossible to verify whether or not these dancers had chondromalacia patella. Of the 68 diagnoses that were listed, 72% appeared to represent clinical chondromalacia patella. If one extrapolates from this, one could roughly approxi-

Table 1. Summary of patellofemoral injury survey

Type of dance	Number of surveys	Knee pain (dance)	3 or more symptoms	Knee pain (nondance)	No injury
Ballet	156	94 (61.5%)	56 (35.9%)	0 —	21 (13.5%)
Modern	206	139 (67.5%)	80 (38.8%)	14 (6.8%)	22 22
Total	362	235 (64.9%)	136 (37.6%)	14 (3.9%)	43 (11.9%)
Aerobics	188	51 (27.1%)	25 (13.3%)	26 (13.8%)	109 (58.0%)

mate that about 27% of ballet and modern dancers surveyed may have had chondromalacia patella. This is quite similar to the author's clinical experience where 31% of 287 dancers exhibited classical signs and symptoms of chondromalacia patella.

Because this survey represents only the serious dancer, the 38% incidence of patellofemoral complaints might be quite similar to that of the distance runner who runs 40 miles per week or more (Aple, 1979; Bierman & Ralston, 1965; Brody et al., 1981; Stanish, 1984). If one considers the aerobic dance population, where only 13% reported they had experienced three of more classic symptoms of chondromalacia patella (see Table 1), it becomes clear that the incidence of reported patellofemoral complaints would be markedly lower if recreational and casual dancers were included in the population under investigation.

In summary, despite the limitations of survey methods, the results suggested that the incidence of patellofemoral complaints in serious dancers is quite high. Differences in reported incidence for either knee pain or patellofemoral complaints between ballet and modern dancers were not significant ($X^2 = 1.7148$ and .2134, respectively, $df = 1$, $p > .05$) and were probably similar to or higher than the serious distance runner. Because many dancers are hesitant to seek medical help and are noted for their tendency to "dance through pain," the incidence of this knee condition may not be adequately represented in the literature.

Etiological Factors Related to the Incidence of Chondromalacia Patella

When questioning the high incidence of chondromalacia patella seen in dancers, consideration must be given to the large patellofemoral compression forces associated with many dance movements.

Patellofemoral Compression Forces

The two most critical factors in determining patellofemoral joint reaction (PFJR) forces are the angle of knee flexion and the force produced by the contraction of the quadriceps femoris (Marquet, 1979; Perry, Antonelli, & Ford, 1975). As knee flexion increases, the center of gravity of the body falls increasingly posterior to the center of rotation of the knee. This shift of the center of gravity enlarges the flexor moment at the knee, which in turn requires greater contraction of the quadriceps in order to maintain an equilibrium (Hungerford, 1983). Furthermore, with increasing knee flexion a greater amount of the force generated by the quadriceps is transmitted into compression of the patella against the femur due to an increase in the angle formed between the quadriceps tendon and the patellar tendon (Hungerford, 1983; Marquet, 1979). Thus, with increasing flexion, both an increasing quadriceps force and an increase in the percentage of this force being directed toward the patellofemoral joint act synergistically to increase PFJR forces.

Knee Flexion During Pliés

To gain a better understanding of the magnitude of the knee flexion accompanying dance movements, knee angles at first, second, and fifth demi- and grand pliés in 52 dancers were measured with a gonimometer. An unexpected finding was the tremendous variation among dancers even when considering the same type and level of dancer (see Table 2). Note the large ranges found in all positions. In comparing the ranges of ballet dancers to modern dancers, much overlap is apparent, although the mean magnitude of knee flexion was slightly greater for five of six positions in ballet than in modern dancers.

The angles of knee flexion seen in Table 2 that occurred during demi-pliés and second position grand pliés would be somewhat similar to those seen with some studies of the activities of daily living. For example, stair descending is accompanied by approximately 90° knee flexion and rising from a chair with 100° knee flexion (Seedham, 1981). PFJR forces for these activities have been calculated to be approximately 3.3 times body weight (Reilly & Martens, 1972; Seedham, 1981). With greater degrees of knee flexion, similar to those seen with grand pliés, PFJR forces have been estimated to be as high as 7 to 9 times body weight (Bishop, 1977).

Thus, the plié in its various positions utilizes quite large angles of knee flexion. As the knee bends, eccentric contraction of the quadriceps occurs, the patella is pushed with great pressure against the femur (Glick, Gordon, & Scheck, 1973; Quirk, 1983), and large PFJR forces are produced. However, since the magnitude of quadriceps force also dramatically affects compression forces, even larger forces would be expected in dance movements requiring greater quadriceps force. A subtle example of this would be the addition of torso movements to grand pliés (as is a common practice in modern dance), which appears to further increase extensor moments at the knee (Lessard, 1980).

A more obvious example would be bending the knee with all the body weight on one leg versus two (e.g., a fondu). In an EMG study, Brewerton (1955)

Table 2. Comparison of degrees of knee flexion accompanying selected pliés in dancers with and without patellofemoral complaints

Type of dance	First-position demi		Second-position grand		Fifth-position demi	
	PF	No PF	PF	No PF	PF	No PF
Ballet						
Adv.-Pro. mean	74	56	123	110	79	56
Ballet mean	68	73	107	106	68	66
Ballet range	45-89	45-97	75-147	80-123	43-97	40-85
Modern						
Adv.-Pro. mean	59	70	92	97	57	70
Modern mean	59	66	89	98	61	68
Modern range	40-77	43-87	67-110	82-109	38-70	55-82
Overall						
Adv.-Pro. mean	67	63	108	104	68	63
Overall mean	64	70	98	102	65	67
Overall range	40-89	43-97	67-147	80-123	38-97	40-85

found that such a movement to 90° knee flexion was accompanied by 50% to 80% maximum voluntary isometric contraction of the vastus medialis and 45% to 85% maximum voluntary isometric contraction of the vastus lateralis. This was approximately 4 times the EMG amplitude seen with stepping up a 6-in. stair. It is also interesting to note that this movement so commonly performed in dance, has been suggested as one of the tests that can be utilized for identification of retropatellar cartilage degeneration (James, 1979).

Additional examples of movements requiring large quadriceps forces are floor work and jumps. The former often requires weight to be on one leg as the dancers lower themselves and then rise from the floor. This frequently is done very rapidly and involves extreme angles of knee flexion, twisting, and sometimes all of the body weight resting on one knee. Large PFJR forces would be expected to accompany such movements.

Jumping may produce the largest PFJR forces in dance. Smith (cited in Dowson & Wright, 1981) found vertical ground reaction forces to be approximately 2 and 6 times body weight when landing from .305 m (12 in.) and 1.07 m (42 in.), respectively. Dowson and Wright (1981) calculated that the PFJR forces associated with this latter jump would be approximately 20 times body weight and would involve the generation of about 9,600 N of force by the quadriceps femoris. In three dancers measured doing a grand jeté, vertical ground reaction forces ranged from 3.0 to 6.3 times body weight (Clippinger & Novak, 1981).

Considering the large forces that appear to accompany dance movements, it is interesting to speculate as to the possible effects of the previously noted large variation among dancers in knee flexion on patellofemoral pathology. The shifting of surface contact areas, lever arms, and quadriceps forces associated with different angles of knee flexion might make such a consideration important. Although further investigation would be necessary to establish a definitive trend, preliminary results suggest that when examining first-position demi-pliés, fifth-position demi-pliés, and second-position grand pliés (see Table 2), modern dancers with patellofemoral complaints tended to exhibit lower values for knee flexion. This trend was most marked at the advanced and professional level. In contrast, with advanced and professional ballet dancers, this trend appeared to be reversed. Lower ballet levels appeared similar to modern dancers.

Although at first these results appear contradictory, it could be that dancers with extremes (i.e., either reduced range or excessive range of knee flexion) might be more vulnerable to patellofemoral complaints. Decreased range could be associated with greater force being absorbed per unit of time in such movements as jumps. Furthermore, pronation is commonly used by the dancer with a tight Achilles tendon in an attempt to gain more ankle dorsiflexion, which results in a deeper plié. The association between pronation and patellofemoral complaints has been previously noted. On the other hand, the dancer with excessive range may need to work for sufficient strength to control that range and may also have an increased tendency for greater genu recurvatum and extensor mechanism laxity. If these noted differences were found to hold with dancers from other schools, it could provide some insight for rehabilitation and injury screening.

Turnout

Considering the large PFJR forces that appear to accompany the previously discussed dance movements, it is not surprising that many of these movements were listed as aggravates of knee pain by dancers suffering from patellofemoral complaints on the previously described survey (see Table 3). Another commonly listed aggravate was turnout. Although technically this rotation occurs at the hip, in reality the direction of the feet versus the knees is often used as a measure of turnout. In the search for perfect turnout, many dancers add rotation from the knee downward. With 90° of knee flexion, which is similar to that used in second-position grand pliés, a maximum of external rotation of the tibia is possible and ranges from 40° to 50° (Caillet, 1977; Frankel & Nordin, 1980; Steindler, 1977). Even with just slight knee flexion of 32°, about 30° of rotation of the tibia is possible (Steindler, 1977). Theoretically, almost no transverse plane motion is possible at full extension (Frankel & Nordin, 1980), but even here many dancers have stretched out soft tissues sufficiently to allow tibial rotation.

When this practice of forced turnout is utilized, excessive torsional stress is borne by the knee (Clippinger & Novak, 1981). Functionally, it produces an increased Q angle and a composite of relative internal femoral rotation, infacing patella, relative tibial torsion, and foot pronation. Thus the components of the miserable malalignment syndrome are functionally created. The role of torsional and angular malalignments of the lower extremity in influencing patellofemoral mechanics and predisposing the individual to chondromalacia patella has already been noted (James, 1979).

Examination of the Second-Position Plié

The implication of forced turnout in patellar pathomechanics led to an investigation of the possible relationship between dance technique, as reflected by the plié, and patellofemoral disorders. An anatomical model was used to ex-

Table 3. Dance movements that were frequently reported to aggravate knees of ballet and modern dancers with patellofemoral complaints

Dance movement	Ballet	Percent reported Modern	Both
Plié	60% (27)	69% (41)	65% (68)
Grand plié	16% (7)	15% (9)	15% (16)
Jumps	27% (12)	22% (13)	24% (25)
Flexion to extension	18% (8)	22% (13)	20% (21)
Turnout	20% (9)	10% (6)	14% (15)
Kneeling/floor work	0% (0)	20% (12)	12% (12)
Number of respondents	45	59	104

amine possible muscle function at the hip during a second-position grand plié. This was followed by a cinematographic and electromyographic evaluation of the plié formed by dancers with and without a history of patellofemoral complaints. The second-position plié was chosen for study in order to avoid the potential danger of sustained maintenance of a first- or a fifth-position grand plié.

Anatomical Model

A model was made by placing screw eyes in a skeleton at the approximate center of proximal and distal attachments of muscles that cross the hip joint. Measurements were taken of the distance between these screw eyes for each muscle under the following conditions: (a) standing in second position, (b) correct second-position grand plié, and (c) incorrect second-position grand plié. It is important to keep in mind that the changes in length were reflective of the axial line of pull of the measured muscles and not of the muscle fibers themselves.

An examination of the transition from standing in second position to a grand plié revealed fairly large changes in length in the adductor brevis, adductor longus, adductor magnus, quadriceps femoris, sartorius, tensor fascia latae, and biceps femoris. All of these changes, excluding the sartorius, involve an increase in length, potentially associated with an eccentric contraction. In bending the knees, as gravity is resisted, one would expect an eccentric use of both knee and hip extensors. Thus it is not surprising to see the large change in the quadriceps or biceps femoris. The biceps femoris could also be utilized in its role of external rotation of the tibia (Basmajian, 1978; Marshall, Girgis, & Zelko, 1972; Rasch & Burke, 1978).

A less commonly noted participant is the adductor group. When considering the turned-out position, where motion ideally occurs in an almost frontal plane, the muscles seem to be in an appropriate position to provide important assistance. This conjecture was given some support by electromyographic recordings taken during standing in first position. A marked adductor activity was noted in three of the four ballet dancers tested (see Figure 1). This activity was much less pronounced in the four modern dancers monitored. The possible secondary actions of the adductor muscles should also be considered when interpreting this apparent activity in some dance movements (Green & Morris, 1970; Jonsson & Steen, 1966; Rasch & Burke, 1978; Vincent, 1978).

Lastly, when normalizing the length changes relative to the length of that muscle in standing, marked changes can also be noted with some of the deep outward rotators of the hip. This is not surprising, but unfortunately these muscles are not readily accessible to surface electromyography recordings.

Cinematography and Electromyography Materials and Methods

Fourteen subjects were chosen and matched according to type and level of dance. All were ballet or modern dancers of an intermediate to professional

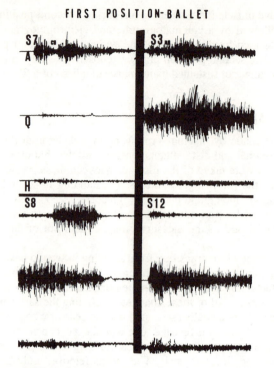

Figure 1. First position of ballet

Electromyography key

A = adductor (adductor longus)
Q = quadriceps femoris (vastus medialis)
H = hamstring (biceps femoris)
S = subject number
CH = subject with chondromalacia patella
NO = subject with no history of chondromalacia patella
N = normal plié
C = corrected plié
MVC = maximum voluntary isometric contraction
O = 0° of knee flexion (straight knee position)
30 = 30° of knee flexion
60 = 60° of knee flexion
F = full knee flexion at depth of plié

level. Each subject performed pliés on a 0.6 by 0.9 m aluminum plate within the space defined by four poles with known (control) points. Two mirrors located at angles to this aluminum plate served as "cameras." A Nikon camera was appropriately placed so that direct linear transformation can be utilized at a later time for three-dimensional analysis. The present report utilized a preliminary two-dimensional analysis from film records taken at 30°, 60°, 90°, and full-knee flexion in a second-position grand plié.

This portion of the testing session was immediately followed by a series of pliés that were monitored with EMG and filmed with a Locam camera at 30 frames/1 s. Taking into consideration the previously described anatomical model, electrode sites were chosen to include the vastus medialis, biceps femoris, and adductor longus. The muscle potentials were connected to Grass P15 preamplifiers. These amplified potentials were monitored on an oscilloscope and simultaneously stored on a seven-channel FM tape recorder. Later the recorded signals were put through a Grass polygraph to produce hard copy for comparative purposes.

Cinematography Results

The film records were examined with regard to trunk lean, lumbar lordosis, pronation, and an angle reflective of Q angle. These measures were chosen because of their influence of patellofemoral mechanics. Due to perspective errors, these preliminary measures are only approximate and relative. However, when used solely for comparison of subjects filmed under the same conditions, they should provide a useful reflection of subject differences. A description of these measures and the results for the five paired subjects appear in Table 4. (Four subjects were unmatched due to loss of their partner or to intermediate chondromalacia status.) Appropriate points (landmarks) taken from the film records of each subject's full second position grand plié were used for analysis (see Figure 2).

Examination of the results (see Table 4) reveals a slight trend for increased trunk inclination and lumbar lordosis in subjects with chondromalacia patella when compared to their matched partners without chondromalacia patella. Incidence and degree of pronation showed no consistent difference between paired subjects. Lastly, P angle appeared to be markedly greater in subjects with chondromalacia. Because of the mirror position, P angle would probably reflect a combination of Q angle and amount of hip rotation.

These results demonstrate that subjects with chondromalacia patella did not as closely approximate the ideal criteria for pliés of a vertical descent and prevention of an anterior pelvic tilt (Lessard, 1980) as did their counterparts without chondromalacia (e.g., see Figure 2). This anterior pelvic tilt could affect knee position, as could muscle use, foot placement, and anatomical limits of hip rotation. A closer evaluation of these factors will have to await further analysis utilizing three-dimensional techniques. However, the initial finding suggest that some consistent differences in technique may be present in subjects with chondromalacia patella.

Electromyography Results

When examining the general pattern of muscle activity that occurred during performance of a normal second-position grand plié, 11 of 14 subjects showed the greatest EMG amplitude in the vastus medialis. In terms of relative magnitude, quadriceps activity was followed in a majority of cases by the biceps femoris, with the adductor longus generally demonstrating the lowest relative magnitude. In some cases there was a rather symmetrical rise and fall of muscle

Table 4. Comparison of selected measures of the second-position grand plié from film records

	Subjects with chondromalacia patella					Subjects without chondromalacia patella			
Subject	Trunk[a] lean	Lumbar[b] lordosis	P[c] angle	Pseudo-[d] pronation	Subject	Trunk lean	Lumbar lordosis	P angle	Pseudo- pronation
1	0	–	37	+1	4	0	–	13	+½
2	8	++	22	+½	3	4	+	0	+½
7	8	+	36	+½	6	7	–	0	+1
13	9	+	42	–	9	6	+	37	–
14	4	++	23	+1	10	5	–	33	+1

[a]Trunk lean: angle of line connecting greater trochanter to mid-shoulder from the vertical as seen in camera 2; positive values indicate forward inclination of the trunk from the vertical.

[b]Lumbar lordosis: + = mild lordosis; ++ = marked lordosis; – = no lordosis (as seen in camera 2).

[c]P angle: angle of line connecting midpoint of patella to tibial tubercle and a line connecting the anterior superior iliac spine to the midpoint of the patella as seen in camera 2 (comparable to the Q angle measured with knee extended).

[d]Pseudo-pronation: distance of tubercle of the navicular from a line connecting the medial malleolus and head of the first metatarsal as seen in camera 1: +1 = drop of ⅓ of the distance from this line to the ground; +2 = drop of ⅔ of this distance.

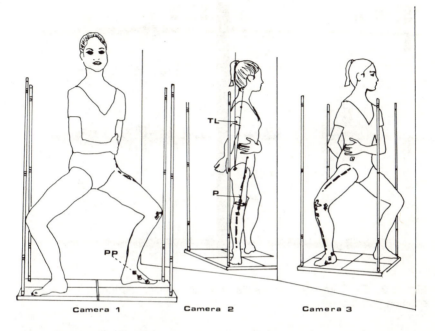

Figure 2. Second position plié of subject without clinical chondromalacia patella s(3)
TL = Trunk lean — P = *P* angle — LL = Lumbar Lordosis — PP = Pseudo Pronation

activity (e.g., *Q* of Subject 7 in Figure 4) while in other cases there were multiple peaks and asymmetric spindles (e.g., *Q* of Subject 3 in Figure 3). Perhaps the most noteworthy observation was the marked variability among subjects. This suggests that activation patterns for a plié clearly reflect differences in individual control.

Normal Versus Chondromalacia

Several differences are apparent when comparing matched subjects with and without chondromalacia patella. In four of five matched pairs, subjects with chondromalacia demonstrated slightly higher peak amplitudes in the quadriceps than their counterparts who were free of knee problems (e.g., see Figure 3). An extreme example of this can be seen with Subject 13 (see Figure 5). The peak amplitude of the quadriceps (vastus medials) in Subject 13 was more than 2 times higher than that seen in her matched intermediate level partner and almost 3 times greater than that in Subject 3 (professional, nonchondromalacia, ballet dancer). When looking at the peak amplitude relative to recorded maximum voluntary isometric contractions (MVC) the difference is even more marked. While Subject 3 utilized only an approximate 25% MVC during a second-position grand plié, Subject 13 utilized an approximate 128% MVC of the quadriceps in the same dance movement.

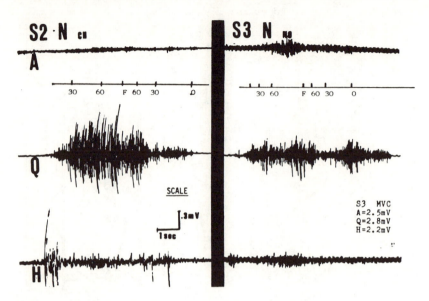

Figure 3. Electromyography results of muscle activity during normal second-position grand plié

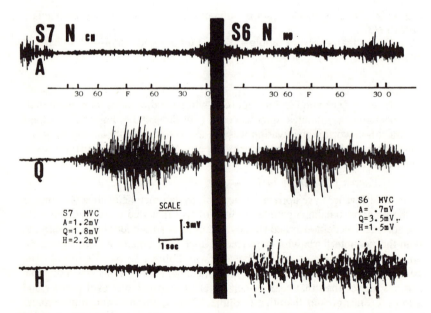

Figure 4. Electromyography results of muscle activity during normal second-position grand plié

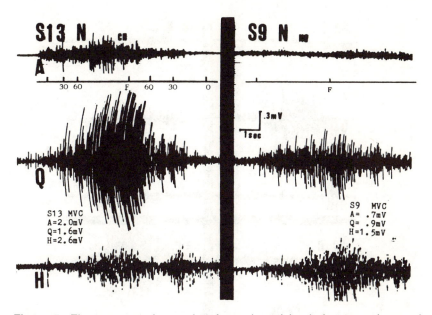

Figure 5. Electromyography results of muscle activity during normal second-position grand plié

Quadriceps activity also appeared to be sightly more dispersed in four of five nonchondromalacia subjects (e.g., see Figure 4). Another trend was the tendency for greater activity in the hamstrings and adductors in the nonchondromalacia versus chondromalacia partners (e.g., see Figure 4). Thus there appeared to be a general trend of greater quadriceps dominance with less co-contraction of the adductors and hamstrings in subjects with chondromalacia patella. An interesting example occurred with Subject 7 (see Figure 4). Marked adductor longus activity was present while standing in second position. However, as soon as knee flexion began there was a rapid cutoff of adductor activity and greater resultant quadriceps dominance. As the plié was completed, marked adductor activity was again present.

Normal Versus Correct Pliés

An attempt was made with several subjects to improve their plié with approximately five minutes of instruction. Four were successful, as evidenced by the knee going more directly to the frontal plane in Locam film recordings. Subjects 3 and 2 were most successful and their EMG records can be seen in Figure 6. In Subject 3 such dramatic increase in adductor activity occurred that the adductors became the most dominant muscle and the quadriceps showed the lowest relative magnitude. A definite although less marked increase also occurred in hamstring activity. Subject 2 showed an increase in activity of

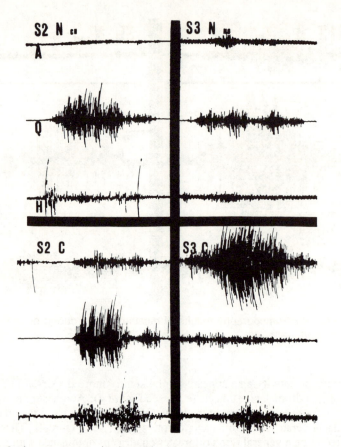

Figure 6. Improvements in the plié with 5 minutes of instruction

all three recorded muscles. Among these muscles there appeared to be a slightly greater increase in adductor and hamstring compared to quadriceps amplitude when performing the corrected plié.

Discussion and Summary

This presentation is not meant to imply that technique is the only factor leaning to the apparent susceptibility of the dance population to chondromalacia patella. Surely such factors as the larger percentage of women in dance (Glick, 1973; Haycock & Gilette, 1976; Henche, 1978), the prevalent aesthetic demand for hyper-extended knees (Howse, 1972), extreme flexibility (Glick, 1973; Powers, 1979), the tendency for quadriceps weakness (Anderson, Cote, Coyle, & Roby, 1979; Haycock & Gilette, 1976; Kirkendall et al., 1984; Mostardi, Porterfield, Greenberg, & Lea, 1983; Powers, 1979), and rampant training errors are likely also to play a role in the genesis of the disorder and could help to explain the high reported incidence obtained by survey methods. However, with the large angles of knee flexion where large quadriceps torques and small patellofemoral contact areas make large patellofemoral compression forces inherent to dance, it seems likely that technique errors that produce patellar pathomechanics provide one important consideration.

Cinematographic analysis demonstrated a slight trend for increased angles of trunk inclination and lumbar lordosis as well as markedly greater P angles in subjects with chondromalacia patella when compared to their matched partners without chondromalacia. Each of these factors could negatively affect patellofemoral mechanics.

Preliminary electromyography findings suggest that dancers with chondromalacia may utilize greater amplitudes and dominance of quadriceps activity. This may have significance in that PFJR forces are directly related to the force generated by the quadriceps. The EMG results also suggest that co-contraction of the adductors and hamstrings during second-position grand pliés may be desirable. Dancers without chondromalacia tended to demonstrate more co-contraction than their matched partners with chondromalacia. Furthermore, attempts at correction were associated with an even greater preponderance of co-contraction with greater reliance on adductor activity. However, care should be taken in drawing definitive conclusions because the number of subjects was small and the variability in muscle activation patterns across subjects prevailed to the point that it would be difficult, simply by inspection of their EMG patterns, to correctly categorize subjects with and subjects without chondromalacia patella.

Perhaps the clearest finding was that the seemingly consistent activation pattern of each dancer was often quite different from that of other dancers. Despite the consistency, with cueing some dancers were able to profoundly alter their pattern. This plasticity suggests the importance of technique and implies that feedback from teachers, kinesiologists, or medical personnel could be effective in altering motor patterns. However, further research will be necessary to more clearly define the ideal that should be replicated to clarify the interplay of technique and injury.

References

Anderson, M.B. Cote, R., Coyle, E.F., & Roby, F.B. (1979). Leg power, muscle strength and peak EMG activity in physically active college men and women (abstract). *Medicine and Science in Sports and Exercise, 11*, 81-82.

Aple, D.F. (1979). Knee pain in runners. *South Medical Journal, 11*, 1372-1379.

Basmajian, J.V. (1978). *Muscles alive*. Baltimore: Williams and Wilkins.

Bierman, W. & Ralston, H. (1965). Electromyographic study during passive and active flexion and extension of the knee in the normal human subject. *Archives of Physical Medicine, 46*, 71-75.

Bishop, R. (1977). On the mechanics of the human knee. *Engineering in Medicine, 6*(2), 46-52.

Brewerton, D.A. (1955). The function of the vastus medialis muscle. *Annuals of Physical Medicine, 2*(5), 164-168.

Brody, D. (1979). *The knee in running*. Paper presented at the 13th Annual Sports Medicine and Conditioning Seminar, Seattle.

Brody, D, Roneche, S., Woodley, S., & Kryder, S. (1981, July). A Study of 4,000 running injuries. *Running Times*, pp. 22-29.

Caillet, R. (1977). *Soft tissue pain and disability*. Philadelphia: F.A. Davis.

Clippinger, K., & Novak, M. (1981). *Comparison of ground reaction forces in landing from a grand jeté with bare feet versus pointe shoes*. Unpublished paper, University of Washington.

Davies, G., Wallace, L., & Malone, T. (1981). Mechanisms of selected knee injuries. In *The knee*. American Physical Therapy Association, Alexandria, Virginia.

Dehaven, D.E., Dolan, W. & Mayer, P. (1979). Chondromalacia patella in athletes: Clinical presentation and conservative management. *American Journal of Sports Medicine, 7*(1), 5-11.

Dowson, D., & Wright, V. (1981). *An introduction to the biomechanics of joints and joint replacement*. London: Mechanical Engineering Publications.

Ficat, P. (1983). Lateral fascia release and lateral hyperpressure syndrome. In J.C. Pickett & E.L. Radin (Eds.), *Chondromalacia of the patella*, (pp. 95-112). Baltimore: Williams and Wilkins.

Ficat, R.P., & Hungerford, D.S. (1977). *Disorders of the patellofemoral joint*. Baltimore: Williams and Wilkins.

Frankel, V.H. (1974). Biomechanics of the knee. In A. Helfet (Ed.), *Disorders of the knee*. Philadelphia: J.B. Lippincott Co.

Frankel, V., Nordin, M. (1980). *Basic biomechanics of the skeletal system*. Philadelphia: Lea and Febiger.

Garrick, J. (1980). *The knee*. Presented at the Bay Area Conference in Sports Medicine, San Francisco.

Glick, F.M. (1973). The female knee in athletics. *The Physician and Sportsmedicine, 2*(9), 35-37.

Glick, J.M., Gordon, R.B., & Scheck, M. (1973). Arthrography of the knee. Presented at the 40th Annual Meeting of the American Academy of Orthopaedic Surgeons, Las Vegas.

Goodfellow, J. (1983). Cartilage lesions and chondromalacia. In J.C. Pickett & E.L. Radin (Eds.), *Chondromalacia of the patella* (pp. 43-48). Baltimore: Williams and Wilkins.

Green, D.L., & Morris, J.M. (1970). Role of the adductor longus and adductor magnus in postural movements and in ambulation. *American Journal of Physical Medicine, 49*(4), 223-240.

Hamilton, W.G. (1978. Ballet and your body: An orthapaedist's view. *Dance Magazine, 8*(6), 84-85.

Haycock, C.E., & Gilette, J.V. (1976). Susceptibility of women athletes to injuries: Myths versus reality. *Journal of the American Medical Association, 236*(2), 163-165.

Henche, H.R. (1978). Patellar shaving: Indications, techniques, results. In D.E. Hastings (Ed.), *The knee* (pp. 157-164). New York: Springer-Verlag.

Henry, J., & Crosland, J.W. (1977). Conservative treatment of patellofemoral subluxation. *American Journal of Sports Medicine, 7*(1), 12-14.

Hlavac, H. (1977). *The foot book* (pp. 232-238). Mountain View, CA: World Publications.

Howse, A.J.G. (1972). Orthopaedists aid ballet. *Clinical Orthopaedics and Related Research, 89*, 52-63.

Hungerford, D.S., & Barry, M. (1979). Biomechanics of the patellofemoral joint. *Clinical Orthopaedics and Related Research, 144*, 9-15.

Hungerford, D.S. (1983). Patellar subluxation and excessive lateral pressure as a cause of fibrillation. In J.C. Pickett & E.L. Radin (Eds.), *Chondromalacia of the patella*, (pp. 24-42). Baltimore: Williams and Wilkins.

Insall, J., Falvo, K. & Wise, D.W. (1976). Chondromalacia patella: A prospective study. *Journal of Bone Joint Surgery,* **58A**, 1-8.

Insall, J. (1979). Chondromalacia patellas: Patellar malalignment syndrome. *Orthopedic Clinics of North America,* **10**(1), 117-127.

James, S. (1982). Acute and chronic conditions of the patella (Tape). Symposium on *The Athletes Knee.* Cincinnati University Sports Medicine and Orthopaedic Center, Cincinnati.

James, S.L. (1979). Chondromalacia of the patella in the adolescent. In J.C. Kennedy (Ed.), *The injured adolescent knee* (p. 205). Baltimore: Williams and Wilkins.

Jonsson, B. & Steen, B. (1966). Function of the gracilis muscle: An electromyographic study. *Acta. Morphologica Neerlando-Scandinavia,* **VI**(4), 325-341.

Kirkendall, D.T., Bergfield, J.A., Calabrese, L., Lomardo, J.A., Street, G., & Weiker, G.G. (1984). Isokinetic characteristics of ballet dancers and the response to a season of ballet training. *The Journal of Orthopaedics & Sports Physical Therapy,* **6**(1), 207-211.

Klein, K.K. (1983). Developmental Asymmetries and Knee Injury. *The Physician and Sportsmedicine,* **11**(8), 67-76.

Larson, R. (1974). Chondromalacia: The patella of the female athlete—Subluxation, chondromalacia and patellar compression syndrome. *Medical Aspects of Sports,* **16**, 12-18.

Lessard, B. (1980). *Biomechanical analysis of the classical grand plié and two stylistic variations.* Unpublished doctoral thesis. Texas Women's University, Denton.

Maquet, P. (1979). Mechanics and osteoarthritis of the patellofemoral joint. *Clinical Orthopaedic and Related Research,* **144**, 70-73.

Maron, D. (1978). Prevention of overuse injuries in the distance runner. In K. Scriber & E.J. Burke (Eds.), *Relevant topics in athletic training.* New York: Mouvement Publications.

Marshall, J.L., Girgis, F.G., & Zelko, R.R. (1972). The biceps femoris tendon and its functional significance. *Journal of Bone Joint Surgery,* **54**(7), 1444-1450.

Meachim, G. (1983). Cartilage lesions on the patella. In J.C. Pickett & E.L. Radin (Eds.), *Chondromalacia of the patella* (pp. 1-10). Baltimore: Williams and Wilkins.

Mostardi, R.A., Porterfield, J.A., Greenberg, D., & Lea, M. (1983). Musculoskeletal and cardipulmonary characteristics of the professional ballet dancer. *The Physician and Sportsmedicine,* **11**(12), 53-61.

Paulos, L., Rusche, K., Johnson, C., & Noyes, F. (1981). Patellar malalignment, a treatment rationale. In *The knee.* American Physical Therapy Association, Alexandria, Virginia.

Perry, J., Antonelli, D., & Ford, W. (1975). Analysis of knee-joint forces during flexed knee stance. *Journal of Bone Joint Surgery,* **57A**(7)), 961-967.

Pickett, J.C., & Radin, E.L. (1983). *Chondromalacia of the patella.* Baltimore: Williams and Wilkins.

Powers, J.A. (1979). Characteristic features of injuries in the knees in women. *Clinical Orthopaedic and Related Research,* **143**, 120-124.

Quirk, R. (1983). Ballet Injuries: The Australian experience. *Clinics in Sports Medicine,* **2**(3), 507-514.

Rasch, P.J., & Burke, R.K. (1978). *Kinesiology and applied anatomy.* Philadelphia: Lea and Febiger.

Reider, B., Marshall, J., & Warren, R. (1981). Clinical Characteristics of Patellar Disorders in Young Athletes. *The American Journal of Sports Medicine,* **9**(4), 270.

Reilly, D.J., & Martens, M. (1972). Experimental analysis of the quadriceps muscle function and patellofemoral joint reaction force for various activities. *Acta Orthopaedica Scandinavica,* **43**, 126-137.

Seedham, B.B. (1981). Knee. In D. Dowson and V. Wright (Eds.), *An introduction to biomechanics of joints and joint replacement.* London: Mechanical Engineering.

Stanish, W.D. (1984). Overuse injuries in athletes: A perspective. *Medicine and Science in Sports*, **16**(1), 1-17.

Steindler, A. (1977). *Kinesiology of the human body*. Springfield, IL: Charles C. Thomas.

Subotnick, S. (1975). Orthotic foot control and overuse syndrome. *The Physician and Sportsmedicine*, **3**(1), 75-79.

Vincent, L.M. (1978). *The dancer's book of health*. Kansas City: Sheed Andrews and McNeal.

Williams, J. (1974). Vastus medialis re-education in the management of chondromalacia patella. *Medical Aspects of Sports*, **16**, 19-24.

6

First Aid, Immediate Care, and Rehabilitation of Knee and Ankle Injuries in Dancers and Athletes

Carol C. Teitz
UNIVERSITY OF WASHINGTON
SEATTLE, WASHINGTON, USA

When considering the rehabilitation of knee and ankle injuries in dancers and athletes, one must first appreciate the differences and similarities between sports and dance. Neither dancers nor athletes want to stop their activities. Both must be strong as well as supple. Athletes are generally strong but need to be more supple. Dancers on the other hand are usually quite supple but often need strengthening. Professional dancers are more likely to be malnourished than professional athletes and this makes the healing of injuries slower and more difficult.

Dance is an art form and must appear effortless. A dancer may not overtly grimace as the hurdler might when achieving equivalent height in a jump. Limping into the wings is not greeted with the same applause that the injured quarterback receives when he struggles to the bench. Moreover, in a small company, there is no bench. Often only one dancer can perform a given role and, if that person is significantly injured, the company must either cancel a performance or change the program. In addition, because of the importance of appearance, supportive knee or ankle braces usually cannot be worn when performing.

Dance is not seasonal. Spring training or a true off-season does not exist. Finding time to rehabilitate an injury is often difficult in dance. Although dancers do have specific performing seasons, they attend classes the year around. When they are performing, their work schedule resembles the Olympic decathlon. Despite the different demands of dance and sport, however, the principles of treatment and rehabilitation of injuries in the two are really quite similar.

Knee and ankle problems and injuries are common in both dance and sports. The types of problems seen in the knee include overuse injuries such as patellofemoral pain, jumper's knee (patellar tendinitis), and medial knee strain, as well as traumatic injuries such as a torn meniscus, ligament tears, and patellar subluxation and dislocation. In the ankle, tendinitis is common in both athletes and dancers. Dancers may also suffer from anterior impingement by talar spurs or posterior impingement by the os trigonum. Traumatic injuries in both groups, however, usually fall into one of two categories: ankle sprains or Achilles tendon rupture. Although this discussion is limited to immediate care and rehabilitation of acute traumatic knee and ankle injuries in athletes and dancers, the principles and many of the specifics apply to the treatment of overuse injuries as well.

In sports, traumatic ankle injuries predominate in volleyball and basketball, and knee injuries predominate in sports that involve cleated shoes and fixation of the foot, such as football and soccer. In dancers, these types of knee and ankle injuries appear to be more prevalent in ballet than in modern or aerobic dance (J. Garrick, personal communication, March, 1984), possibly because of the required rotation. The data may be skewed, however, because of the dearth of data on modern dancers. Quirk's (1983) study of 2,113 ballet dancers revealed an incidence of 22% ankle injuries and 17% knee injuries. In the study by Washington (1978) of 1,662 dance injuries, knee injuries accounted for 14% to 34% and ankle injuries for 13% to 21%. In these particular studies, tendinitis and chondromalacia were also included as injuries, accounting for the high incidence. Washington's series included seven verified meniscal tears, nine "dislocations and chondromalacia" of the patella, and three fractured patellae. In the ankle he found three fractures and 38 ligament injuries, which included three Achilles tendon ruptures.

First Aid

In all cases of significant injury to either the knee or the ankle, the athlete or dancer will note sudden pain during execution of a movement. Pain will increase during attempts to bear weight, and in some cases bearing weight may not be possible. Significant swelling usually occurs within the first 12 hours after injury.

Immediate care should include rest, ice, compression, and elevation (RICE). Rapid application of ice and compression wrapping of the injured area will minimize hemorrhage and swelling. Elevation of the leg, preferably above heart level, will also markedly decrease the amount of swelling after injury. If one can minimize swelling and bleeding immediately following an injury, the body will need to do less "clean up" before the healing process begins. The injured area should be rested to avoid further trauma and a diagnosis should be made as soon as possible so that treatment can proceed quickly.

Knee Injuries

Much information about a knee injury can be obtained by a careful history and physical examination. Mechanism of injury, the time it took for swelling to occur, the ability to bear weight, and previous injury are all important historical factors. Physical examination includes determining the presence or absence of effusion, localizing the site(s) of tenderness, and assessing patellar and ligamentous stability. In addition, anatomic factors predisposing to injury should be noted. Arthroscopy is sometimes indicated to confirm the diagnosis.

Tears of the Menisci

The most common acute traumatic injuries in the knee are tears of the menisci. The menisci are small semilunar cartilages in the knee that provide some stability to the knee joint by acting as spacers, increase the congruity between the femur and the tibia and thus distribute the load in the knee, act as shock absorbers, and also aid in nourishment of the articular cartilage by helping to distribute the synovial fluid. The medial meniscus is most commonly injured by twisting and the lateral meniscus by hyperflexion. In dance, meniscal tears are less common than in sports. The dancer is usually performing rehearsed movements in a controlled fashion. The athlete may be starting or stopping or rotating in an unpredictable fashion in response to movements of an opponent. In addition, in sports involving cleated shoes the foot is planted when rotation of the body occurs.

In dancers the most common mechanism for tearing a meniscus is screwing the knee to increase turnout. Screwing the knee involves planting the feet on a 180° line when the knees are flexed. The dancer then tries to straighten the knees and, if external hip rotation is limited, the knee is forced to rotate abnormally. The lateral meniscus is also in jeopardy during plié and more so during Russian folk dancing involving a great deal of forced, hyperflexion movements. When a history of pain during twisting or squatting is followed by swelling, a tender joint line, and pain on attempted rotation of the knee, one must suspect a torn meniscus.

The menisci are important structures that should not be removed unless absolutely necessary. Initially, one should rest the knee by wrapping it with an Ace bandage or using a knee immobilizer for about 5 days. Applications of ice two to three times per day during this period will decrease the swelling. Quadriceps setting exercises should be initiated as soon as possible to prevent the atrophy that occurs whenever pain or swelling are present in the knee. In patients who are unable to recruit their vastus medialis muscles or who have pain when trying to do quadriceps setting exercises, we have had a great deal of success with electro-galvanic stimulation of the quadriceps muscle.

After 5 days' rest, the isometric quadriceps strengthening exercises are increased to include straight-leg raises with gradual addition of weight, and then short-arc isotonic exercises are added. Isometric exercises are usually tolerated better than isotonic exercises because of the limited range of motion in the post injury period. Isokinetic rehabilitation on a Cybex machine may be added if necessary. Ultimately full-arc isotonic quadriceps exercises are recommended if the patient has no preexisting patellar problems. The adductor muscles also need to be strengthened.

Range of motion is regained by actively moving the knee in warm water. Swimming also maintains cardiovascular endurance but the whip-kick must be avoided. Stretching exercises are encouraged. During all of these exercises, the knee must be warmed up prior to activity, wrapped during activity, and iced down after activity. We then encourage gradual return to specific training, initially omitting torsional activities. Patients can return to normal sport or dance activities when they have regained full range of motion and normal strength in the knee and when limited participation has resulted in no aggravation of knee pain or swelling. This entire program usually takes 4 to 6 weeks. If pain or effusion persist or recur in the first few weeks after injury, or if the knee locks, either partial meniscal removal or meniscal repair are indicated. Postoperative rehabilitation is exactly the same as treatment not involving surgery except that meniscal repair requires 6 weeks of cast immobilization.

Finally, if a technical fault such as screwing the knee contributed to the meniscal injury in a dancer, this fault must be corrected prior to returning to dance. After analyzing a few commonly used movement patterns, we often recommend practicing barre exercises lying on the floor to learn to use the lower extremities correctly. In addition, we emphasize use of the hip short external rotators to obtain turnout, and abdominal muscle strengthening and stretching of the hip flexors to control the pelvis. Proper use of the muscles will decrease knee torsional stresses.

Anterior Cruciate Ligament Tear

Another common knee injury in sports is the anterior cruciate ligament tear. The anterior cruciate ligament is one of two central pivotal ligaments in the knee responsible for anteroposterior and rotational stability. It can be torn in concert with other ligaments or menisci or as an isolated injury. Injury can occur from rotation with the foot planted, during hyperextension of the knee, or from contact. This is fortunately uncommon in dancers, although I have seen an anterior cruciate tear in a dancer who hyperextended his knee when landing from a jump.

In the event that an anterior cruciate ligament injury is identified, the arguments over repair, reconstruction, or nonoperative treatment must be considered. These discussions are the subject of week-long seminars and will not be dealt with here. Suffice it to say that the principal goal is to produce a stable knee. If the knee cannot be sufficiently stabilized by a rehabilitation program to allow return to activity, ligament reconstruction must be considered. Special considerations in dancers are that most reconstructions result in small, 5° to 10° flexion contractures of the knee, which are unacceptable in dancers. An additional problem is that derotational braces, which are especially useful in returning athletes to sports after anterior cruciate ligament rehabilitation or reconstruction, cannot be worn by dancers because of costuming constraints. Hence, the dancer with an anterior cruciate ligament injury usually has only one option and that is intense rehabilitation. The athlete can choose from rehabilitation, bracing, and operative reconstruction.

Rehabilitation emphasizes hamstring strengthening. The hamstring muscles are crucial in controlling the excessive motion of the tibia following an anterior cruciate ligament injury. Dancers' hamstrings are often lax because of frequent knee extensions. Hamstring strengthening is usually isotonic with gradually increasing weights, or isokinetic with gradually increasing speeds. Cybex testing of quadriceps and hamstring muscles for strength and power is useful for setting goals and for assessing progress during the rehabilitation period. Prior to returning to full activity, the strength of the injured knee should at least equal and preferably exceed that of the uninjured knee by about 10%.

Patellar Injuries

Patellar injuries are more common in dancers than in athletes. Both injure their patellae either in falls or during rotational movements. In modern dance movements involving falling onto the knees or rotating on the floor while on the knees, it is possible to produce not only patellar contusions but also actual fractures of the articular cartilage or bone. Patellar subluxation and dislocation usually are due to abnormal rotatory stresses at the knee, when the feet are planted. These injuries are more common in people whose anatomical alignment is inconsistent with natural turnout; that is, they have increased femoral anteversion. Whereas we are unlikely to find this degree of malalignment in the professional dancer, it is certainly rampant in the adolescent dancer.

Usually a significant patellar injury produces a hemarthrosis, and diagnostic arthroscopy is done initially to assess the damage. Patellar fracture, chondral injury, or complete medial retinaculum tears may require additional procedures. When none of these is found, the patient's knee is placed in a knee immobilizer for about one week to allow resolution of swelling. Rehabilitation is then initiated and emphasizes strengthening of the vastus medialis obliquus, which is the key to patellar control.

Electrical stimulation is especially useful in these patients to initiate quadriceps contractions. Again, we progress from quad sets to straight-leg raises. The straight-leg raises should be done with the limb in external rotation to overwork the vastus medialis and to strengthen the adductors. In dancers, the adductors should control flexion and extension during plié to avoid increasing the compressive forces on the patella. Short-arc isotonic exercises are added to the program but we never recommend full-arc isotonic exercises to patients with malalignment or patellar injury, as these exercises produce additional patellar damage and are poorly tolerated in those patients.

Patients who have suffered patellar dislocation are often found to have tight lateral retinacular structures, particularly where the iliotibial band attaches to the patella. Hence, iliotibial band stretching should be added to the quadriceps rehabilitation program. Since hyperextension of the knee can also lead to patellar subluxation or dislocation, hamstring strengthening is recommended. Excessive use of quadriceps muscles during plié increases patellofemoral forces, and screwing the knee increases the tendency for lateral patellar subluxation or dislocation. We therefore recommend the supine barre and learning to use hip short external rotators, as previously mentioned, for correcting these technical faults. Well-trained movement analysts can be extremely helpful in assessing and correcting poor mechanics that contributed to the injury. Patellar restraining braces, useful in providing additional support to the returning athlete, can be used by the dancer during class or rehearsal but usually cannot be worn in performance.

Ankle Injuries

Sprains

Ankle sprains are most common in sports such as volleyball or basketball, which involve a great deal of jumping activity and the risk of landing on someone else's foot. In dance, ankle sprains may also occur during jumps or turns, especially when the foot is in the demi-pointe position. When the foot is in a complete pointe position the posterior part of the calcaneus is locked against the tibia, and the potential is less for lateral ankle sprain. The incidence of sprains is also a function of the choreography and the floor. The latter can be too slippery or too sticky. Ankle sprains occur commonly in rehearsal, when the dancer is trying new steps and is tired (Hamilton, 1982).

Immediate care of an ankle injury should include icing, elevation, and compression wrapping, as well as the use of crutches. One must then rule out fractures and determine the degree of injury and instability. Patients are encouraged to use crutches and to put only partial weight on the injured limb for the first 4 to 5 days. During that time we recommend range of motion exercises, contrast therapy, and isometric peroneal strengthening if painless.

Range of motion is increased by attempting to "write the alphabet" with the injured foot suspended in warm water. Alternately plunging the ankle into cold and hot water (contrast baths) improves the circulation in the area and decreases the swelling more quickly. Peroneal strengthening can be initiated isometrically by everting the foot and pushing against an immobile object.

The ankle is supported in an Ace wrap or air cast between rehabilitation sessions. Swimming or biking are recommended to maintain aerobic endurance. In the first week after an ankle sprain we often recommend the ballet barre in the pool so that dancers can maintain their flexibility while the water relieves the ankle of its weight-bearing function.

Peroneal strengthening and proprioceptive training are crucial following a ligamentous injury. After initial isometric peroneal strengthening, isotonic exercises with tubing and finally with weights are added. In the dancer, the peroneals must be strengthened both in plantar flexion and in neutral because many of the dance steps take place with the foot plantar flexed. In addition, the peroneal muscles may be stretched and weakened from malpositioning and poor balance in relevé. Pointe work, in particular, stretches the anterior tibial muscles and strengthens and tightens the posterior tibial muscles, calf muscles, and heel cord. These must be balanced and body mechanics and positioning evaluated and corrected so that any problems with positioning that led to the original sprain can be corrected. Proprioceptive training encourages recruitment of the peroneal muscles. Using a wobble board, one alternates controlled inversion, eversion, plantar flexion, and dorsiflexion.

Athletes with ankle injuries advance from peroneal strengthening and proprioceptive training to a gradual running program, first running straight, then running figure 8s, and finally cutting sharply and quickly. Ultimately, they practice movements that simulate what they will be doing in their sport. Dancers advance from the wobble board and pool barre to barre exercises in class, initially without relevé, finally adding relevé and jumping. We usually ask dancers to avoid demi-pointe position and jumping for the 6 weeks needed for ligaments to heal.

Ankle braces and taping, useful in athletes when returning to full activity, can be used in dance class but they prevent the full pointe position and can present costuming problems. Ligament healing requires 6 weeks, and remodeling of the scar tissue continues for about 1 year. The rapidity with which the athlete and dancer return to full activity depends on the degree of damage and instability present.

Moderate sprains with uniplanar instability are immobilized for about 3 weeks prior to initiating rehabilitation. Air casts are useful because they allow swimming. Athletes with severe biplanar or rotatory instability are usually treated in casts from 4 to 6 weeks, and in some cases surgical ligament reconstruction is necessary for late instability. The peroneus brevis muscle is used in the reconstruction and in a dancer leaves a functionally compromised ankle. Hence, some have recommended primary repair of severe sprains in dancers (Hamilton, 1982). Rehabilitation after immobilization or operation is the same as that previously described.

Achilles Tendon Ruptures

Achilles tendon ruptures are found in the third decade in dancers and in the fourth decade in nondancers. Rupture is often but not always preceded by at least one episode of Achilles tendinitis. Failure to rest an Achilles tendinitis as well as routine failure to get the heels on the ground when landing jumps both contribute to tendon rupture.

When the Achilles tendon ruptures the patient reports a sensation of being shot or kicked in the back of the leg. A subsequent loss of push-off strength is followed, within 24 hours, by swelling and ecchymosis. Tenderness and sometimes a palpable defect occur at the site of the tear. Active plantar flexion does not rule out Achilles tendon rupture, as the toe flexors and posterior tibial tendons can perform plantar flexion. Producing foot plantar flexion by squeezing the calf (Thompson test) is a fairly reliable sign for an intact Achilles tendon (Thompson & Doherty, 1967). Some difference of opinion exists about operative versus non-operative treatment of Achilles tendon ruptures in the general population (Inglis, Scott, Sculco, & Patterson, 1976; Listor, 1981). The general trend, however, is for competitive athletes and dancers to be treated with operative repair of the Achilles tendon. In either case, the ankle will be immobilized in plantar flexion from 4 to 8 weeks. Healing and remodeling of the Achilles tendon are slow because of its relative avascularity.

The keys to rehabilitation following Achilles tendon rupture are gaining strength while restoring flexibility of the tendon. Toe raises (relevé en demi-pointe) while carrying gradually heavier weights will strengthen the musculotendinous unit. Stretching initially must return the foot to neutral. Gradual lowering of the heel is accomplished by wearing street shoes with a series of heel lifts that are removed one at a time. The next step involves both gastrocnemius and soleus stretching. The patient leans forward against a wall and places the injured ankle behind, gradually lowering the heel to the ground. The farther the foot is from the wall, the greater the stretch incurred. These exercises should be performed both with knees flexed (soleus) and knees extended (gastroc).

Additional stretching can be gained by standing with the toes on the edge of a box or stair and gently lowering the heels, holding the stretched position for 20 seconds and then returning to the neutral position. As in all stretching exercises, the stretching should be slow and sustained rather than ballistic in order to avoid reflex contraction of the muscle. In the dancer, slow pliés in second and fourth positions are a good way of stretching the Achilles tendon but these often cannot be initiated for several months after repair. During this interval aerobic conditioning should be maintained by bicycling, swimming, or rowing. Flexibility and strength elsewhere can be maintained by stretching and strengthening exercises or by limited participation in dance class.

Rehabilitation Principles

Principles involved in the rehabilitation of injured dancers and athletes are as follows:

1. The injured joint must be protected while it is healing to avoid chronic problems or recurrence. This may mean limited activities or complete rest for a certain period of time, followed by partial return to activity at first. Muscles surrounding the injured joint need to be strengthened to make up for weak and damaged ligaments. Intraligamentous or tendinous scar tissue is never quite as flexible or strong as the original tissue; hence, dynamic strength must make up for loss of static strength.
2. Range of motion about the injured joint should be maintained or regained. Until the range of motion is normal the dancer or athlete will have a predisposition to recurrent injury as a result of substituting and overusing incorrect muscles or demanding greater-than-normal motion in nearby joints to make up for the lack in the injured joint.
3. Total body endurance, flexibility, and strength must be maintained while avoiding stress on the injured area. Endurance can be maintained by swimming, bicycling, walking, or rowing. Flexibility can be maintained with stretching exercises and, for dancers, use of barre exercises. Lifting weights can maintain strength elsewhere.
4. Any technical problems that led to the original injury must be corrected. Sports medicine is unique in the sense that the physician is returning patients to the activities in which they were originally injured. Furthermore, these activities demand a great deal more flexibility, strength, and endurance of the musculoskeletal system than nonphysically strenuous activities. Hence, we must make sure not only that patients are fully rehabilitated but

also that potentially injurious technical faults or anatomical problems can be corrected.

5. Rehabilitation must be activity specific so that the patient will be able to return to preinjury performance levels. Although we initially recommend general rehabilitation, we must ultimately devise a specific rehabilitation program that utilizes some of the motions that will be required of patients in their desired activities.

6. During a period of activity restriction, keeping injured athletes or dancers in their normal practice environments will minimize the psychosocial stresses that also occur following injury. We would like to avoid deconditioning not only physically in aerobic ability, flexibility, and strength, but also in the psyche of the athlete and dancer. When a team or company member has been injured and is removed from the usual environment, not only does the individual suffer but the other team or company members suffer as well. They may have to increase their workload under the additional threat of knowing that injuries occur in their environment.

During the rehabilitation period a great deal of cooperation between the patient, the physician, the physical therapist, and the coach or dance administrator is required if the goals of optimal healing, return to maximal performance levels, and prevention of additional injury are to be achieved. Usually, if the physician or therapist explains the rationale of the treatment program to those involved, they are quite cooperative in trying to meet the ultimate goal of returning the athlete and dancer to full activity.

References

Hamilton, W.G. (1982). Sprained ankles in ballet dancers. *Foot and Ankle, 3*(2), 99-102.

Inglis, A., Scott, W.N., Sculco, T., & Patterson, A. (1976). Ruptures of the tendon Achilles. *Journal of Bone and Joint Surgery, 58-A*, 990-993.

Listor, L. (1981). Surgical and non-surgical treatment of Achilles tendon rupture. *Journal of Joint and Bone Surgery, 63-A*, 394-399.

Quirk, R. (1983). Ballet injuries: The Australian experience. *Clinics in Sports Medicine, 2*(3), 507-514.

Thompson, T., & Doherty, J. (1967). Spontaneous rupture of tendon of Achilles. A new clinical diagnostic text. *Anatomical Research, 158*, 126.

Washington, E.L. (1978). Musculoskeletal injuries in theatrical dancers: Site, frequency, and severity. *American Journal of Sports Medicine, 6*(2), 75-98.

7

Diagnosis and Management of Dance Injuries to the Lower Back: An Osteopathic Approach

Richard M. Bachrach
THE CENTER FOR DANCE MEDICINE
NEW YORK, NEW YORK, USA

During my 30 years of dealing with dance-related injuries it has become apparent that, although most seem to involve the foot, ankle, and knee, some relationship to dysfunction or derangement of the lower back or pelvis almost always exists. The location of the initial complaint depends largely on the stage of pathologic development at which the dancer is first seen. Often the low back-pelvis involvement is obviously primary; less frequently, it is secondary to compensations necessitated by primary involvements of the lower extremities.

The injured dancer must be considered holographically. The observed clinical picture is essentially not reducible to the individual elements manifested in different parts of the body. To consider one a cause of another may be teleologic thinking and thus, therapeutically, nonproductive. Distinctions between body regions in consideration of dance injuries thus become blurred.

Construction of the Lower Back and Pelvis

The bony skeleton involved consists of five lumbar vertebrae, the 12th thoracic vertebra, and the pelvis—consisting of the fused ilium, ischium, and pubis along with the sacrum and coccyx. Because of the profound bony, muscular, and ligamentous interrelationships, the proximal femora must be included.

The lumbar vertebrae are progressively larger from cephalad to caudad and the intervertebral discs progressively thicker (up to the one between L4 and

L5) in order to withstand increasing weight-bearing demands. The normal lumbar lordosis (curvature with concavity posteriorly) is a response of the developing body to weight bearing. In the erect position, the major possible motions are flexion (forward bending), which normally results in decreasing the lordosis, and backward bending or extension, which results in increasing lumbar lordosis. The range of the latter exceeds that of the former for reasons we will explain shortly. Most of the extension and flexion in this area occurs in the lower lumbars, primarily between the fifth lumbar vertebra and the sacrum.

Between vertebral bodies are the intervertebral discs (IVDs). These fibrocartilaginous rings surrounding a soft jelly-like center function as shock absorbers and facilitate intervertebral movement.

Ligaments are relatively inelastic fibrous structures that connect bone to bone. In the lumbar spine, the posterior longitudinal ligament is closely adherent to the posterior aspect of the bodies of the lumbar vertebrae and their intervertebral discs. Flexion in this region is limited by the inelasticity of this ligament. The posterior longitudinal ligament narrows as it descends to terminate at the sacrum, thereby allowing for flexion but weakening the posterior support of the IVDs. Primarily for this reason, disc herniations usually occur dorsolaterally in the lower lumbar spine. The effect of this disc herniation may be pressure on the nerve roots as they exist between the vertebrae, causing radiating pain syndromes.

The ventral or anterior parts of the vertebral bodies are connected, much more loosely, by the anterior longitudinal ligament. The vertebral arches are connected by the strong and elastic ligamentum flavum. The intertransverse ligaments connect the transverse processes, and the interspinal and supraspinal ligaments connect the spinous processes.

The lumbar vertebrae articulate directly with each other via the articular facets (right and left), which are like any other synovial joints having a synovial membrane, articular cartilage, and a capsular ligament. The capsular ligament in the lumbar spine is quite taut, permitting little movement.

Muscles of the Lower Back and Pelvis

The principal muscles involved in the movement of the low back are divided into intrinsic and extrinsic groups. The intrinsic muscles, the erector spinae, are situated on the dorsal surface of, or behind, the vertebral column. There are two main groups in the lumbar area. The lateral and medial tracts have fibers connecting the pelvis to the posterior surface of the ribs; the transverse, spinous, and costal processes of the lumbar vertebrae; the transverse and spinous processes of the thoracic vertebrae; and each other. They are innervated by the dorsal rami of the spinal nerves. When acting bilaterally, these muscles serve to maintain erect posture by extending the spine. Acting unilaterally, their contraction will bend the spine to the same side as the contraction.

The erector spinae are invested by two layers of fibrous connective tissue called the lumbodorsal or thoracolumbar fascia. This fascia not only encapsulates the erector spinae group but also is a source of origin for superficial back muscles and the muscles of the abdominal wall. The extrinsic muscles are not, per se, necessarily back muscles. They are located anterior to the vertebral column and, therefore, their contraction flexes the spine or bends the torso forward on the pelvis; unilaterally, they pull the spine to the side of the contraction.

The quadratus lumborum is a quadrangular sheet of muscle arising from the iliac crest and extending to the 12th rib and the costal processes of the lumbar vertebrae. Its function is to lower the 12th rib and flex the body to the side of its contraction. It is a deep abdominal muscle.

The abdominal musculature consists of three basic groupings: (a) lateral, including the external and internal obliques and the transversus abdominus; (b) medial, including the rectus abdominus and pyramidalis; and (c) deep. These muscles serve to support the abdominal contents by forming the anterior wall of the abdominal cavity. They lower the ribs and elevate the anterior brim of the pelvis and aid in flexing the trunk on the hips. They help to rotate the trunk when the lower extremities are fixed and, most importantly, during respiration their contraction elevates the intra-abdominal pressure, thus supporting the trunk.

The hip flexors, primarily the psoas and its companion the iliacus, are among the most important postural muscles. They serve to direct movement anteriorly. The iliopsoas is the muscle most vitally involved in low-back mechanics and thus is of primary concern in injuries of the low back.

The hamstrings (the semimembranosus, the semitendinosus, and biceps femoris) by virtue of their connection from the ischial tuberosity to the tibia and fibula, cross two major body joints, the hip and knee. They act as extensors of the thigh on the pelvis and also counter the psoas by pulling the posterior pelvis downward. In this action, the hamstrings complement the abdominal muscles, while opposing the erector spinae and psoas groups. They also act as flexors of the knee.

The gluteus maximus is an extensor of the hip and a powerful external rotator of the thigh and also helps prevent excessive lateral tilting of the pelvis. It acts both as an abductor (through the iliotibial tract, of major importance to dancers with low-back problems) and adductor of the hip. The gluteus medius acts through its anterior fibers as an external rotator and extensor. The gluteus minimus acts similarly but is a weaker abductor.

The deep outward rotators of the hip (the three gamelli, the obturator externus and internus, the quadratus femoris, and the piriformis) are stronger than the internal rotators and thus, in the erect position, the foot is normally slightly turned out.

The rectus femoris is one of the quadriceps group on the anterior aspect of the thigh. By virtue of its proximal attachment to the anterior inferior iliac spine, it acts to flex the thigh on the pelvis and extend the pelvis on the lumbar spine; that is, a tight rectus will act in concert with the shortened iliopsoas to pull the pelvis into hyperextension. This is an action of great importance to the dancer, because many dancers achieve greater turnout by increasing the hyperextension of the lumbar spine. It is also a major source of low-back injury.

Movement, however slight, occurs at both the pubic and sacroiliac joints. Maintenance of that movement is of vital importance to the functional integrity of the lower back and pelvis.

Dance Injuries of the Lower Back and Pelvis

Dance injuries to the low back are seldom related to one single trauma or physical factor; rather, they are usually the result of repeated microtraumata super-
imposed on multiple interrelated pathologic biodynamic factors. Repeated
hyperflexion-hyperextension in the presence of maladaptive alignment can
produce stress on the articular pillars with resultant fracture—a condition
referred to as spondylolysis. This, for example, is often produced in adolescent dancers by the repeated improper execution of arabesques or lifts, particularly in the presence of hyperlordosis when external rotation of the hips is
also restricted. The attempt to force the turnout results in increasing the lordosis
with consequent facet impingement. The dancer may complain specifically of
pain in the lower back of a pinching nature occurring regularly with arabesque
or any extension to the back on the affected side.

Spondylolisthesis is a progression of bilateral spondylolysis in which repeated
flexion-extension trauma combined with the forward pull of the psoas on the
vertebral body results in a forward slippage of the body of L5 on the sacrum
or, more rarely, of L4 on L5. It is notable that spondylolysis and spondylolisthesis appear to be more prevalent in the dance and gymnastic population than
in the at-large group. This suggests confirmation of the theory that the etiology
lies in the repeated hyperflexion-hyperextension movement that takes place
during developmental years. In my experience, this lesion is also more common
in females, corresponding to the generally earlier onset of their dance training.

The majority of low-back injuries among dancers are overuse-related and
secondary to alignment-technique defects. Primarily they are the result of the
failure of the compensatory mechanisms for contracture, shortening of, or
failure of adaptive lengthening of, the psoas muscle. The psoas arises from
the bodies, intervertebral discs, and transverse processes of the last thoracic
and the five lumbar vertebrae. It courses downward and forward and slightly
outward, passing across the front of the hip joint and running downward to
join the iliacus in its insertion into the lesser trochanter of the femur. It is innervated by branches of the first to third lumbar nerves that pass through its
substance.

With the lower extremities fixed, these muscles act to pull the lumbar vertebrae forward (increasing the lordosis). They extend the pelvis and bring the
trunk forward on the hips as in port de bras to the front. Acting in the opposite
direction—that is, from above downward—the iliopsoas will externally rotate
the thigh, flex it, and adduct it, as in battements to the front. Acting from
above downward, with the leg fixed, however, the iliopsoas is an internal rotator
of the entire hip. Thus a tight psoas restricts turnout. Unilateral psoas contraction will result in unilateral downward deviation of the innominate on that
side. This produces an increased load on the iliotibial band and consequently
on the gluteus maximus and hamstrings. Operating in the opposite direction—
that is, from below upward—the unilateral psoas pull on the thoracolumbar
spine will cause a list of the spine and a scoliosis, or lateral spinal convexity,
in the direction of the pull with rotation of the vertebral bodies in the opposite
direction.

The reasons for iliopsoas shortening in the human are multifold, even having to do with the age at which the erect posture becomes dominant. Rapid

bony growth often outstrips the rate of muscle lengthening. If we sleep in the fetal position, the iliopsoas is contracted on both sides. If one leg is drawn up, the iliopsoas is shortened. When we sit, it is the iliopsoas that flexes our hips and it stays short as long as we are in that position. In walking, the iliopsoas contracts to advance the leading leg. In fact, since most of our activities are oriented to the front, there is almost constant iliopsoas contraction or shortening on one side or the other—frequently both. Add dance movements, most of which are directed forward, and require active iliopsoas contraction for their performance (battement tendus, développés, port de bras, extension, etc., to the front) and small wonder this muscle tends to be tight.

Under normal conditions our muscles must perform some work to maintain the erect position against the force of gravity. However, with optimal alignment —ear over shoulder, over hip, over knee, over midtarsals—only the iliopsoas and the calf muscles show significant electrical activity at rest. When the iliopsoas is tight, however, the pelvis is rotated downward (i.e., extended) and the lumbar lordosis is increased. This loads the hamstrings, causing the knees to tend toward partial flexion. In order to keep the knee straight, the quadriceps are statically contracted. This pull is transmitted to the calf muscles with resultant hypertrophy, tightness, and thus decreased range dorsiflexion at the ankle (i.e., plié). As a further consequence, there is an increased dorsal kyphosis and compensatory tightening of the erector spinae. This, in turn, causes tightening of the thoracolumbar fascia. Eventually shortening of the posterior longitudinal ligament as well as the erector spinae in the lumbar area limits forward-directed movements. The abdominal muscles have become stretched and therefore weaker, less able to support the trunk, and less efficient in flexing the trunk on the pelvis.

More problems arise when movement is attempted. Muscles already in a state of contraction respond inefficiently to instructions from the brain; they use more energy and fatigue more easily. Développés and battements to the front, for example, are limited by the aforementioned concentric rather than eccentric (shortening versus lengthening) contraction of the extensors (hamstring and erector spinae) which makes flexion (forward movement) more difficult.

Dancers often attempt to increase their turnout by tilting the pelvis downward (hyperextending). Although this may to a certain extent decrease the tension in the iliofemoral or Y ligament, the net effect is to increase the lumbar lordosis, thereby compromising the lower back; and, because of the hamstring counter-contraction, efficient flexion is facilitated by simultaneous lengthening of the opposing extensors, diminishing the range of flexion at the hip. This is further limited by the encroachment of the femur on the down-tilted innominate with impingement of the intervening soft tissues.

Movements to the rear, such as arabesque, are limited because the extensors (hamstrings) are opposed by the already contracted flexors, that is, the psoas and rectus femoris. Efficient extension is facilitated by simultaneous lengthening of the flexors. The increased lordosis, produced by the iliopsoas shortening, approximates the spinal joints. To attempt further extension is painful and is resisted by the body.

Low-back pain in dancers resulting from intervertebral disc compression, protrusion, degeneration, or herniation is less common. However, repeated lifting trauma in the presence of maladaptive spinal movement patterns may cause disc degeneration if continued over a long period of time, particularly in the presence of predisposing factors such as spondylolysis or spondylolisthesis.

Lower extremity malalignment may result in low-back problems. Leg-length inequality, when associated with either scoliosis convex to the short side (and consequent psoas shortening) or with flexion of L3 on L4 or L4 on L5 to the long-leg side, should be corrected by use of a lift. This is a delicate procedure and requires a good deal of trial and error, but can result in prevention of many knee, ankle, and low-back problems.

Pronation of one foot may occur, in cases where there is a leg-length discrepancy, on the side of the long leg. This may be an attempt on the part of the body to level the pelvis. Treatment here involves correction of the pronation *and* the leg-length deficit, if needed. Not all cases of foot malalignment need correction, but low-back dysfunction in the presence of pronation usually indicates the necessity for orthoses. Likewise, excessive inversion, bilateral or unilateral, often causes compensatory dynamic overpronation as well as an overload of the iliotibial bands. This is often associated with genu varum and tibial torsion. Leg length inequality may also be unconsciously compensated for by the tendency to partially flex the knee on the long-leg side.

Discrepancies in hip external rotation range may also be a factor in low back problems. Quite commonly, in order to equalize turnout, the dancer will hyperextend the pelvis on the side of lesser turnout, thus producing torsion at the sacroiliac and lumbosacral joints as well as impingement of the lumbar apophyseal joints. Often turnout can be somewhat improved simply by repeated psoas stretching.

Recurvatum (or hyperextension) of the knees is usually accompanied by hyperlordosis and also causes low-back problems, particularly when a discrepancy exists between the amount of recurvatum on the two sides, resulting in a functional leg-length deficiency. Valgus deviation of the knee is usually associated with pronation at the foot and ankle and loads the lateral thigh and leg with the attempt by the body to self-correct.

In an overwhelmingly large percentage of dancers with complaints regarding the lower back and hip, the following historical picture is found after careful investigation. The dancer complains of pain and restricted motion of the lower back or hip: battements, développés, and extensions to the front are labored or painful. Sitting on the floor in second position, they find difficulty in stretching down over the involved side. The arabesque and other extensions to the rear may be painful and are usually tighter and lower on the side of the complaint. Often the dancer will describe intermittent, vague knee discomfort, particularly at the bottom of grand plié or when fully extending the knee, especially with weight bearing.

Either the dancer or the teachers, or frequently both, will have noted pronation of the foot and ankle in the first or fifth position demi-plié; and the complaint may indeed be tendinitis of the flexor hallucis longus secondary to forcing turnout to compensate for tightness at the hip. Physical examination of the lower back usually reveals restricted sacroiliac motion on the side of primary involvement (although this may not be the side with pain). Commonly found are a lumbar scoliosis convex to the same side; downward rotation of the innominate with resultant restricted flexion; extension at that hip; and consistent tightness of the iliopsoas, as determined by Micheli's test, as well as the iliotibial band, as determined by Ober's test. Effective prevention and treatment of these injuries is highly dependent on early recognition. This, in turn, depends to a great extent on the dancer's awareness of his or her body and ability to suspend denial.

Treatment

Once chronicity of the injury is established, the dancer begins to make compensations, and what was once a relatively simple problem with a nonsurgical solution has become far more complex and threatening. A dancer complains of pain in a hip and inability to perform extensions to the front or the side. She readily acknowledges a year-old injury to the knee but says, "It's fine now." Not so. She still does not straighten her knee in balances or extensions and will not do so because it would hurt. However, she has learned to make compensations that allow her to continue to dance. She does not even recognize that her hip problem is related to her knee injury.

The first step in the treatment of an injury is to recognize and acknowledge its existence as early as possible. Denial is a universal brain ploy but need not victimize the injured. The key is to recognize that a movement that used to come easily no longer does so. This is the cue to say, "Something is wrong." Not everything, just something. Admitting a problem does not mean the end of the job, getting out of shape, losing the edge, the end of a career. It is a simple acknowledgment that something is not working. At this point, probably the teacher will have the answer, which is likely to be found in a technique or alignment correction. If not, many movement analysts are available.

Warm-up is a major factor in injury prevention. Suffice it to say that the warm-up should involve aerobics plus the range of motion for all joints that will be involved in movement. A 5- to 10-min run around the studio is excellent preparation for a class. Stretches should always follow a warm-up and are most useful after class as part of a warm-down. As a rule (because of the marked tendency to shortening or contraction of these muscles), the psoas or hip flexor stretch should be done at least four or five times a day. Generally speaking, dancers manifest tight quadriceps, hamstrings, hip flexors (psoas), and calf muscles. These groups are regularly in need of stretching. The hamstrings, quadriceps, peroneals, and especially the abdominals are frequently weaker than they should be and often need strengthening.

Treatment is multifaceted. In our practice we combine osteopathic manipulation, including correction of the specific somatic dysfunctions, with neuromuscular repatterning and ideokinesis. The latter has proven to be an effective method of dealing with alignment problems. As previously noted, orthotic correction of biomechanical dysfunctions of the feet and ankles is carried out when indicated. We manufacture orthotics for all types of footwear except pointe shoes.

There is little indication for injection therapy except in cases where, because of ligamentous laxity, repeated subluxation of the sacroiliac or lumbar-apophyseal joints results in profound low-back instability. The ligaments involved can effectively be injected with a sclerosing solution but, during the course of this treatment, it is not possible to continue full dance activities.

All of these treatments are complemented by the use of nonsteroidal anti-inflammatory drugs when necessary, and of physiotherapeutic modalities such as high- and low-volt electrogalvanic stimulation, ultrasound, and acupuncture. We do a noninvasive form of acupuncture utilizing a micro-electric current to treat acupuncture points.

Clinical experience involving thousands of dancers has led to the following conclusions:

1. Only a few apparently discreet dance-induced injuries or pathologic conditions occur.
2. Upon careful analysis, these injuries are seen to be profoundly interrelated rather than distinct or discreet.
3. With few exceptions, dance related injuries, including most of those labeled acute, are ultimately traceable to repeated microtraumata secondary to maladaptive movement patterns or defective dance techniques.
4. Usually they are associated with chronic somatic dysfunction of the lumbosacral spine and pelvis and related alignment problems.
5. These dysfunctions are characterized by uni- or bilateral shortening of the psoas—the consequence of either (a) chronic contracture due to weakness or overuse or (b) the failure of adaptive lengthening.
6. Effective prevention and management of these maladaptive technique-related injuries and conditions depend largely on correction of the related somatic dysfunctions.
7. This, in turn, often depends not only on correction of the dysfunction and stretching the psoas by means of osteopathic manipulative techniques but, even more important, on maintaining those corrections through active stretching, exercise, and visualization by the dancer.

8

Back Injuries in Dancers

Lyle J. Micheli and Elisabeth R. Micheli
CHILDREN'S HOSPITAL
BOSTON, MASSACHUSETTS, USA

Back injuries are encountered among dancers of all ages and at all levels. The length of dancing experience, although a factor in other types of dance injuries such as those of the lower extremities, is not a factor in back-injury patterns. Male and female dancers both incur back injuries; however, males may have more occurrences because of their lifting activities. The back is the fourth most common site of dance injury, according to 1979 statistics from our Sports Medicine Clinic. Often back injuries are more severe than other types of injuries and require long periods of time off from dancing.

Types of Injuries

Back injuries may be of the single macrotrauma type, resulting from a single twist or fall; more commonly, they are of the repetitive microtrauma type. In either case, examination should include not only the dancer's back but an evaluation of the relative strength, flexibility, and range of motion of the entire body, including the upper and lower extremities. Assessment of the dancer's technique and style is necessary in order to understand the mechanism of injury and to successfully work toward preventing reinjury.

The four categories of back problems most common among dancers are mechanical low-back pain, discogenic back pain, spondylolysis, and upper back strain. Mechanical low-back pain, the back disorder most frequently encountered in young dancers, is usually associated with hyperlordotic posturing of the low back during moving, lifting, and turning. Hyperlordosis in a dancer is almost always an acquired posture, observable during barre or floor work. It is often the result of poor technique, as the dancer attempts to increase turnout at the hip by swaying the back. This should be stopped as soon as it is observed because, besides being aesthetically displeasing, it increases the chance of back injury.

The diagnosis of hyperlordotic posture should be made only after more specific entities—such as discogenic back pain, spondylolysis, or even neoplastic or inflammatory processes, all diseases of the young—have been eliminated. Management of the condition usually consists of a directed exercise program to strengthen the abdominal muscles; at the same time the teacher emphasizes the avoidance of hyperlordosis while dancing. In mechanical back pain with lumbar lordosis that does not respond to exercises alone, we have used an anti-lordotic brace in addition to the exercise program, with results that have been pleasing. Treatment usually lasts 4 to 6 months, with the dancer wearing the brace full time except during dance activities.

The second type of low-back pain is discogenic back pain, with or without associated sciatica. This is usually encountered in the male dancer and is associated with hyperlordosis during either free dancing or lifting. Every attempt is made to treat it nonoperatively. An approach involving relative rest while using a modified Boston brace permits the dancer to continue dancing on a limited basis while avoiding lifting. A directed exercise program is also prescribed including abdominal strengthening, gentle resisted lower extremity stretching exercises, and swimming.

A dancer with a serious disc herniation, involving disabling pain and progressive neurologic loss, requires a more drastic treatment program of complete bed rest, local heat, analgesics, and muscle relaxants. A Chymopapain injection added to the treatment may be effective and certainly should be considered before surgery. If a discetomy is absolutely necessary, the dancer must be informed that he or she will be unable to perform fully for 12 months, that an extensive rehabilitation program will be required, and that the possibility of further professional dancing will depend totally on the extent of recovery.

The third category of back injury in the dancer is spondylolysis. The incidence of spondylolysis among dancers perhaps equals that of gymnasts, which appears to be greater than that of the general population. Dance and gymnastics both require repetitive flexion and extension of the spine, which may result in a stress fracture of one or more pars interarticularis of the lumbar spine. Spondylolysis should be strongly suspected in dancers with persistent low-back pain who do not respond to the treatment for mechanical low-back pain.

Pain during hyperextension of the back while standing on one foot, as in the arabesque, is often the first sign of a spondylolytic stress fracture. Physical examination usually reveals a limitation of motion in the lumbar spine on forward bending, and pain with hyperextension of the back. These characteristics are frequently accompanied by tight hamstrings but, except for rare occasions of associated sciatica, the neurological examination of the lower extremities is usually unremarkable.

Oblique radiographs of the lumbosacral spine often are needed to diagnose a pars fracture. However, if the radiograph does not reveal a fractured pars, a bone scan should be done, because radiographic change may not be evident at the site of a stress fracture, including stress fractures of the pars interarticulars, until a significant period of time after injury.

Spondylolysis in a young dancer, associated with pain of less than 6 months' duration, should be treated as a fracture, and an antilordotic brace should be used to achieve reduction and immobilization. In addition, we recommend an antilordotic exercise program. Dance training may be continued through the bracing period, as long as there is no pain.

Spondylolytic lesions that do not heal do not necessarily end a dancer's career. Often a directed antilordotic and abdominal strengthening program, coupled with the avoidance of painful technique and jumping activities, eliminates pain and allows for dance participation. This type of spondylolysis is a stable condition and usually does not result in futher forward slipping, or spondylolisthesis. The dancer has a stable back and, although not always able to dance comfortably, he or she may dance safely. A dancer with spondylolysis, unresponsive to treatment, may be relieved of pain through fusion of the unstable segment.

The fourth type of back injury is upper back strain. Injuries to the soft tissue of the upper back and periscapular musculature occur in both male and female dancers. Female dancers usually injure this area while performing movements requiring elevation and rotation of the upper arm. The male dancer is prone to acute muscle-tendon strains from lifting, especially if a lift is attempted while the dancer is off balance.

The management of both types of strain is similar. A cold spray or ice massage will provide immediate symptomatic relief, permitting completion of a performance. Immediate mechanical massage may reduce limitation of motion and associated muscle spasms. Use of mild nonsteroid antiinflammatory medications helps to speed recovery and relieve muscle stiffness. Ice massage before rehearsal helps eliminate pain, while heat and massage after class appears to limit the extent of stiffness. Simple strengthening exercises, using a dumbbell or hand resistance, have been useful in speeding recovery and preventing recurrence in both male and female dancers.

Risk Factors for Injuries

In diagnosis and management of all of these types of back injuries, a list of risk factors is useful. The first risk factor to be considered is training error, including changes in intensity, frequency, and style of dancing. Sudden increases in amount of dancing time may bring on injuries even in a fit dancer. Poor dance technique is another risk factor often associated with back injuries. Avoiding excessive lumbar lordosis or pelvic flexion, especially during such movements as attitude, arabesques, and lifts, is part of good technique.

Musculotendinous imbalances such as hyperlordosis, affecting strength or flexibility or both, are a third risk factor and are often acquired through poor technique. The fourth risk factor, anatomic malalignment of the lower extremities, includes leg-length discrepancies, abnormality of rotation of the hips, kneecap position, bowlegs, knock-knees, or flat feet. These must also be detected, as one or another injury may contribute to back pain. Shoe styles and dance surfaces have been described by dancers as factors related to the onset of back pain. Dancing in high-heeled jazz dance shoes, or on a hard stage, are common examples.

The final risk factor is related to the growth process. Especially during the adolescent growth spurt, the accelerated growth of the bones results in a decrease in overall flexibility, with relative tightening of the muscle-tendon units. This growth-related syndrome is expressed in the back as increased tightness of the lumbodorsal fascia, hamstrings, and anterior hip structures, resulting in a tendency to increased lumbar lordosis and dorsal roundbacking. A combination of factors usually contributes to back pain or injury. Discovering and ultimately removing them or compensating for them is the key to diagnosis and management of the injuries.

Prevention

The prevention of back injuries among dancers requires particular attention to the dance education of the young boy or girl dancer. The instructor should check for lordotic posturing at the barre and during floor exercises and correct it promptly, stressing that the dancer should "pull up" on the torso. Specific exercises to strengthen the abdominals and to increase the flexibility of the lumbodorsal fascia will also help to counteract hyperlordotic tendencies. An adolescent dancer should be watched closely during periods of intense growth to prevent development of this incorrect posture.

The older dancer must also pay strict attention to technique and possibly use supplementary exercises to avoid a hyperlordotic posture. The male dancer should always use proper lifting technique—using strong quads and gluteii, while avoiding a lordotic sway in the back. Weight training of the entire body is a helpful step toward protecting the back and, if done properly, does not interfere with dance technique.

Finally, a 20- to 30-min period of slow progressive stretching should always be done before a class or performance. While most dancers and dance teachers realize the role that a proper warm-up plays in the prevention of injuries, this point must be always emphasized.

Additional Reading

Micheli, L.J. (1979). Low back pain in the adolescent: Differential diagnosis. *American Journal of Sports Medicine, 7*, 362-364.

Micheli, L.J. (1984). *Pediatric and adolescent sports medicine*. Boston: Little Brown Publishing.

Micheli, L.J. (1985). Sports following spinal surgery in the young athlete. *Clinical Orthopaedics and Related Research, 198*, 152-157.

Micheli, L.J., Hall, J.E., & Miller, M.E. (1980). Use of the modified Boston brace for back injuries in athletes. *American Journal of Sports Medicine, 8*, 351-356.

White, A.A., III, & Purjabi, M.M. (1978). *Clinical biomechanics of the spine*. Philadelphia: Lippincott.

PART II

Nutritional, Physical, and Physiological Considerations in the Dancer and Athlete: Similarities and Differences

Ever since *Sports Illustrated* ran a story in 1971 on New York City Ballet's Edward Villella (Kram, 1971), matching his strength and agility to world-class athletic contemporaries, dancers have increasingly become the subjects of studies comparing them to athletes. About the same time the Western world began comparing Villella with the equally agile and stunning defector from Russia's Kirov Ballet, Rudolf Nureyev. Both Villella and Nureyev moved with unprecedented range and control; their uniquely individual styles of movement provided the observer pleasing examples of power on and off the ground, endurance, and (let's admit it) beautifully defined musculature.

The result was studies—mostly longitudinal in design—on dancers and their training that substantiated low body-fat levels (Dolgener, et al., 1980), high measures of power and strength in specific patterns of movement (Bushey, 1966; Chass, 1974), and an endurance capacity equal to many athletes (Cohen, et al., 1980; de Guzman, 1979; Jette & Inglis, 1975; Novak et al., 1978; Van Zile, 1980; Rimmer & Rosentsweig, 1981-1982). Ultimately, the combined results of those studies have aided in answering the ongoing question, "If dancers are such good athletes, what makes them so?" The answers thus far are based primarily on physiological data, and indeed dancers have been shown to amass and display physiological characteristics similar to world class athletes; however, dancers have not been shown to be necessarily superior athletes (Kirkendall & Calabrese, 1983).

With the increased interest in studying dancers, Mostardi felt it was necessary to introduce into the scientific literature certain quantitative measures on dancers that would serve to characterize or describe their anatomic and physiologic peculiarities. To date little data-gathering has been performed on dancers, unlike athletes, and physicians have nothing to use to comparatively evaluate dancers' injuries. In his article, Mostardi describes how he compiled the physical profiles of dancers as athletes, using X rays and Cybex measures.

Physiological research usually consists of measuring certain functions of the body and quantifying strength and endurance capacities, as in Mostardi's study. Although Van Gyn's article is not about measuring or quantifying, it is included in this section because it deals with a physiologically based topic of prime importance to the performance of both dancer and athlete: flexibility. Van Gyn describes and assesses four techniques for developing flexibility and offers a strong case favoring proprioceptive neuromuscular facilitation (PNF), or the 3-S method. She points out that PNF contributes to strength gains as well as increased range of motion, both of which are requisite to excellent performance. Mostardi confirms that female dancers have less leg strength than some female athletic groups—specifically, lower peak torque generated by the quadriceps. Thus we might conclude than any and all strength-building alternatives should be added to the training programs of dancers.

One wonders how dancers can compete at all on the same plane as athletes, considering the differences in their nutritional habits. Today there is virtually no athlete or coach who does not apply the latest physiological and nutritional findings to the enhancement of athletic performance. On the other hand, too few dancers and their teachers are aware of the benefits of specific food groups to a given performance or of suggested schedules for food intake to prepare and maintain the body for optimal training results and performance.

Until Calabrese conducted research on professional dancers' nutritional needs (Calabrese et al., 1982), knowledge of dancers' poor eating habits was generally unknown and unmonitored. Dancers' habits are loosely based on misinformation, misunderstanding, myth, and often missing funds. Peterson attempted to ascertain the differences in dancers' and athletes' nutritional habits and reported the findings in her article. A feature of her report is her conclusion that dancers may in fact have different nutritional requirements than athletes because of the anaerobic nature of dance.

In spite of their unorthodox nutritional practices, dancers are able to garner the necessary forces to perform explosive sequences as well as to prolong temporally uniform phrases of balance and imbalance. This ability to seemingly defy basic laws of physics, like all of the other scientific aspects of dance, contributes to the dancer-as-athlete mystique. Like the athlete, the dancer capitalizes on physical laws to achieve measurable success in each movement; however, dancers also strive for an aesthetic quality in that movement. The dancer may not fully comprehend the physical law that applies to a given turn, leap, or balance, but the highly skilled dancer understands what "feels right" within the body in order to achieve and accurately repeat the turn, leap, or balance on command.

Kenneth Laws is perhaps the most active researcher in physics and dance (Laws, 1978-1979, 1979, 1980, 1984). Undeniably, his work is only a half step away from kinesiological inquiry; but, unlike the kinesiologist, he endeavors to apply physical principles to reveal, measure, and improve the qualitative rather than the quantitative aspects of performance. In his article, he writes from two viewpoints: that of the theorist and that of the practiced artist. He is both physicist and dancer, having initiated ballet study 8 years ago in order to experience the problems that dancers face in learning to control and generate a variety of forces during movement. Laws' studies are equally useful to athletes who are involved in artistic sports (such as, diving, gymnastics, and ice skating), for he cautions us to keep our pursuit of quantitative measures in perspective lest we lose sight of our pursuit of quality in movement.

References

Bushey, S.R. (1966). Relationship of modern dance performance to agility, balance, flexibility, power, and strength. *Research Quarterly, 37*, 313-316.

Calabrese, L. et al. (1982). Menstrual abnormalities and body composition in professional ballet dancers. *Medicine and Science in Sports and Exercise, 14*, 145.

Chass, M. (1974, August 18). Gut issue: Who shapes up best, athletes or dancers? *New York Times*, pp. 5, 25.

Cohen, J.K., et al. (1980). The heart of a dancer: Noninvasive cardiac evaluation of professional ballet dancers. *American Journal of Cardiology, 45*, 959-965.

de Guzman, J. (1979). Dance as a contributor to cardiovascular fitness and alteration of body composition. *Journal of Physical Education and Recreation, 50*(4), 88-91.

Dolgener, F.A., et al. (1980). Body build and body composition of high ability female dancers. *Research Quarterly, 51*, 599-607.

Jette, M., & Inglis, H. (1975). Energy cost of square dancing. *Journal of Applied Physiology, 38*(1), 44-45.

Kirkendall, D.T., & Calabrese, L.H. (1983). Physiological aspects in dance. *Clinics in Sports Medicine, 2*, 525-537.

Kram, M. (1971, September 27). Encounter with an athlete. *Sports Illustrated*, pp. 93-100.

Laws, K. (1978-1979). An analysis of turn in dance. *Dance Research Journal, 1, 2*, 12-19.

Laws, K. (1979). Physics and ballet: A new pas de deux. In D.T. Taplin (Ed.), *New Directions in Dance* (pp. 137-146). Waterloo, IA: University of Waterloo.

Laws, K. (1980). Precarious aurora: An example of physics in partnering. *Kinesiology for Dance, 12*, 2-3.

Laws, K. (1984). *The physics of dance*. New York: Schirmer.

Novak, L.P. et al. (1978). Maximal oxygen intake and body composition of female dancers. *European Journal of Applied Physiology, 39*, 277-282.

Rimmer, J.H., & Rosentswieg, J. (1981-1982). Maximum oxygen consumption in dance majors. *Dance Research Journal, 14*(1-2), 29-31.

Van Zile, J. (1980). Energy use: An important stylistic element in dance. *CORD Research Journal, VIII*, 85-86.

9

Musculoskeletal and Cardiopulmonary Evaluation of Professional Ballet Dancers

Richard A. Mostardi
AKRON CITY HOSPITAL
AKRON, OHIO, USA

The heart, lungs, and muscular system of athletes have intrigued scientists for years and have been the subject of intense research. For example, what are the physical attributes that enable a man to run 1,500 meters in less than 4 minutes or 100 meters in less than 10 seconds? These are remarkable athletic accomplishments and cannot be achieved by the average man or woman. The little anatomic and physiologic data available indicate that special attributes in runners, gymnasts, and football players to a large extent predict excellence in performance.

Unfortunately, the ballet dancer has not been a focal point of such research efforts and there is a paucity of data in the literature relative to measurable anatomic and physiologic qualities that could be useful in describing performance. One of the purposes of the Physical Fitness Testing Center at Akron City Hospital is to generate data on a variety of types of athletes in an attempt to characterize or describe their extraordinary physical qualities. These data can then be used to comparatively evaluate injuries. For example, the lower legs and feet of both male and female ballet dancers, although normal, are anatomically peculiar and considerably different from what is usually thought of as normal. Such anatomic and physiologic differences are found in all types of highly skilled performers but, again, the ballet dancer has received little attention. Additionally, baseline data on world-class athletes are extremely useful to the physician or physical therapist because each class or type of physical process differs markedly in subtle forms of function and structure. It is these subtle differences that are of extreme interest in this laboratory.

The purpose of this study was to carry out detailed evaluations of the cardiac, pulmonary, and musculoskeletal system of competent ballet dancers in order to profile such an athlete. It is also our intent to describe their nutritional status and dietary habits in order to identify any peculiar commonalities which might affect performance. This will enable the medical community to better understand the normal functions of these individuals from a physical profile point of view and also permit more effective treatment in case of injury.

Methods

The evaluation will be broken down into (a) history, physical, lower extremity X rays and Cybex testing, and (b) cardiopulmonary testing. The history, physical examination, and X rays, done by Barry J. Greenberg, MD, served two purposes. One was to screen each dancer from a cardiovascular point of view, permitting stress testing. The second was to examine, via X ray, the skeletal anatomy of the lower extremity. For the Cybex tests, the dancer was asked to change into shorts and to sit alongside the dynamometer. Cybex isokinetic testing was then performed on various muscle groups or movements, including one-plane movements at the hip, knee, and ankle. The testing protocol for each joint follows.

Hip

The Cybex II Isokinetic Dynamometer[1] was set at 30°/s. It was placed and turned so that the axis of rotation was at the posterior aspect of the hip. The pad was placed on the distal end of the femur and the patient was asked to do abduction and adduction in a side-lying position. Two warm-up bouts of exercise preceded testing. The testing protocol for the hip was three contractions for all testings. The right and left side were tested. The patient was then asked to lie in a supine position and the axis of rotation was aligned at the greater trochanter. The pad was placed on the anterior aspect of the distal femur and the patient was asked to do isokinetic flexion and extension of the hip. The patient was asked to do two warm-up bouts of exercise, and then three bouts of exercises were recorded. The patient was then asked to sit facing the dynamometer with the center of rotation aligned at the center of the patella. Proper femoral stabilization was carried out and the patient was asked to do femoral internal and external rotation. Two bouts of exercises were carried out for warm-up and three bouts were recorded. A digital work integrator measured each set of contractions.

Knees

The dynamometer was turned so that the knees could be tested. The center of rotation was aligned one thumb width above the head of the fibula and mid-

---

[1]The Cybex unit is an instrument that measures strength, power, and endurance of various muscle groups.

way between the anterior and posterior aspects of the knee. The subject's femur was strapped to the table and the pad was placed at the distal aspect of the tibia. The patient was asked to do two bouts of exercise at 30°/s. Maximal effort was encouraged. The lever arm speed was then increased to 180°/s and the patient was asked to kick hard and fast until told to stop. Criteria for ceasing the test were two or more quadriceps torque curves 50% below the peak torque at that speed. The procedures were repeated on each leg.

Ankles

The Cybex was positioned so that the plantar flexion and dorsiflexion of the ankles could be tested. The testing protocol consisted of three contractions at 3 rpm and 10 contractions at 7 rpm. The patient was given a warm-up exercise as before, and both legs were tested. The inversion and eversion were tested by placing the patient so that the femur was at 90° flexion and the tibia was horizontal to the ground. The patient's foot was secured into the device and specific stabilization by the examiner at the proximal distal ends of the tibia was done. Inversion and eversion, two contractions, were done for a warm-up. The recorder was placed at the 30 ft/lb scale and the patient was asked to do three maximal contractions at 3 rpm. Both legs were done. In order to ensure random design, the legs were alternated. This was to randomly rule out any type of learning process by the patient during testing.

Graded Exercise Test

The next series of tests, cardiopulmonary function, was carried out on another day because of the time and energy expended on Cybex testing. The female dancers found it difficult, if not impossible, to run for this test. Their customary drastic external rotation of the lower extremity and their aversion to running necessitated a fast walk to complete the test. The speed of the treadmill was set at 6.4 kph without elevation for the initial phase and was then elevated 3% every 3 min until exhaustion. After this effort the subject recovered for 5 min while the $\dot{V}O_2$ max was calculated.

The subject was then asked to perform an additional workload at an elevation 3% higher than the last. This workload was preceded by a 5-min warm-up so that the heart rate was similar to that during the last stage of the earlier effort. The treadmill was elevated the final 3%, and the subject again walked to exhaustion, which usually took about 2 min. If the $\dot{V}O_2$ of these last two efforts was within 2%, we assumed that maximal aerobic levels had been achieved. The technique was the same for the men, but the treadmill speed was 9 to 10 kph.

At each 3-min segment the heart rate was recorded on a Quinton Model 662 ECG, and oxygen consumption ($\dot{V}O_2$) was determined by the open circuit method. Inspired air was determined using a Parkinson-Cowan CD-4 dry gas meter, and the expired air was collected in previously evacuated Douglas bags. Expired oxygen was determined on a Beckman E2 analyzer and carbon dioxide on a Beckman Spinco LB-2 analyzer. Calibration gases for these instruments were previously verified on a Lloyd Haldane chemical analyzer.

The nutrition component of the physical fitness program was provided by a registered dietitian and consisted of a detailed nutrition assessment based on a computer analysis of a patient-reported 3-day food intake record, a patient profile, laboratory data, and patient diagnosis. Actual weight versus ideal weight was discussed. Cholesterol, sodium, alcohol, vitamins, and minerals consumed daily in foods were assessed in relation to the recommended daily allowance (RDA) and the U.S. Dietary Goals.

This information was then translated into a nutrition plan detailing foods that should be increased, decreased, or added to a daily meal plan, specific recommendation for kilocalories, and distribution of kilocalories as protein, carbohydrate, and fat. Also available was the nutrition counseling option. This entailed instruction and guidance through the recommended nutrition plan on a group and individual basis. Subjects covered during nutrition counseling included explanation of the exchange lists for meal planning, various aspects of food selection and preparation, eating away from home, and behavior modification techniques.

Results

Table 1 shows the vital data for the participating dancers. All were found to be in good health.

X Rays

All dancers examined had varying degrees of flattening of the head of the first metatarsal associated with osteophyte formation at the cortical-cartilage border of the metatarsal head as well as the base of the proximal phalanx. Significant superior notching with varying degrees of aseptic necrosis was observed at the neck of the talus in most of the dancers, as well as varying degrees of osteophyte formation of the superior and posterior aspects of the talus and tibia. Lateral standing X rays revealed varying degrees of volar sag of the naviculocuneiform joint—the so-called flexible flatfoot deformity—in most dancers.

Cardiopulmonary Testing

Table 2 shows the mean metabolic values for both men and women. Maximal heart rate and $\dot{V}O_2$ max were higher in the male dancers. Both men and women had higher aerobic power than nonathletic counterparts, although their values were in the range of nonendurance athletes.

Table 1. Vital data for ballet dancers (mean ± sd)

Variable	Women (n = 11)	Men (n = 5)
Weight (kg)	50 ± 4	64 ± 6
Height (cm)	165 ± 6	175 ± 5
Age (yr)	25 ± 5	28 ± 4
Resting heart rate	68 ± 6	69 ± 9

Table 2. Summary of cardiopulmonary data for ballet dancers (mean ± se)

Variable	Women (n = 11)	Men (n = 5)
$\dot{V}O_2$ max (liters·min^{-1})	2.4 ± 0.01	3.83 ± 0.09
$\dot{V}O_2$ max (ml·kg^{-1})	48.6 ± 1.3	59.3 ± 2.0
$\dot{V}E$ max (liters·min, BTPS)	94.8 ± 5.2	142.6 ± 3.9
HR max (beats·min^{-1})	188.0 ± 4.2	200.0 ± 2.6
$\dot{V}E/\dot{V}O_2$	39.7 ± 1.9	37.3 ± 0.7

Cybex Testing

The Cybex data are shown in Table 3, which indicates the various modes of motion as well as the speed of the lever arm. The endurance values for the knee are reported as the number of contractions required to reach 50% contractile height compared with the control value. In addition, the values for knee flexion were expressed per kg of body weight so that we could compare dancers with other athletes. The men's values were 2.73 ± 0.38 and 2.58 ± 0.26 (N-meter·kg^{-1}, mean ± SE) for right and left legs, respectively, and for women the values were 1.56 ± 0.11 and 1.52 ± 0.07 (N-meter·kg^{-1}, mean ± SE).

Discussion

X Rays

The X rays were normal except for several morphological changes in the skeletal and ligamentous elements of the feet and ankles. The hallux valgus associated

Table 3. Summary of isokinetic cybex data for ballet dancers (peak torque in n-meter, mean ± se)

Variable	Women (n = 11)	Men (n = 5)
Right leg		
knee flexion 30°/s	64.5 ± 3.6	87.5 ± 10.3
knee extension 30°/s	107.3 ± 7.3	162.0 ± 11.2
knee flexion 180°/s	40.6 ± 1.5	58.3 ± 6.0
knee extension 180°/s	54.8 ± 2.4	97.7 ± 9.5
endurance[a]	27.7 ± 8.8	27.6 ± 1.7
Left leg		
knee flexion 30°/s	61.6 ± 2.6	89.9 ± 7.0
knee extension 30°/s	103.3 ± 4.4	157.0 ± 7.5
knee flexion 180°/s	40.8 ± 2.2	60.6 ± 6.7
knee extension 180°/s	54.2 ± 2.4	91.3 ± 9.8
endurance[a]	27.8 ± 7.7	31.5 ± 4.3

[a]Number of contractions required to reach 50% contractile height compared with the control value.

with metatarsus adductus and cortical thickening have been described before. It has not been determined whether the hypertrophy of the metatarsals is due to repeated stress fractures with subsequent healing or a physiological hypertrophy of the diaphysis of the metatarsus secondary to stress imposed by walking and standing on pointe. These abnormalities were not associated with pain or disability and were interpreted as positive adaptive changes. This statement is based on past clinical experience because such changes have not yet appeared in a number of 10- to 12-year-old ballet dancers. It is suggested that such changes occur after initiating pointe position exercising and that they are an example of Wolff's law. Such structural changes are not often observed in nonathletic persons.

Cardiopulmonary Data

Apparently, years of ballet training dictate that running is contraindicated for the development of structurally and functionally sound muscles in female dancers. Even in these conditions of walking and steep degrees of elevation, it is believed that the dancers achieved true levels of maximal aerobic capacity as indicated principally by the high rate and the level of fatigue. Furthermore, each dancer performed an additional workload at a grade 3% higher than the last completed workloads. The criterion for maximal oxygen consumption was that these two workloads should be within 2% of each other. Male dancers, on the other hand, had no problem with running and each subject ran at a comfortable speed of between 9 and 10 kph.

The female dancers had excellent levels of maximal aerobic capacity, as indicated in Table 2, when compared with other athletic women except for elite distance runners and speed skaters. Recent data by Cohen et al. (1982) showed that women from the American Ballet Theater had maximal oxygen consumption values that were considerably below the values of the Ohio Ballet dancers. The male dancers also had a high maximal oxygen consumption. Again, in comparing these data with data by Cohen et al., the Ohio Ballet dancers have statistically significantly higher levels of maximal aerobic capacity. Also, their mean maximal oxygen consumption would rank them well above other professional athletes such as professional basketball players and football players.

Cybex Data

It is difficult to compare Cybex data among athletic groups because of the lack of standardization of Cybex testing protocols in research laboratories and clinics. We chose the testing protocol at the lower lever arm speeds for all joints so that we could test the muscle's ability to perform maximal contractions. The slow lever-arm speeds stimulate muscle contraction as the contraction changes from isometric to isokinetic. We believe that this gives the best picture of the muscle's ability to shorten forcibly. We realize that the slower lever-arm speeds do not correlate with the joint motion that takes place during ballet dancing. However, we were mainly interested in the force with which the muscle can contract.

Peak torque of the quadriceps at 180°/s was lower for female dancers than female national basketball champions. Additionally, recent work using elite

Alpine ski racers shows that the ballet dancers also have significantly lower peak torque generated by the quadriceps. These differences are probably due to the weight-lifting and weight-training programs of basketball players and ski racers. Ballet dancers almost never lift weights because bulky musculature is not aesthetically desirable in this art form.

Nutritional Data

The caloric intake by the female ballet dancers averaged 1,200 calories. Types of foods consumed varied considerably and made comparison difficult. We did not place emphasis on the nutritional data because we felt (a) that the forms were filled out improperly because of poor supervision on the part of the investigators and (b) that dancers have a tendency to understate the amount of food consumed during a 24-hour period. New attempts are being made to analyze dietary habits of female dancers.

In conclusion, these data show that the professional ballet dancer requires extraordinary neuromuscular capabilities and, in certain professional groups, aerobic capacity. This activity appears to require a most interesting variety of talents, and we suggest that the ballet dancer is an athlete of considerable ability and compares favorably with other professional groups.

Reference

Cohen, J.L., Segal, K.R., Witriol, I., et al. (1982). Cardiorespiratory responses to ballet exercise and $\dot{V}O_2$ max of elite ballet dancers. *Medicine and Science for Sport and Exercise,* **14,** 212-217.

10

Contemporary Stretching Techniques: Theory and Application

G.H. Van Gyn
UNIVERSITY OF VICTORIA
VICTORIA, BRITISH COLUMBIA, CANADA

Sherbon (1975) has stated that artistic expression is dependent upon the technique and control of a given instrument of expression. For the dancer, of course, the instrument is the body. Extending the range of motion through which the body can move will increase the possibilities in the dancer's expressive movement. This paper will describe the concept of flexibility, discuss its physiological bases, describe techniques for developing flexibility, and assess the effectiveness of each of these stretching techniques.

Flexibility Defined

Flexibility is usually defined as the range of motion around a joint or series of joints (as in the case of the spine). This is the definition for static flexibility, whereas the ability to move a joint quickly with little resistance to the movement is dynamic flexibility. Little is known about dynamic flexibility, even though it may be extremely important to physical performance (de Vries, 1980).

Additional categories of flexibility—active and passive—have been suggested (Van Gyn, 1983). Dance demands not only extension of body parts but that the extension be controlled and usually held. An example is the position achieved during a développé. This position necessitates active flexibility, which requires strength development throughout the range of the extension. Passive flexibility, on the other hand, involves the extension of a body part without the control of the terminal position or the controlled return of the limb to its original position. This type of movement is usually initiated by the development of momentum in a body part or by resistance against an immovable surface (e.g., the floor or barre), and is controlled by gravity. Flexibility without control is of little use to the dancer. Flexibility training should therefore be combined with strength development throughout the range of motion to achieve active flexibility.

Limits to Flexibility

The major limiters to flexibility are the bones and the soft tissue. One of the functional reasons for turnout in dance is to allow for greater range of motion in the hip joint. Turnout of the leg positions the head of the femur so that bony contact of femur and pelvis is reduced. Repositioning of body parts is the only way to overcome limitations resulting from bony structure. The soft tissue (muscle tissue, fascial sheath, and the connective tissue of tendon, ligaments, and joint capsule) is modifiable by physical methods and is thus of most concern when assessing stretching techniques. The greatest resistance to stretch results from the fascial sheath that covers the muscle and the contractile elements of the muscle fiber (Ramsey & Street, 1941).

Functions of Flexibility

Often the question is asked, What are the advantages of flexibility other than that it gives greater range of motion? For the dancer, as has already been stated, it contributes to the expressiveness of movement. Extension also contributes to the line of the movement, making it aesthetically more pleasing. On a more functional level, a greater range of motion may contribute to the biomechanical efficiency of specific movements. For instance, flexibility in the gastrocnemius allows for increased dorsiflexion in the ankle joint. Therefore, during a demi-plié preceding a jump, this flexibility will allow the foot to remain in contact with the floor longer and generate more force. The equal and opposite force (Newton's third law) generated from the floor is increased and will contribute to a higher jump.

Flexibility also leads to a physiological advantage with respect to the functioning of the muscle itself. Cavagna, Dusman, and Margaria (1968) showed that lengthening or stretching the muscle before contraction (negative work) results in the accumulation of elastic energy that is used to augment the following positive work of the contraction. In other words, greater force can be produced by a muscle if it is stretched first.

A possible benefit from the development of flexibility is in the prevention of injuries, although this has not been well documented. Stretching as a warm-up may result in an acute state of muscle relaxation and increased blood flow to the muscle, which then may reduce the probability of injury. Some stretching techniques may, however, contribute to muscle injury. Techniques used in the development of passive flexibility, such as the ballistic stretch method, may result in muscle soreness and injury. At the same time, certain types of stretching are used to relieve muscle soreness as well as for warm-up when the acute effects of stretching will be beneficial to the activity to follow.

Physiology of Stretching

Evaluating stretching techniques is difficult unless the physiological mechanisms in the muscle that will contribute to the development of flexibility are understood. The *musculotendinous unit* is structured so that the contractile units (the muscle fibers) are encased in connective tissue called the endomysium. The bundles of muscle fibers, the fasciculi, are further surrounded by the perimysium; and the whole muscle, made up of these muscle bundles, is encased in the epimysium. Because muscle fibers do not necessarily run the length of the muscle or even through a fasciculus, the force of contraction must be transmitted from the muscle fiber to connective tissue and eventually to the bones in order to initiate movement. It is these three types of connective tissue, collectively called the fascial sheath, that offer the greatest resistance to stretch. This is logical because it is the connective tissue that gives stability to the joint. As de Vries (1980) has stated, in the pursuit of flexibility, the major focus must be on this connective tissue.

The *functional unit* of the muscle is the sarcomere, the number of them determining the length of the muscle. It is this unit that contracts and causes movement.

Embedded in the musculotendinous unit are two major *intrinsic receptors* that have a direct effect on the ability to stretch: the muscle spindle and the Golgi tendon organ. The muscle spindle lies between and parallel to the extrafusal or contractile fibers of the muscle. It is sensitive only to the length of the muscle and when stretched responds to the rate of change (phasic response) and ultimate length achieved (tonic response). Most muscle spindles receive two types of innervation. The primary afferent fiber (Type I) is more sensitive than the secondary (Type II), as it has a lower threshold to stretch. Actually it responds to the speed of the stretch; therefore, the faster the stretch the greater the response. The response is the monosynatic stretch reflex or myotactic reflex, which results in a contraction of the muscle in which the muscle spindles are embedded (the agonist) and a relaxation of the antagonist or opposing muscle. The secondary, or Type II, fibers are smaller and conduct impulses at a slower rate. They respond only to the final stretched length of the muscle and act to relax the agonist and provide facilitation of the stretch. However, since the speed of conduction of these fibers is relatively slow, this facilitation will not occur unless the stretch is done slowly.

Motor innervation to the spindle is in the form of gamma motor neurons and their function is to reset the sensitivity of the spindle. In passive stretching, the firing of primary afferents increases at first but returns to its resting frequency as the sensitivity of the spindle is reset. This means that the spindle will respond briefly to oppose a change in length but if the terminal position is held, the spindle will reset to its resting level and the contraction caused by the stretch reflex will cease.

The Golgi tendon organ (GTO) is located at the musculotendinous junction and is in series with the muscle fibers. It will, therefore, discharge when the muscle is stretched or contracted; that is, it responds to tension rather than length. The GTO is a protective device. It evokes an inverse myotactic reflex that inhibits the contraction of the muscle of origin as well as the entire functional muscle group. The GTO is much less sensitive to stretch than the muscle spindle and is not unloaded by contraction.

Presumably, to be effective, any stretching technique should take advantage of the aspects of the system that will contribute to the stretch and avoid activating those aspects that will inhibit stretching. Stretching can result in two types of effects: acute, or short-term, and chronic, or long-term. Perhaps more descriptive terms are those used by Sapega, Quendenfeld, Moyer, and Butler (1981). They refer to two types of stretching as (a) elastic stretch, which represents spring-like behavior and is described as temporary and recoverable, and (b) plastic stretch, which occurs when the linear deformation produced by the tensile stretch remains and is described as nonrecoverable or permanent.

Sapega et al. (1981) describe connective tissue as having viscoelastic properties. The viscous property allows for chronic or plastic change and the elastic property permits acute or recoverable change. The acute effects are those that will contribute to the enhancement of flexibility over a series of training sessions. The acute effects include the results of the elastic properties of the connective tissue as well as the action of the muscle spindle and the tendon organ on the muscle.

Chronic physiological changes of flexibility training are not well documented. The current thinking is that connective tissue that is subjected to stretch of sufficient frequency and duration adapts to this overload and is remodelled to accommodate the stretch. The amount of remodelling or lengthening is dependent on how and under what conditions the stretching is performed. Principal factors are the amount and duration of applied force and the temperature of the tissue when stretching is performed (Sapega et al., 1981).

This means that as an individual stretches he will find that his range of motion becomes greater in that training session due to acute changes. As the training continues, more stable changes will occur that contribute to a relatively permanent increased range of motion. The effects of a stretching program may persist for at least 8 weeks (McCue, 1953). The amount of change, either acute or chronic, will depend on the type of stretching technique chosen.

Stretch Techniques and Their Effects

Traditionally, the dancer has relied on three methods of stretching: ballistic stretch, slow stretch, and static stretch. A fourth method widely used in clinical applications is proprioceptive neuromuscular facilitation (PNF) or the 3-S method (Holt, 1978). There has been some controversy as to the acute and chronic effects of the four approaches.

Ballistic Stretching

Ballistic stretch relies on the speed and the weight of the moving body part to lengthen the muscle group (e.g., a battement initiated from lunge position with the intent of stretching the hamstrings of the moving leg). Because of the speed of the movement, the stretch reflex is very strong. Therefore, two opposing forces act on the muscle group: the force generated from the fast stretch that is attempting to lengthen the muscle and the reflexive contraction of that same muscle group. This combination of opposing forces may result in fiber tears in the muscle group being stretched.

The acute effect of this method may be a relative shortening of the muscle group being trained. Type II afferent fibers do not respond to a fast stretch and thus no facilitation is gained from this source. Because the range of stretch is limited within a single session, the training effect will not be as great. The principle of overload implies that the improvement will be related to increase in the range of motion achieved at each training session.

As Holt, Travis, and Okita (1970) have shown, chronic gains in flexibility using ballistic stretch are not as good as from the other methods. In addition, research has shown that the proportion of tissue elongation that remains after tensile stress is removed is less for high-force, short-duration methods of stretching (Warren, Lehmann, & Koblanski, 1971, 1976). Warren et al. also showed that this method produces more structural weakening than low-force, long-duration techniques. Muscle soreness is another negative side effect.

Slow Stretching

Slow stretch involves a gradual lengthening of a specific muscle group until it is in a maximally stretched state. The dancer then releases and returns the body part to its resting state. Generally this is used as a passive technique in that the terminal position is held against an immovable object. Because of the slowness of the stretch, this technique takes advantage of the Type II facilitating response. It thus follows that a greater range can be achieved in any one session and the technique should result in a better training effect over sessions.

Static Stretching

Static stretching, also known as the stretch-and-hold technique, has been popular and is regarded as one of the most effective stretching methods. The acute effects are the same as for the slow method but, because the terminal position is held, the sensitivity of the muscle spindle is reset and the initial stretch reflex contraction diminishes. This is in addition to the facilitation of the secondary afferents. The low-force, long-duration static method is effective in promoting chronic changes in passive flexibility. It certainly is safe in terms of maintaining the integrity of the structural support system and will not cause undue muscle soreness.

PNF or 3-S Stretch

The PNF or 3-S stretch is derived from Kabat's (1965) clinical technique for rehabilitation. Holt's modification has made the technique applicable to the sport and dance setting (Holt et al., 1970).

Generally, this technique requires a partner but can be done using a barre or wall for some specific stretches. The method involves (a) placing the muscle group to be stretched in an elongated position, (b) gradually contracting the stretched muscle group isometrically until a near maximum effort is attained, (c) sustaining this contraction for approximately 4 seconds, (d) relaxing that muscle group, and (e) concentrically contracting the opposing muscle group and extending the position of stretch (this can be aided by slight, gentle pressure from the partner). The process is repeated three or four times in order to fully stretch the muscle group of concern.

Physiologically the technique takes full advantage of those systems that will enhance stretch. As the stretch is initiated, the muscle spindles fire, causing a myotatic stretch reflex. The muscles being stretched will then contract. However, since the elongated position is maintained and the stretch is slow, the sensitivity of the muscle spindle is reset and the Type II afferents are stimulated, causing the muscles being stretched to relax. The second phase, the isometric contraction, stimulates the Golgi tendon organ, evoking an inverse myotactic reflex. This causes further relaxation of the elongated muscle group.

The final phase, the concentric contraction of the opposing or antagonist muscle group, causes additional relaxation in the elongated muscle group through reciprocal inhibition. This process is a phenomenon associated with a spinal-level reflex that acts to prevent the extensor muscles from contracting, thereby ensuring relaxation of the antagonist muscle during the completion of the movement. These acute effects lead to the development of a greater range during the training session and therefore may lead to overload and greater plastic or chronic effects.

In addition to the flexibility effects, Holt et al. (1969) found that the PNF method resulted in strength gains in both the stretched muscle group and the opposing muscle group. In a practical sense, by using the PNF method, the dancer's active range of motion, which involves extending the limb and holding it in the extended position, would be enhanced. This active stretch capacity is obviously preferable to an improved passive range of motion. As with the other low-force, long-duration methods, the stability of the joint is not reduced. Tanigawa (1972) indicated that PNF not only develops a greater range of motion than other methods but rates of improvement are better.

Although the way PNF occurs still is not totally clear, it does appear that the number of apparent benefits for the dancer in his or her training makes it the most desirable method. There are two negative aspects. First, it is necessary to have informed personnel to aid in the stretch. The person helping with the stretch must understand the technique and be sensitive to correct alignment and the amount of force that needs to be applied. Second, this method takes considerable time and therefore is not suitable as part of a class.

Further Considerations

Regardless of the stretching technique chosen, several other factors should be considered. The first is temperature, which appears to have a significant influence on the mechanical behavior of connective tissue under tensile stress.

Lehmann, Masock, Warren, and Koblanski (1970) have shown that raising the temperature of a tendon increases the amount of permanent elongation. Sapega et al. (1981) suggest, therefore, that flexibility training sessions be preceded by at least 5 minutes of light but gradually progressive muscular exercise. They maintain that raising body temperature should make stretching safer and more productive.

Frequency and duration are two other important factors. For the dancer, the stretching that takes place during the technique class generally is not of sufficient intensity to result in any major change. Specific flexibility sessions should occur at least three times per week. Duration refers not to the length of the session but rather to the length of the hold phase of the static and PNF methods. Earlier reference was made to the benefits of two low-force, long-duration methods. Typically, both have used a 6- to 10-second hold phase. Although this may be adequate, maximum benefits in terms of plastic changes will occur with a hold phase of 30 seconds or greater. That this will make the training sessions fairly long is a small consideration in light of the safety and effectiveness of the static and PNF methods using this extended hold phase.

The last consideration in stretching is correct body alignment. Since flexibility is so specific to both the joint and type of movement, the placement of the body becomes critical. The PNF technique in particular requires that there is no postural deviation. It should be the responsibility of the partner to watch for deviations or ''cheating'' on the part of the dancer who is stretching, especially in the contraction phase.

Conclusion

Increasing flexibility, an aspect of fitness, requires specific training techniques. Of the four techniques reviewed, the static and PNF methods utilize facilitation from physiological sources most effectively. PNF, in addition to increasing the range of motion in a joint, contributes to strength gains. It is, therefore, effective in developing active flexibility, which is most desirable for dance training.

References

Cavagna, G.A., Dusman, B., & Margaria, R. (1968). Positive work done by a previously stretched muscle. *Journal of Applied Physiology,* **24**, 21-32.

de Vries, H.A. (1980). *Physiology of exercise* (3rd ed.). Dubuque, IA: Brown.

Holt, L.E. (1978). *Static stretching for sports (3-S)*. Halifax, Nova Scotia: Sport Research.

Holt, L.E., Kaplan, H.M., Okita, T., & Hoshiko, M. (1969). The influence of antagonistic contraction and head position on the responses of antagonistic muscles. *Archives of Physical Medicine and Rehabilitation, 50,* 279-280.

Holt, L.E., Travis, T.M., & Okita, T. (1970). Comparative study of three stretching techniques. *Perceptual and Motor Skills,* **31**, 611-616.

Kabat, H. (1965). Proprioceptive facilitation in therapeutic exercise. In S. Licht (Ed.), *Therapeutic exercise*. New Haven, CT: Williams and Wilkins.

Lehmann, J.F., Masock, A.J., Warren, C.G., & Koblanski, J.N. (1970). Effect of therapeutic temperatures on tendon extensibility. *Archives of Physical Medicine and Rehabilitation, 51*, 481-487.

McCue, B.F. (1953). Flexibility of college women. *Research Quarterly, 24*, 316.

Ramsey, R.W., & Street, S. (1941). The isometric length tension diagram of isolated skeletal muscle fibers of the frog. *Journal of Cell Composition Physiology, 15*, 11.

Sapega, A.A., Quendenfeld, T.C., Moyer, R., & Butler, R.A. (1981). Biophysical factors in range of motion exercise. *The Physician and Sportsmedicine, 9*(12), 57-65.

Sherbon, E. (1975). *Modern dance methods* (2nd ed.). Palo Alto, CA: Mayfield.

Tanigawa, M.C. (1972). Comparison of the hold-relax procedure and passive mobilization on increasing muscle length. *Physical Therapy, 152*(7), 725-735.

Van Gyn, G.H. (1983, Spring). Sing the body elastic. *Dance in Canada*, pp. 17-19.

Warren, C.G., Lehmann, J.F., & Koblanski, J.N. (1971). Elongation of rat tail tendon: Effect of load and temperature. *Archives of Physical Medicine and Rehabilitation, 52*, 465-474.

Warren, C.G., Lehmann, J.F., & Koblanski, J.N. (1976). Heat and stretch procedures: An evaluation using rat tail tendon. *Archives of Physical Medicine and Rehabilitation, 57*, 122-126.

11

A Comparison of Nutrient Needs Between Dancers and Other Athletes

Marilyn S. Peterson
THE SPORTS MEDICINE CLINIC
SEATTLE, WASHINGTON, USA

Athletes, whether dancers or runners, are eager for nutritional information. They will change their eating habits if a change has been demonstrated to be an advantage to performance. The runner or any other athlete will consider factors such as percentage of lean body mass, $\dot{V}O_2$ max, and training schedules, and adjust calories and carbohydrate composition of the diet up or down to meet the challenge of competition (American Dietetic Association, 1980; Bentivegna & Kelly, 1979). The dancer, however, has not caught up with this body of knowledge and is still bound by the desire to continually maintain the dance "look" or image. And this desire dictates, throughout the entire span of the dancer's career, the quantity and frequency of food intake.

If the major difference between dancers and other athletes is simply the caloric intake, which in turn influences the quality of the diet, it is possible to aid the dancer in selecting foods that will encourage sound lifelong eating habits, perhaps prevent some of the more common health problems, and prevent eating disorders. The dancer's diet needs to be carefully planned and structured to allow the meals and snacks that can realistically fit into rigorous rehearsal and class schedules and other demands.

Data from Calabrese and others has already examined the diets of female dancers and athletes in great detail. The most prevalent observation for this data is that while performance and training expectations are great for all athletes, the caloric intake and the quality of the diet is consistently lower for the dancer. The estimation for caloric needs considers resting or basal metabolic needs, daily activity levels, training needs, and growth needs. Caloric levels of the elite female runner have been reported to be three times that of the reference female, while case studies of the elite dancer report caloric levels below 75% of the Recommended Dietary Allowances (Calabrese et al., 1982; Caldwell, 1984). There are many reasons for this, of course, but some of them center around the training, self-image, and future expectations of the athletes in each field.

Several interesting comparisons of data (see Table 1) were gathered from a questionnaire offered to Olympic-caliber track and field athletes preparing for the 1980 trials and to advanced ballet students preparing for professional dance.

This information was taken from a food frequency form and, while not detailed, again shows the trend of the female track and field athlete to maintain

Table 1. Nutritional comparison between ballet dancers and track and field athletes

Dancers	Track and field athletes
Age: 21-33	19-33 years
Weight: 98-125 lb	105-180 lb
Height: 5'1''-5'8''	5'2''-6'
Race: white	5 black, 6 white
Occupations: student, dancer	coach, teacher, waitress, student, "athlete"
Training duration: 7-9 years	8-12 years
Reported injuries: lower extremities	knees, feet
Nontraining activities: quiet time, laundry, cleaning, homework	other workouts, time with family and friends, dancing, fun.
Favorite food: cookies, candy, ice cream, popcorn, black licorice	breakfast, fruit
Preevent meals: some carbohydrate	high carbohydrate, low fiber
Food frequency: 5/day/dance, 2/day/nondance	3 meals plus one snack
Location of meals: home, sack lunch	everywhere
Low nutrients: protein, calories, calcium, vitamin D	vitamin D, E, A, Iron, Zinc, and calcium
Calories: below 75% of RDA	69%-33% of RDA
Supplementation: inconsistent use	iron, vitamin A and C
Changes in diet during past year: lost weight, skipped meals frequently, ate less at night, tried Weight Watchers, Women's Ski Team Diet	increased calories, carbohydrates
Individual observations: high coffee, diet soda use, infrequent water consumption	paid attention to fluid needs

body weight by increasing exercise and calories simultaneously and to follow dietary advice specific to her sport, and shows her high activity pattern off the field (Peterson, 1977).

Regardless of the "scientific attempt" to collect information on the dietary habits of the dancer, it is well to remember that our world is in the midst of an unprecedented dance boom, reflected in the number of people engaged in some form of dance activity—classical, modern, native, or aerobic. A growing and now shared body of research is identifying the relationship between diet and physical activity, particularly how the body uses nutrients in both aerobic and anaerobic exercise. This accumulating research has influence on how the athlete and dancer train and develop, and on the type of diet followed for maximum performance and to prevent the dangers of poor nutrition (Costill & Miller, 1980; Diehl, Lohman, Smith, & Kertzer, 1982; Hargreaves, Costill, Coggan, Fink, & Nishibata, 1984). At a slower pace, research is also dispelling the myths surrounding the relationships between nutrition and quality performance. Coaches, dance instructors, and health educators encourage long-term performance that is as injury-free as possible, yet somehow forget that present nutritional status is the most influential factor in rehabilitation of athletic injuries (Katch & Behnke, 1980).

Unfortunately, serious interest in nutrition for dancers is partially an outgrowth of concern for the prevalence among dancers of anemia, amenorrhea, early-onset osteoporosis, bulimia, anorexia, and failure to heal, rather than of the observation of nutrients found on the training table (Nutrition Concerns, 1982). These frequently occurring revelations of poor health shed an entirely different medical light on the dancer who so gracefully moves through various routines. Yet while these observations are very well documented, emphasis now must turn to methods of introducing nutrition to the very young dancer and his or her parents. This is the time in the dancer's life when the growth spurt normally occurs and nutritional requirements simultaneously increase. Calories, adequate fluids, protein, carbohydrate, calcium, iron, and folic acid are of particular concern. Failure to meet such nutritional requirements compromises the health of the young dancer (Nutritional Enhancement, 1984; Pate, Maguire, & Van Wyk, 1979).

The dancer's long-term nutritional needs resemble those of any age-matched athletic group. The dancer needs an adequate supply of fluids, calories matched to work demands, good quality protein, and vitamins and minerals in correct amounts. And this balanced diet, using a wide variety of foods, applies to any phase or condition of the dancer's life, whether it be early growth, injury, chronic or acute illness, pregnancy, lactation, aging, training, or the demands of the performance itself.

If a specific diet were recommended for dancers, it would be a diet calorically balanced to activity, including a wide variety of foods and a pattern of frequent snacks chosen from the highest quality of nutrient-dense foods available. Using the food groups (see Table 2) as a guideline for choice provides one way of food planning.

The body's first need is for energy. It takes energy to provide for growth needs, inevitable tissue repair, and three to four hours of dance each day. (At least 30 calories/pound per day are needed during rapid growth and 15

Table 2. Food groups

Milk or Dairy: at least 3 servings for children, 4 servings for teens, and 2 servings for the young adult (and this may be increased to 3 with supplementation of calcium for the dancer). One serving equals 8 oz of milk or yogurt or 1½ oz of cheese. This group is frequently omitted by the dancer and often is replaced by diet soda.

Meat Group: at least 2 servings. A serving equals 2 oz of lean meat, poultry or fish, 2 eggs, ½ cup cottage cheese, or 4 tbsp of peanut butter. As cheese and peanut butter are used so frequently by the dancer to supply the protein group, it is not unusual to find fat intake contributing over 40% of the dancer's daily calories.

Fruit and Vegetable Group: 4 servings. 1 cup raw or ½ cup juice equals a serving. Dancers and athletes include this group frequently, as fruits and vegetables are portable and low-calorie.

Grain Group: 4 servings. 1 slice of bread, 1 cup of dry cereal or ½ cup of cooked cereal, pasta, or rice equals a serving. The dancer frequently omits this group, while other athletes will have as many as 10 servings a day from this group.

The Other Group: wine, cookies, soft drinks, candy bars, and chips provide as much as 25% of the dancer's total calories according to two diet surveys, and are often classed as the dancer's "favorite food" (Calabrese et al., 1982; Peterson, 1977).

A balanced meal includes one serving from each group and provides ¼ to ⅓ of daily nutrient needs.

calories/pound per day thereafter.) Actual energy expenditure is difficult to measure during dance, but it seems reasonable to estimate not more than 200 calories/hour or class would be used in the most active of situations. The total daily energy needs of the dancer could thus be calculated simply as:

$$\text{body weight} \times 15 \ (30) + 400 \ \text{kcal} = \text{Total Energy Requirement}$$
$$\text{(e.g., 100 lb} \times 15 + 400 \text{ equals 2,050 kcal/day).}$$

Most female dancers are energy deficient by this calculation. One dilemma the female dancer has is that by lowering her daily energy intake she eventually lowers her basal metabolic requirements. Her other caloric requirements are based on age, body size, and other activities. At this point it takes only one analytical observation to question the type of diet that provides the female dancer with the power her performance demands.

In recording heights and weights of level-four dancers during a personal health profile, it was interesting to note that the very young dancer has already established the slim look of the professional. Of the 20 dancers measured, 19 were in the 80th and 90th percentile of height for age; all were below the 40th percentile for weight. While each of these dancers had performed professionally, all were students living at home. They were not experiencing the harsh realities of a low-income job with high competition for roles. They were still, like their audience, enchanted with dance.

The slender lines of the very young dancer are possible because of the higher caloric needs covering both growth and dance. It becomes increasingly more difficult for dancers to remain at dance-ideal body weight as age increases because dancers do not use the energy of age-matched counterparts in other sports. Most dancers have moderate aerobic profiles, low body fat, and low muscle mass. One cannot help but suggest that if more aerobic training were introduced to dance training, and other activities such as biking and running were allowed, energy demands would be higher. If these higher caloric needs were then met, perhaps the quality of the dancer's diet would improve. More fat would be used in activity, rather than glycogen and lean body tissue being depleted. In summary, until we honestly admit that at least 50% of our dancers are malnourished according to athletic standards, or until the supply of talented youth diminishes, or we arrive at a point where American dance companies must compete against other countries for principals, we most likely will encourage more difficult routines and choreography and ignore for our dancers the basic physiological need of nutrition which our "other" athletes long ago accepted (Peterson, 1982).

References

American Dietetic Association. (1980). Position paper on nutrition and physical fitness. *Journal of the American Dietetic Association, 76*, 433-437.

Bentivegna, A., & Kelly, J. (1979). Diet, fitness, and athletic performance. *The Physician and Sports Medicine, 7*, 99-105.

Calabrese, L., Kirkendall, D., Floyd, M., Rapoport, S., Weiker, G., & Bergfeld, J. (1982). Menstrual abnormalities and body composition in professional female ballet dancers. *Medicine and Science in Sport and Exercise, 14*, 145.

Caldwell, F. (1984). Light boned and lean athletes. Does the penalty outweigh the reward? *The Physician and Sportsmedicine, 9*.

Costill, D.L., & Miller, J.M. (1980). Nutrition for endurance sport: Carbohydrate and fluid balance. *International Journal of Sports Medicine, 12*.

Diehl, D.M., Lohman, T.G., Smith, S.C., & Kertzer, R.J. (1982). The effects of physical training on the iron status of female athletes. *Medicine and Science for Sport and Exercise, 14*, 164.

Hargreaves, M., Costill, D.L., Coggan, A., Fink, W.J., & Nishibata, I. (1984). Effects of carbohydrate feeding on muscle glycogen utilization and exercise performance. *Medicine and Science for Sport and Exercise, 14*, 219-222.

Katch, F.I., & Behnke, A.R. (1980). The underweight female. *The Physician and Sportsmedicine, 8*, 55-60.

Nutrition concerns of women. (1982, October). A Symposium for Health Professionals. University of Washington Continuing Dental Education.

Nutritional enhancement of athletic performance. (1984, August). From Nutrition Abstracts and Reviews (1984, January), *Sports Nutrition News, 3*(2).

Pate, R., Maguire, M., & Van Wyk, J. (1979). Dietary iron supplementation in women athletes. *The Physician and Sportsmedicine, 7*, 81-85.

Peterson, M.S. (1977). *Measurements taken on elite distance runners.* Squaw Valley: USOC.

Peterson, M.S. (1982). Nutritional concerns for the dancer. *The Physician and Sportsmedicine, 3*, 137-143.

12

The Application of Physical Principles to Dance

Kenneth Laws
DICKINSON COLLEGE
CARLISLE, PENNSYLVANIA, USA

Scientific principles must be applied to dance with great care. As an aesthetic art form that depends largely on subjective judgments of quality rather than objectively quantifiable measures, dance may seem to be an activity not conducive to scientific scrutiny. In this article I wish to reflect on the ways science can be applied to dance, and on the state of the science of dance kinesiology at this time.

Physical laws apply to human body movement whether the objective is dance or athletic activity. These principles have been applied to athletic endeavors with increasing success in the recent past. Why have we not seen a similar rate of progress in the study of dance? One characteristic of athletic activity is that the quality of performance is often easily measured. Developing a technique for achieving a higher high jump is obviously a positive accomplishment. Understanding the trajectories of a basketball as it approaches a basket, if that understanding improves the probability of scoring baskets, is clearly useful. But using principles of science to improve the quality of dance is more subtle because the measures of success, improvement, or quality of performance are generally not directly quantifiable.

The best dancers have an integrated combination of two talents—a knowledge of what is to be expressed, and the physical and mental tools to accomplish that expression. A dancer who is able to jump higher, balance longer, achieve more turns in a pirouette, or create illusions such as that of floating, is not necessarily a better dancer, but does have the advantage of a greater range of tools with which to create the desired images. And there is no doubt that science has much to offer dancers who find that understanding the physical bases of human movement can help improve technique. Such understanding is also clearly beneficial to teachers of dance.

Dancers use several means to learn technique: comments and corrections from teachers and others, trial and error, and observation of other dancers. Understanding some relevant physical principles adds another way of thinking that can supplement these traditional means of learning.

Dance Kinesiology as a Science

A science develops as an inverted pyramid of knowledge. A few basic assumptions about the role of observation, the relationship of the science to other fields, and the vocabulary to be used for communication provide the foundation. Then an expanding framework is established above that foundation, in which many qualitative observations are made, some crude analyses are carried out, and people become increasingly attuned to the new orientation of thinking. The framework is then filled in by the painstaking work of those who make very careful quantitative observations and analyses that gradually build the fund of knowledge on which further advances depend.

Of course the process of scientific progress is never that neat. The careful quantitative measurements sometimes precede the framework that makes them most useful. And, in the case of Einstein's theory of special relativity early in this century, the very foundations of a well-established science were significantly modified.

The science of dance kinesiology (the physics of dance movement specifically) may currently be out of balance in the various ways progress can be made. There are good, careful quantitative studies being carried out with emphasis on statistical validity and control of variables. There are increasing uses of technology—computer analyses and computer graphics, force platforms, and photographic or video techniques. But there are perhaps some fundamental issues at the apex of this inverted pyramid that involve the applicability of science to the art form and the use of terminology. And is there sufficient work being done on the "framework"—research that involves the development of physical insight, careful identification of the questions asked, and consideration of the significance of those questions and the usefulness of the results and conclusions?

An increasing number of people are becoming active in the field of dance kinesiology. Articles are appearing that represent careful observation and analysis of different dance movements. Good examples are the analyses of leaping turns, including the saut de basque, by Wiley (1981) and the fouetté sauté, by Shea (1981). A more limited scope of investigation is represented by the study of the movement from demi-plié to relevé, pointe, or sauté, reported recently by Clarkson, Kennedy, and Flanagan (1984).

Consider now an example of the way asking a specific question can make progress in understanding easier. It is possible to study the angular momentum of a dancer performing a pirouette. This can be done in detail by determining body segment lengths and masses, and using three-dimensional photographic analyses to determine velocities, and thereby linear and angular momenta, of the body segments. That procedure is clearly a difficult and time-consuming one. Another approach is to ask the question, How does a dancer develop torque against the floor to achieve the required angular momentum for a particular type of pirouette? (We assume that the pertinent physical quantities are rigorously defined and understood.) Understanding the mechanism by which a torque is exerted against the floor can enhance a dancer's ability to control the turn. The question leads to a technique of observation that is considerably simpler, in that the total angular momentum of the dancer as a function of time is the quantity needed rather than a detailed analysis of where in the body that angular momentum resides. This total angular momentum can be easily measured by techniques described elsewhere, with results that provide interesting and useful answers to the specific questions asked (Laws, 1978-1979).

Another example illustrates the value of developing physical insight into mechanisms before making the careful measurements that provide a more detailed and quantitative understanding. It is a type of analysis that is primarily qualitative. Fouetté turns are a continuous series of pirouettes, in which the gesture leg extends and revolves front to side once during each rotation of the body. The reason for that movement of the leg is not just because it is the way a good fouetté turn is done; it allows for a temporary transfer of angular momentum from the body as a whole to the gesture leg. During the time the angular momentum resides in the gesture leg, the body can stop rotating, allowing it to exert some torque that maintains the turn and regain balance and position. That qualitative understanding alone is useful to dancers, in that it demonstrates the importance of certain aspects of the movement. A crude *quantitative* analysis shows that the time for each revolution is split roughly equally between the rotation of the body as a whole and the quarter revolution of the gesture leg while the body is stationary. A more detailed analysis of this movement and the tour jeté described next can be found in Laws' recent book (1984).

A qualitative analysis of the tour jeté, or grand jeté en tournant, provides a further example of the value of physical insight without detailed quantitative analyses. This leaping turn may be performed in two different ways that not only emphasize different visual aspects of the movement, but use two entirely different physical principles. In one case, the moment of inertia of the body is controlled so as to create the illusion that the body is rising off the floor, flipping over in the air, then returning to the floor. There is some angular momentum of the body established while the take-off foot is still on the floor. That angular momentum is constant once contact with the floor is lost. Henceforth, if the body's moment of inertia is decreased, the rate of rotation will increase while the body is airborne. To create that appearance, the dancer must concentrate on creating a body configuration that is aligned along the rotation axis during that time of maximum rotation rate.

An entirely different effect is created if the torso, head, and arms are rotated in the air while the legs are still in the original kicking position. After that rotation is complete, the legs are reversed front to back to complete the tour jeté movement, in which the landing is on the leg opposite to the take-off leg. In this case, the dancer must concentrate on leaving the legs in the kicking position, where they contribute a large amount of moment of inertia to the body, while the rest of the body is rotating. Both the appearance of the movement and its "feel" are distinctly different.

Stretching Science Further

One can take a further step in analyzing dance scientifically by attempting to quantify aspects of the dance accepted as being totally aesthetic—an attempt eliciting a response ranging from surprise to outrage. As an example, imagine trying to describe a good arabesque position over the telephone. Without confidence that the verbal imagery used translates into the same visual images, two communicating people may have a totally invalid presumption of good communication. The imagery *is* often valid because there is a strong tradition in dance, particularly in classical ballet. An admonition about "sitting in the hip" probably means something very similar to two communicating dance teachers. But communication would be more dependable if it were based on one crucially important aspect of the physical sciences—the agreement on rigorously and objectively defined meanings for the terminology used.

Suppose we suggest that one aspect of a good arabesque position involves the orientation of the pelvis. Specifically, if one defines a Z axis as the axis attached to the pelvis and originally vertical when the body is in a standing position, that axis will tilt forward as the leg is lifted into the arabesque position, and some rotation about that axis will occur as the gesture leg is turned out. But if the Z axis also moves out of the sagittal plane when the body reaches the final position, the arabesque line becomes distorted. If the classical ballet community accepts this pelvic position as one criterion for a good arabesque, then it becomes a criterion that is objectively and rigorously defined, not subject to the potential vagaries of verbal imagery. And such a criterion *can* be communicated in our hypothetical telephone conversation.

Summary

The science of dance kinesiology can progress in different ways. As a relatively recently developing field, it can fruitfully use qualitative and descriptive studies that emphasize physical insight and understanding. As the field matures, careful quantitative studies become increasingly useful. These studies can involve detailed analyses of body movement, or, more dangerous, attempts to quantify aesthetic characteristics of movements or positions. It will be important for the modest number of people involved in dance kinesiology research to maintain a perspective of the field as a whole, maintaining valid communication of ideas and observations, and maintaining a recognition that the scientific aspects of human body movement represent merely one approach to understanding the inherently human and creative activity called dance.

References

Clarkson, P., Kennedy, T., & Flanagan, J. (1984). A study of three movements in classical ballet. *Research Quarterly for Exercise and Sport, 55,* 175-179.

Laws, K. (1978-1979). An analysis of turns in dance. *Dance Research Journal,* **11**, 12-19.

Laws, K. (1984). *The physics of dance.* New York: Schirmer Books.

Shea, M. (1981). *A kinematic and descriptive study of the rotation of major body parts in the performance of the fouetté sauté.* Master's thesis, University of Wisconsin-Madison, Department of Physical Education.

Wiley, H. (1981). *Laws of motion controlling dance movement: A qualitative and kinematic analysis of saut de basque.* Master's thesis, New York University School of Education, Health, Nursing, and Arts Professions.

PART III
Dance for Fitness

It is impossible to separate the topic of fitness from physiology. Yet, as the titles of the ensuing articles suggest, some aspects of fitness have little to do with the physiological condition of the dancer. Articles were selected that would reflect the breadth of the impact of the fitness surge in dance. Just how fit are dancers? Davidson's article serves as an excellent resource for readers who seek a thorough review of the research literature. No clear answers exist as to which dance form(s) provides the greatest aerobic benefits (it depends on a myriad of circumstances), but the literature clearly suggests that dancers need supplementary exercise conditioning outside of the studio to enhance their fitness and endurance.

If dancers elect one of the aerobic dance alternatives, then proper footwear and floor structure are essential to the prevention of injuries. This was stressed in Hardaker's article, "Pathogenesis of Dance Injuries," presented in the first section of the proceedings, and again in Rosenberg's article on footwear for aerobic dance. Because of the repetitive impact loading of the lower extremities during aerobic dance activities, it is essential that the shock absorber and lever systems of the body be protected from potential breakdown by wearing shoes especially designed to accommodate that activity. Running shoes, jazz shoes, ballet slippers, and barefeet cannot possibly protect the dancer from injury in an aerobic dance class.

If a student sustains an injury from a poorly prepared environment or instructor, then litigation may erupt. Social scientists have ways of explaining this as a function of human behavior within organized contexts; and in his article, attorney-at-law Caffray shows how the functions of today's complex society have afforded opportunities for consumers of dance fitness to legally seek compensation for injuries. Litigable consequences of negligent training practices and environments in dance and athletics may have become more likely today with the advent of malpractice lawsuits in the medical profession. Dance teachers and athletic coaches are equally plausible targets.

What can teachers of dance for fitness do to protect themselves from litigation? Caffray sums it up by advising careful documentation of all efforts to provide safe and beneficial instruction. In addition, Johnson urges a thorough knowledge of the instructional materials, and in her article she outlines the theoretical and practical bases of dance for fitness. Furthermore, the prudent teacher of dance for fitness will seek to maintain current knowledge by searching the literature regularly for updated information. Davidson's review of the literature and the articles by Rosenberg, Caffray, and Johnson are a worthwhile beginning for the conscientious teacher.

13

Dance and Cardiorespiratory Fitness

Dennis M. Davidson
UNIVERSITY OF CALIFORNIA
IRVINE, CALIFORNIA, USA

Although global assessment of physical fitness in dancers includes cardiorespiratory capacity, strength, endurance, flexibility, healthy nutrition, weight maintenance, and smoking abstention, this report will focus only on the effects of the various forms of dance on cardiorespiratory fitness.

Determinants of Cardiorespiratory Fitness

Cardiorespiratory fitness, one of the major determinants of a dancer's endurance and efficiency, can be defined in terms of oxygen consumption (aerobic capacity), ventilation, heart rate, and blood pressure responses to physical activity.

The amount of oxygen used by the body's tissues (including working muscles) is termed oxygen consumption ($\dot{V}O_2$). Endurance capacity can be expressed in terms of heart rate (HR), blood pressure (BP), and ventilation rate ($\dot{V}e$) responses to a given workrate. For example, endurance time varies in an inverse exponential manner with $\dot{V}O_2$ consumption expressed as a percentage of the individual's maximal capacity. The degree of cardiovascular conditioning is indicated by values of HR and BP at rest and by the degree to which they rise during physical activity. Similarly, ventilation rates during exercise reflect respiratory conditioning.

Supported in part by a Preventive Cardiology Academic Award (NIH HL01243-01) from the National Institutes of Health.

Oxygen consumption is traditionally measured in liters of oxygen consumed per minute. To provide $\dot{V}O_2$ comparisons among persons of different size, one divides $\dot{V}O_2$ by body weight (in kg). This calculation yields VO_2 in ml/kg/min. However, even after normalizing in this manner for body weight, men have higher values of maximal $\dot{V}O_2$ than women at all ages. Therefore, further adjustment can be made for the higher percentage of body fat noted in most women by expressing $\dot{V}O_2$ max as ml O_2 consumed/kg lean body mass/min. This narrows the oxygen consumption differences between men and women to within 10% to 15%.

Oxygen consumption so measured allows us to calculate other cardiorespiratory parameters. For example, $\dot{V}O_2$ is the product of the rate of oxygen extraction by the tissues (arteriovenous oxygen [a-$\bar{v}O_2$] difference) and cardiac output. In turn, cardiac output equals the product of heart rate and left ventricular stroke volume (ml of blood ejected with each contraction). Although both stroke volume and a-v oxygen difference increase slightly with exercise, the largest contributor to increases in oxygen consumption is the rise in heart rate. Therefore, we can use heart rate to estimate oxygen consumption in dancers while in class or on the stage.

Fitness in Dancers

Dance, in its many forms, has positive effects on cardiorespiratory fitness. The magnitude of such effects in an individual dancer is related to the intensity, frequency, duration, and type of habitual activity.

Studies to date have been of several types: (a) physiological profiles of dancers, (b) comparisons of dancers and controls, (c) monitoring of previously sedentary persons who begin dancing, (d) echocardiographic studies, and (e) supplemental training for dancers.

Physiological Profiles

Heart rate and $\dot{V}O_2$ responses during dance have been studied in many dance forms, including tap, social, folk, aerobic, and ballet. Noble and Howley (1979) studied 15 college women, ages 17 to 26, taking beginning and intermediate tap classes. While doing soft-shoe and slow-buck routines (tempo, 112 beats/min), subjects consumed a mean of 16.7 ml/kg/min.

Various forms of social and folk dancing involve similar rates of energy expenditure. Passmore, Thomson, and Warnock (1952) noted an energy cost of 12-20 ml/kg/min during execution of the waltz, rhumba, foxtrot, petronella, and eightsome reel. Jette and Inglis (1975) studied four couples whose mean age was 37. These subjects engaged in Western square dancing and expended approximately 16 ml/kg/min during their activity.

Examining a newer dance form, Leger (1982) measured oxygen consumption of eight male-female couples immediately after disco dancing 135 beats/min. Using a retroextrapolation method, he calculated an oxygen consumption value (in ml/kg/min) of 31.2 for men and 28.1 for women, with mean heart rates for the two genders of 133 and 135, respectively.

Traditional folk dancing, however, can be more vigorous. Wigaeus and Kilbom (1980) investigated the Swedish folk dance, hambo. Six men and 6 women, ages 22 to 32, had oxygen uptakes (ml/kg/min) of 38.5 and 37.3, and heart rates of 179 and 172, respectively.

Aerobic dancing studied by Foster (1975) involved 4 women aged 20 to 38. He found peak $\dot{V}O_2$ values from 42.7 to 46.3 (mean, 43.6) ml/kg/min during routines averaging 4 min in length. Igbanugo and Gutin (1978) studied heart rate responses at low, moderate, and high levels of aerobic dance intensity, noting 110, 137, and 149 beats/min as activity level increased.

In a study of female ballet dancers in the Stockholm Opera Ballet, Åstrand (1973, cited in DeGuzman, 1979) found peak $\dot{V}O_2$ ranged from 41 to 56 ml/kg/min (mean, 48), while maximal heart rate during performance ranged from 190 to 212.

Micheli, Gillespie, and Walaszek (1984) studied 9 adult women who were professional ballet dancers. They reported a mean $\dot{V}O_2$ max of 41.8 ml/kg/min, and $\dot{V}e$ values (in L/min) ranging from 6.5 at rest to 79.4 during peak tread-mill exercise.

Cohen, Segal, Witriol, and McArdle (1982) performed treadmill testing of 4 female dancers from the American Ballet Theatre company. They found a mean peak $\dot{V}O_2$ of 43.7 ml/kg/min and noted $\dot{V}e$ values ranging from 72.1 to 99 L/min. Mean blood pressures rose from 99/68 to 149/65, while mean heart rate increased from 55 to 179 in these dancers with a mean age of 27. The same investigators monitored heart rates during ballet class, finding mean values for men and women of 134 and 117 during barre and 153 and 137 during center floor exercise. Other members of the same company allowed radiotelemetry monitoring of their heart rate during entire acts of evening performances of the classical ballets *Swan Lake*, *Giselle*, and *La Bayadere*. During allegro, mean heart rate for men was 178 and for women was 158 beats/min (Cohen, Segal, & McArdle, 1982).

Dancers and Controls

Comparisons of dancers to controls have been limited by poor selection of the control groups. Novak, Magill, and Schutte (1978) investigated 12 female college students who had danced 10 to 15 hours per week for 6 to 7 years. They found peak $\dot{V}O_2$ values of 41.5 ml/kg/min during treadmill testing of their subjects. Their control subjects achieved a mean peak $\dot{V}O_2$ of 36.8 ml/kg/min, but they were 2.4 years older, 4.5 kg heavier, and 4.3 cm taller.

One study compared 6 professional female jazz dancers to 17 women who weighed an average of 12 kg more. Peak $\dot{V}O_2$ values were 41.5 and 35.9 ml/kg/min in dancers and controls, respectively. Male professional jazz dancers in the same study achieved peak $\dot{V}O_2$ values of 49.2 ml/kg/min, with no report of controls (Lavoie & Lebe-Neron, 1982).

Studies in New Dancers

Oxygen consumption values have also been measured in sedentary students who begin dancing. Lavoie and Lebe-Neron (1982) studied 8 college women who took 3 hours of jazz class per week for 8 weeks. Peak $\dot{V}O_2$ rose minimally from 36.1 to 37.0 ml/kg/min. Similarly, DeGuzman (1979) noted no sig-

oxygen consumption

nificant changes in peak $\dot{V}O_2$ in 18 college women taking their first course (14 weeks) in modern dance as compared with 19 matched control women.

Rockefeller and Burke (1979) noted slightly more improvement in students taking aerobic dance (34.3 to 38.8 ml/kg/min). Vacarro and Clinton (1981) noted a rise in peak $\dot{V}O_2$ from 31.1 to 38.2 ml/kg/min in 10 college women who took 2 hours of aerobic dance class per week for 10 weeks.

Echocardiographic Studies

Debate continues regarding the relative contribution of dynamic (isotonic) and isometric work to cardiac fitness in dancers. Endurance athletes such as marathon runners have very high $\dot{V}O_2$ values, yet athletes who do primarily isometric work (e.g., weightlifters) may have no greater $\dot{V}O_2$ values than control groups.

Another physiological adaptation to chronic exercise is a change in the thickness and volume of the cardiac chambers, particularly the left ventricle, which performs the greatest amount of work. Ultrasound techniques to image the heart noninvasively (echocardiography) allow detection of increased thickness or enlarged volume of the heart chambers. Increased myocardial wall thickness is a feature particularly prominent in athletes who do isometric work. Because the left ventricle is assumed to be concentric, this can be translated into a measure of increased cardiac muscle mass. In contrast, athletes who engage in endurance events (such as long-distance running) display smaller wall-thickness changes, but they do develop relatively larger changes in stroke volume (Davidson, Popp, Haskell, Wood, Blair, & Ho, 1981).

Cohen, Gupta, Lichstein, and Chadda (1980) used echocardiography to study 30 full-time professional ballet dancers in New York City. Compared to 15 control subjects of similar size and age, the dancers had greater volume and thickness measurements. Interventricular septum and posterior left ventricular wall thicknesses were 10% to 20% greater in dancers, as were estimates of left ventricular mass. Left ventricular internal diameters were also greater in dancers, reflecting their higher stroke volume.

Cohen et al. (1980) further correlated echocardiographic parameters with intensity of training (number of ballet hours per year) and duration of training (total lifetime ballet hours). They found significant ($p < .05$) correlations between (a) volume and mass indices and (b) intensity and duration measures of training, thus reflecting cardiac adaptation to both isometric and isotonic demands of the dancer's art.

Supplemental Training for Dancers

To investigate the possible benefits of nondance exercise conditioning to cardiorespiratory parameters, Berney, Davidson, Caiozzo, and Plastino (in press) studied female dance majors who were allocated into dance-only or dance-swim groups during a summer semester at their university. All subjects performed a bicycle exercise test to exhaustion before and after the 12-week semester. Both groups continued to take ballet classes at least 5 hours per week. Only the dance-swim group trained by swimming 30 to 40 min three times weekly at target heart rates equal to 70% to 80% of the peak heart rate achieved on their initial bicycle test.

The investigators found two major benefits of the additional training. First, heart rates at all workrates on the treadmill test were significantly lower in the dance-swim group at the end of the training period. Second, ventilation rates at the upper levels of exercise were significantly lower in the dance-swim group. These observations were accompanied by subjective reports by the dance-swim participants that their dance classes produced less fatigue by the end of summer. Thus it is likely that the addition of swimming to dance training would have several benefits: (a) improve overall endurance, (b) offer the physiological and aesthetic benefits of breathing with less labor during performance, and (c) add very little risk of musculoskeletal injury during the supplemental training.

Summary

Although dance forms vary in their cardiorespiratory demands, most seem to require both isometric and dynamic exercise capacity greater than sedentary controls. Professional dancers display high levels of cardiorespiratory fitness, reflecting long-term positive adaptations to the requirements of their art. Echocardiographic studies reveal improved function and appropriate hypertrophy of myocardial tissue to meet these demands. Finally, pilot studies suggest that additional cardiorespiratory training outside the studio may enhance the fitness and endurance of the dancer.

References

Berney, D.E., Davidson, D.M., Caiozzo, V.J., & Plastino, J.G. (in press). Cardiorespiratory effects of swim training on dance students. *International Journal of Sports Medicine*.

Cohen, J.L., Gupta, P.K., Lichstein, E., & Chadda, K.D. (1980). The heart of a dancer: Noninvasive cardiac evaluation of professional ballet dancers. *American Journal of Cardiology, 45*, 959-965.

Cohen, J.L., Segal, K.R., & McArdle, W.D. (1982). Heart rate response to ballet stage performance. *The Physician and Sportsmedicine, 10*(11), 120-133.

Cohen, J.L., Segal, K.R., Witriol, I., & McArdle, W.D. (1982). Cardiorespiratory responses to ballet exercise and the VO_2 max of elite ballet dancers. *Medicine and Science in Sports and Exercise, 14*, 212-217.

Davidson, D.M., Popp, R.L., Haskell, W.L., Wood, P.D., Blair, S., & Ho, P. (1981). Echocardiographic changes during a one year exercise program in previously sedentary middle-aged men. In H. Rijsterborg (Ed.), *Echocardiology* (pp. 167-170). The Hague, Netherlands: Martinus Nijhoff.

DeGuzman, J.A. (1979). Dance as a contributor to cardiovascular fitness and alteration of body composition. *Journal of Physical Education, Health and Recreation, 50*, 88-91.

Foster, C. (1975). Physiological requirements of aerobic dancing. *Research Quarterly, 46*, 120-122.

Igbanugo, V., & Gutin, B. (1978). The energy cost of aerobic dancing. *Research Quarterly, 49*, 308-316.

Jette, M., & Inglis, H. (1975). Energy costs of square dancing. *Journal of Applied Physiology, 38*, 44-45.

Lavoie, J.M., & Lebe-Neron, R.M. (1982). Physiological effects of training in professional and recreational jazz dancers. *Journal of Sports Medicine, 22*, 231-236.

Leger, L. (1982). Energy cost of disco dancing. *Research Quarterly for Exercise and Sport, 53*, 46-49.

Micheli, L.J., Gillespie, W.J., & Walaszek, A. (1984). Physiologic profiles of female professional ballerinas. *Clinics in Sports Medicine, 3*, 199-209.

Noble, R.M., & Howley, E.T. (1979). The energy requirement of selected tap dance routines. *Research Quarterly, 50*, 438-442.

Novak, L.P., Magill, L.A., & Schutte, J.E. (1978). Maximal oxygen intake and body composition of female dancers. *European Journal of Applied Physiology, 39*, 277-282.

Passmore, R., Thomson, J.G., & Warnock, G.M. (1952). A balance sheet of the estimation of energy intake and energy expenditure as measured by indirect calorimetry, using the Kofranyi-Michaelis Calorimeter. *British Journal of Nutrition, 6*, 253-264.

Rockefeller, K.A., & Burke, E.J. (1979). Psychophysiological analysis of an aerobic dance programme for women. *British Journal of Sports Medicine, 13*, 77-80.

Vacarro, P., & Clinton, M. (1981). The effects of aerobic dance conditioning on the body composition and maximal oxygen uptake of college women. *Journal of Sports Medicine and Physical Fitness, 21*, 291-294.

Wigaeus, E., & Kilbom, A. (1980). Physical demands during folk dancing. *European Journal of Applied Physiology, 45*, 177-183.

14

Proper Footwear for Dance for Fitness

Steven L. Rosenberg
PROFESSIONAL DANCE SOCIETY
SANTA MONICA, CALIFORNIA, USA

In today's health world, one pair of athletic shoes is not expected to serve as a shoe for all seasons. Specific shoes are made for specific fitness activities—running, racquetball, volleyball, aerobic dance, and many others. It is important to know what type of shoe to wear because each is designed for the different types of stress the body will encounter. An aerobic dance shoe can probably be worn to play racquetball or volleyball because these sports require side-to-side jumping movements. However, I would not recommend running in an aerobic dance shoe, nor aerobic dancing in a running shoe. Many aerobic dancers work out on concrete surfaces covered by a thin carpet and must wear proper shoes to protect their feet.

The Evolution and Anatomy of the Aerobic Dance Shoe

The aerobic dance shoe evolved from a combination of three different types of performance shoes. They were designed to have the style and flexibility of a jazz shoe, the shock-absorbing qualities of a running shoe, and the durability and support of a court shoe. The aerobic dance shoes on the market today are first- and second-generation shoe designs. As does wine, they will improve with age.

Last

The last (see Figure 1) is a three-dimensional mold, made of wood or plastic that determines the size, shape, and style of the shoe (Califano & Davis, 1983).

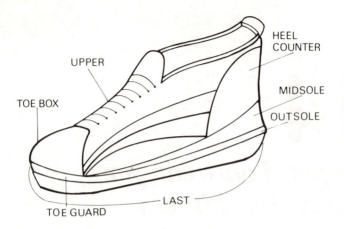

Figure 1. Anatomy of the Aerobic Dance Shoe

Aerobic shoes are made on two different types of lasts. C-shaped lasts—also known as adducted, inflared, or banana type—are designed for an adducted or C-shaped foot. Straight-shaped lasts are designed for a rectus or straight foot (Schuster, 1981, 1982a, 1982b). Once an aerobic-dance enthusiast determines his or her type of foot shape, it will be easy to choose the right type of shoe. Shoes that do not fit properly cause unnecessary foot injuries.

The Upper

The upper (see Figure 1) supports and protects the upper part of the foot (Califano & Davis, 1984). It is usually made out of leather, suede, nylon, or a combination of the three (Califano & Davis, 1983; Schuster, 1982b). An added reinforced support panel, sewn into both sides of the shoe, is designed to give extra support to the feet during the side-to-side movements required in aerobic dance routines (Califano & Davis, 1983; Schuster, 1982b). The reinforcement panel is attached to the toe guard at the front of the shoe and to the heel counter in the back of the shoe.

Lacing System

The lacing system (see Figure 1) aids in the overall support of the foot. The two types are the basic tie and a newer velcro strap.

Tongue

The main function of the tongue (see Figure 1) is to protect and pad the vital structures present in the dorsal area of the foot-the veins, arteries, and nerves.

Innersole

The function of the innersole (see Figure 2) is to give the foot added shock absorption during foot impact and aid in supporting the foot. It is composed of high-density thermoplastic preformed shock-absorbing materials with a protective nonirritating top cover (Schuster, 1981, 1982a, 1983). The purpose of the top cover is to absorb moisture and to reduce the frictional shearing

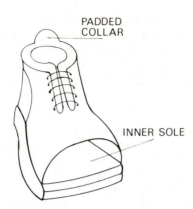

PADDED
COLLAR

INNER SOLE

Figure 2. The inner sole

forces that occur from the horizontal and vertical aerobic-dance movements. The innersole material may be cemented to the floor of the shoe or left freely removable and replaceable.

Midsole

The main function of the midsole (see Figure 1) is to absorb most of the impact shock the foot encounters during aerobic-dance exercise. It is usually a full-length thickness of rubber or rubber-like material between the upper and the outer sole. The midsole is composed of plastic material such as ethylene vinyl acetate (EVA), polyethylenes, or urethanes. These materials expand and contract to foot impact but eventually lose some of their shock-absorbing quality over time. Some midsoles are now made with combination EVA densities so that one layer is much firmer and can absorb more shock than the other layer. Placing this material under the ball of the foot will help reduce impact shock. Midsole flexibility is important in aerobic dance shoes because of the toe, ball, and heel movements required. Midsole material that is too thick will not flex at the ball of the foot (metatarsal phalangeal joints), and injuries such as shin splints may occur.

Outsole

The outsole (see Figure 1) makes the initial contact with the dance surface. It is composed of high density rubber compounds and has varied tread designs for traction and flexibility (Schuster, 1981, 1982a, 1983). The outsole too aids in reducing impact shock. It must be flexible enough at the ball of the foot to permit the metatarsals and small toe joints of the foot to flex freely. This will allow for the normal toe, ball, and heel movement during aerobic-dance routines.

Heel Counter

The heel counter (see Figure 1) is made of a firm material such as leather, suede, or a combination of the two. Its functions are (a) to provide rearfoot stability by limiting excessive heel motion in the shoe, and (b) to center the heel perpendicular to the supporting dance surface (Schuster, 1981, 1982a, 1983). A proper heel counter should extend to the navicular bone in the foot medially and to the calcaneal-cuboid joint in the foot laterally. A padded collar above the counter of the shoe aids in protecting the Achilles tendon.

Toe Box

The toe box (see Figure 1) protects the dancer's toes (Califano & Davis, 1983). It should be wide enough for toe movement and deep enough to prevent unnecessary shoe pressure, which can cause corns and toenail damage. Properly fitting aerobic dance shoes should have at least a ½-in. of space between the dancer's longest toe and the tip of the shoe. The toe box is made out of either leather with perforated air holes or a nylon mesh material that allows for aeration.

Toe Guard

The horseshoe-shaped toe guard (see Figure 1) is made of rubber. It wraps around the toe box to aid in supporting the front part of the foot and also contributes to shoe flexibility (Califano & Davis, 1983).

Running Shoes Versus Aerobic Dance Shoes

Running is a linear progression movement; aerobic dancing requires horizontal, diagonal, and vertical movement. Running shoes are similar to aerobic-dance shoes, with the major differences found in the midsole, outsole, and heel-counter areas. The midsole in the running shoe is much thicker because of the varied and continuous pounding the runner experiences. The outsole is composed of materials with greater wear resistance. It also has different tread designs to encourage flexibility and shock absorption. In the heel counter, additional pieces of firm material are found around the lower part of the counter, giving it greater stability against impact shock (Schuster, 1981, 1982a).

Summary

Aerobic dance shoes should be worn at all times during aerobic-dance exercise because of (a) the increased stress on the dancer's body during the performance of dance routines and (b) the hard, unyielding dance surfaces that can cause injuries to the dancer. A complete understanding of aerobic dance-shoe anatomy will provide the dancer with enough information to select the proper shoe.

References

Califano, R., & Davis, K. (1983, September). Aerobic shoes. *Shape Magazine,* pp. 55-56.

Califano, R., & Davis, K. (1984, May-June). Aerobic shoes update. *Idea Newsletter,* pp. 1-7.

Schuster, R. (1981, November). Explaining shoe features and functions. *The Runner,* pp. 66-68.

Schuster, R. (1982a, November). New features for 1983. *The Runner,* pp. 66-67.

Schuster, R. (1982b, December). The sole of the matter. *The Runner,* p. 22.

Schuster, R. (1983, November). The Runner magazine's 1984 guide to running shoes. *The Runner,* pp. 70-80.

15

Legal Considerations in the Dance for Fitness Environment

Donald B. Caffray
ATTORNEY AT LAW
LONG BEACH, CALIFORNIA, USA

Why should we touch upon legal considerations at all when the subject, dance for fitness, should be devoid of controversy and alive with human, positive enthusiasm? The reason is that we are living in an organized society. To achieve organization means the enactment and implementation of rules for human behavior. Every time someone does something that in any way involves other people, rules of conduct come into play. The more organized we become, the more rules we have. This may be the price that we must pay for our form of civilization. As society becomes more sophisticated, citizens have more and more protection both from the government and from their fellow citizens. In addition, citizens seem to be expecting more and more, not only in terms of protection but also in compensation when they become injured.

At a time when life was far simpler and goods were made by hand with great pride, with a signature on every pair of shoes and everything that was produced, the rule of thumb in the market place was "let the buyer beware." Goods were produced or services rendered with the greatest skill that the artisan could possibly get together, and the buyer was supposed to inspect them and then purchase them at his own peril. Transactions were more personalized; buyers and artisans knew each other. We have now moved into an extremely complex society where transactions are less personal. One does not always know the manufacturer or provider of goods or services with whom one deals on such an intimate basis.

Furthermore, the government has taken over in an effort to develop the utopia of which philosophers have dreamed. In an effort to protect the citizen who is the consumer of goods and services, the rule has been changed to correspond to the philosophy "let the seller beware." We have entered the age of consumerism. The consumer is the voter who elects legislators, judges, and officials to public office, and everyone is trying to please this consumer-voter. The entire philosophy is dominated by the idea of consumer protection. In turn, this philosophy dominates the development of the law that applies to providing goods and, in this case, services.

Considerations

Where in the dance-for-fitness environment do legal considerations arise? They arise in any circumstance when something is being provided for someone else. If a fee is charged, it is of even greater certainty that legal considerations will be present.

Screening

Everyone seeking to receive instruction in exercise of the dance, or any fitness-type activity, must be screened as to experience and physical capabilities. The screening will describe to the instructor where emphasis is needed and where caution should be exercised. Screening can be simplified by having applicants fill out a form wherein they themselves set forth their level of experience and any medical problems they are having. Instead of receiving a written warning, applicants may instead sign an acknowledgment that they understand the dancing-for-fitness training will involve strenuous exercise and could result in serious physical harm if they are not acclimated. In this way applicants acknowledge that they are aware that they themselves must be cautious.

Instructors

Instructors must be screened for experience and qualifications. In general, the more qualified they are in terms of certification, education, and experience, the better they will be. Also, their credentials may be taken into account in the event that anyone makes a claim. Because fitness training involves strenuous effort, instructors should have cardiopulmonary resuscitation (CPR) licenses. A program for monitoring instructors should check both their work and their attentiveness to students' progress. Systems of qualifying people and of monitoring their work are important not only for instructors but also for students.

Place

The location where the instruction occurs is an area where many legal liabilities could arise. The floor, if not state of the art, should at least have some degree of flexibility in consideration for the people who will be exercising on it. When bodies are engaged in fairly stationary vigorous exercise involving movements of feet, arms, and legs, the flooring must be different from that used for other purposes.

Next to moving around, the second active thing that people will be doing is breathing. The air-conditioning system must be adequate because students will be drawing in large amounts of air. Crowding must be avoided. The more people in a given area, the more oxygen that will be used up, and one of the main reasons students attend is to increase their oxygen intake through vigorous exercise. In areas affected by smog, strenuous exercise in the presence of the unfiltered pollutants is a factor to be considered. In the screening process, any applicant with any sort of breathing difficulty should be seriously checked and, if admitted, carefully watched.

Checking on Students

The activities and progress of students must be carefully monitored at all times. This ensures that the students will derive maximum benefits from their exercise experience. It also will enable instructors to detect symptoms before they are out of control and lead to a severe injury. To an extent, both the environment and the entire training program encourage maximum effort. Fragile students must be prevented from becoming injured. Further, some students will say that they feel fine when they are actually showing symptoms of not feeling fine, but want to keep up with their peers. This is particularly true of younger or intensely competitive people or those who have a need to prove something. Someday they may be in court proving that an instructor did not take adequate care of them.

What the Students Do

A well-planned program, tailored to student needs, capabilities, and abilities, should describe the activities and how strenuously they will be performed. Each exercise period must start with a warm-up and conclude with a cooldown period. Of the two, the warm-up is probably more important because many people tend to overlook this and expose themselves to greater injury. The instructor should orchestrate and, like a coach, leads the students through the entire exercise program.

The Law

When consumer protection is at issue, the law of torts applies. A tort action can be broken down into (a) duty and breach of that duty, (b) causation, and (c) damages. All must be tested when considering the right of recovery against a provider of goods or services.

Duty—and Breach of Duty

The heart of the consumer-protection philosophy is the idea of duty. Each person has a duty, or obligation, to all others with whom he or she comes in contact. Thus a group of people charged a fee for instruction in dance and exercise have various rights. They go beyond a mere contract, arising by operation of the law requiring the exercise of ordinary care toward other people. Ordinary care sometimes turns out to be something that one would not ordinarily think of as a duty. In medicine, for example, the physician's duty to obtain consent from his patient before he does a surgical procedure involves more than a signature. He must also see that the patient is informed, prior to giving the consent, and has a full understanding as to what he or she is consenting to. Moreover, if the patient refuses to consent to a medical procedure, then the doctor has a further duty to warn of the risks of refusing.

The extension of this idea of duty brings to mind a case in California involving a client who visited his lawyer in a new office building. Leaving the office, he went down to the parking lot where he had left his car. He surprised two robbers in the process of a holdup. One turned and, in his excitement, shot and killed the innocent person. In the wrongful death action that ensued, the Appellate Court said that the family of the deceased had a right to sue the owners of the building, because they had a duty to people using the building as business visitors to see that they were afforded a reasonably safe place to get into their cars. The problem will be submitted to a jury for a decision. A fairly good chance exists that they will award damages against the owners of the building after considering the adequacy of the building's security system.

Cause

Once duty is established, it is necessary to prove that a breach of duty actually caused damages. Causation may or may not be difficult to prove. If a student receives an injury while engaging in dance exercises, however, it would not seem too difficult to prove that the exercise itself was the cause of the injury. Injuries themselves, which may or may not be difficult to prove, may range from broken bones to emotional trauma to unrealized expectations as to what one hoped would happen if certain other things occurred, such as the fulfillment of a contract or the attainment of goals.

The burden of minimizing the various risks is on the provider of the dance-for-fitness program. This provider cannot guarantee everything but should be aware of as many risks as possible and do his or her best to guard the student against them. Safeguards include careful screening of applicants, careful selection and supervision of instructors, monitoring of students during the program, instructing students about the right kind of shoes and equipment, and providing the proper kind of flooring, ventilation, breathing space, lighted stairways, and safe parking lots. Potential liability can be partially guarded against by obtaining adequate insurance.

Realizing that the burden is on the provider of such a program poses quite a challenge. The best response is to think the entire program through and make sure that it is as well organized and as well executed as possible, giving a maximum amount of attention to the welfare of the participants.

All of these efforts should then be recorded and documented. Documentation is important because it acts as a checklist of safeguards and also promotes the welfare of the participants moving through the program. Finally, it is a demonstration of pride in the program.

Documents include the applications of persons seeking admission to the program and the records of the qualifications of the instructors and of the efforts to employ highly qualified people. Also important are records of the progress of the students or of their difficulties and what has been done about them. Documentation, important to the running of a good program, also provides a summary of past performance on which to build and continue to improve in the future.

16

Do's and Don'ts of Aerobic Dance and Dance for Fitness

JoAnne Johnson
UNIVERSITY OF OREGON
EUGENE, OREGON, USA

Approximately 9 years ago, Jackie Sorensen did what many of us could have done then, and what most of us do now. She integrated basic principles of physical fitness with simple dance steps and locomotor patterns to develop what became known as aerobic dance. Aerobic dance has since become a phenomenally popular alternative to running and other aerobic activities. Most physical educators are familiar with the term *aerobic dance*, and many have had some experience with an aerobic dance class. Unfortunately, many people suffer from misconceptions of what aerobic dance is all about, either because of stereotypic prejudices based on ignorance (e.g., "It's only for women and it's dance, so it can't be that tough," or "It's just jumping-jacks done to music and that's not dance") or because of instructors' lack of training in dance and/or fitness, resulting in unimaginative, awkward, ineffective, and potentially dangerous experiences. Additionally, there hasn't been a plethora of research done on aerobic dance until recently, so good information has not always been available.

Like many new things, especially new dance forms (remember the reaction to modern dance and the ongoing attitude toward jazz, popular dance, and breakdancing), aerobic dance has suffered from rigidly established traditional interpretations. This is changing, however, as the presence of these discussions on dance and fitness at the 1984 Olympic Scientific Congress demonstrates.

Dance fitness is a hybrid field, which like most hybrids, has the potential to incorporate the best of both worlds. Fitness information regarding aerobic dance is important for the skeptical but curious dancers, the dance teachers who would like to include aerobic dance in their repertoire or incorporate fitness principles in their regular class, and the aerobic dance teachers who are admirably attempting to stay on top of the latest information. The consumers or potential students also need this information because standardization in instructor training is lacking and it is up to them to determine the competence of the instructor.

Why Aerobic Dance?

What can aerobic dance do for you, *the dancer* and/or the *skeptic*? The following physiological benefits are covered briefly in this "catch-all" paper in the hope that these benefits are already familiar.

- More efficient gas exchange
- Increased O_2 uptake
- Stronger heart muscle
- Greater stroke volume and cardiac output
- Increased blood supply to muscles
- More mitochondria in the cells
- More efficient use of O_2
- Greater venous return
- Decreased resting heart rate
- Decreased resting blood pressure
- Faster recovery rate after exercise
- Increased glucose tolerance
- Faster and more efficient breakdown of sugars
- Greater storage of glycogen
- Reduced serum low density lipids, especially triglycerides ("bad" cholesterol)
- Increased levels of high-density lipoproteins or "good" cholesterol
- Reduced risk of hardening of the arteries
- Improved fat metabolism
- Increased caloric expenditure
- Facilitated release of endorphines
- Better management of adrenal secretions
- Improved maintenance of bone calcium level
- Possible retardation of the aging process

To the dancer, these benefits mean increased endurance, enabling a longer workout without tiring, which is important after several hours of technique, followed by rehearsal. Thus, the dancer can increase the amount of work (e.g., practice the petit or grand alegro much longer) without fatiguing. Because many injuries are the result of fatigue, the chance of injury is logically reduced. Furthermore, due to a lowered heart rate and regulation of adrenal secretions, the dancer's ability to handle stress in a performance situation is improved. At the end of the day, an aerobic dance class can enhance the body's waste disposal process, eliminating residual adrenal secretions due to the unfulfilled fight or flight syndrome and providing release from tension. In addition, calories are burned and sleep might be better. Although hard to quantify, there are indications that chemical and personality changes occur that contribute to emotional well-being. A final important advantage is that aerobic dance provides an overall workout, utilizing all of the major muscle groups and incorporates strengthening exercises, providing complete conditioning for the dancer and compensating for muscular imbalances due to choreography.

Why should you, *the dance teacher*, become involved in aerobic dance? Teaching aerobic dance, structuring a regular class around fitness guidelines, or recommending an aerobic class to students also benefits the dance teacher. Your students will have greater endurance, improved performance, fewer injuries, sunnier dispositions, and better class attendance. Because aerobic dance is lucrative and so popular, it will help support a studio; it will also bring students into service course programs in higher education, which will help to support smaller service classes. Aerobic dance is a great addition or alternative to a regular conditioning program in secondary physical education and helps build rapport with students by using their music preferences. It is also a great way to introduce people to dance. Any movement or dance form can be incorporated, staying with 4/4 music (unless teaching dance students adept at rhythmic variation) and utilizing the basic fitness principles. Dance teachers make great aerobic dance teachers because they can contribute an intimate understanding of movement and rhythm, an understanding of the use of music, correct technique and alignment, and choreography—providing fluidity and imagination.

Structure and Content of an Aerobic Dance Class

Included in the do's and don'ts of aerobic dance and dance for fitness are discussions of the warm-up, stretching, strengthening, the aerobic workout, and the cool-down.

The Warm-up

The majority of researchers agree that even before stretching some form of a warm-up should occur for the following reasons. The warm-up

- raises the core temperature of the body;
- raises the heart rate and increases the blood flow to the muscles;
- increases the release of O_2 from myoglobin;
- reduces muscle viscosity, thereby improving mechanical efficiency;
- facilitates nervous impulses and augments the sensitivity of the nerve receptors, leading to stronger contractions and indirectly to better coordination;
- lubricates the joints;
- reduces the chance of muscle and joint injury;
- prepares the heart and skeletal muscles for the more strenuous conditioning phase; and
- increases muscle elasticity, which depends on blood saturation. (Stretching cold muscles, which have low blood saturation, is less effective and potentially harmful.)

The warm-up process remains debatable. Authors have recommended anywhere from 30 seconds to 20 minutes for warm-up, most agreeing on around 5 minutes. One compromise is to have students, especially in the morning when they are more likely to be colder, take three laps around the gym (the first slow, the second moderate, and the third slow to a walk), or do a low-activity, low-stress routine for the duration of one song. At the end of the day and on warm days less concern is needed with the initial core temperature, assuming it is already elevated. Keep in mind, most of the "don'ts," such as flinging the extremities, are especially to be avoided during warm-up. If movement is preferred to running laps, it should foreshadow what is to come, that is, it should resemble the full-scale movement used during the aerobic section but should be slower, on a smaller scale, and void of the "don'ts."

Stretching

After warming-up, move on to the stretching section of the class. There are several valid reasons for stretching. For example, by stretching a muscle to its functional long point, there is greater range of motion (ROM) about the joint; more muscle fibers are then recruited for subsequent contractions, and the muscle can be put on a greater stretch prior to an individual contraction, resulting in a greater contraction (like a rubber band). The result is a more efficient use of the muscles during strength and cardiovascular work. Also, stretching helps us tune into our bodies, developing kinesthetic perception and helping us concentrate on correct alignment. Stretching helps us relax and ease unnecessary tension, and it *may* help initiate more right brain involvement in subsequent movement.

How to stretch is even more highly debated than how to warm up. However, after extensive research, here are some recommendations and suggestions. Bouncing is out because (a) it is less effective and more painful; (b) there is the possibility of damage to muscles (e.g., microtears), tendons, and ligaments; (c) it activates the protective stretch receptors, causing the muscle to contract; and (d) it contracts on the way out of the bounce (this is the opposite to a stretch). Proprioceptive Neuromuscular Facilitation (PNF) is apparently the most effective method; however, there is some question as to whether the second phase of PNF, the isometric contraction of the muscle to be stretched, inhibits the desired relaxation of the third phase, limiting the stretch and potentially causing harm. Also, PNF takes a partner or barre, can be harmful if done incorrectly (e.g., partner pushes too hard), and is more time-consuming and less simple than static stretch (my preference).

If done correctly the static stretch should not hurt (there is a difference between discomfort and pain). Emphasize breathing and relaxation and utilize a slow, gentle, progressive approach (i.e., after a few seconds, reach farther and relax again) to achieve a better stretch. It has been claimed that 6 seconds is enough for an effective stretch; however, a muscle stretched to its functional longpoint is more mechanically effective, and though 6 seconds may be enough physiologically to prevent injuries, it may not be enough to truly relax and therefore gain the best stretch. Furthermore, the previously mentioned benefits cannot be achieved in 6 seconds.

If limited by time and music, work with the music; for example, hold for 16 slow counts before moving to the next stretch. If time is a factor, keep stretches simple and do fewer. At the minimum, stretch the erector spinae (the spinal muscles), the adductors (the groin), the hamstrings, the gastrocnemius, the quadriceps, and the iliopsoas. If jumping is involved, warm up the ankles. Encourage students to relax by keeping the head lowered, which releases tension and stretches the spine. After holding the stretch for a while, have them take a deep breath and then attempt a slightly greater stretch as they exhale.

Start on the floor as this reduces the effect of gravity; that is, you do not have to worry about the postural muscles of the leg; it helps to lubricate the weight-bearing joints prior to weight bearing; you can concentrate on alignment of the spine; and you can begin stretching the spine without trauma. At the beginning of a term, start with 13 to 15 minutes of stretching and reduce it to about 8 minutes over a period of time (in a 45- to 60-minute class). In a shorter class it is possible to get by with a 5-minute stretch. Provide some variation, but keep the stretching routine consistent so the students can relax and tune into their bodies without concentrating on the instructor and on memorization. (Again, it is hypothesized that this enables the involvement of the right brain.) In addition, make sure that it is the belly of the muscle being stretched rather than the inelastic tendons and ligaments so that the stretch is effective, pain is reduced, and the stability of the joint is maintained.

Strength Training

A third and important component of an aerobic dance class is strength training. Flexibility should be balanced with strength in order to control the ROM about a joint, again to prevent stress on the tendons and ligaments. When actively working, emphasize control; it is less damaging and more effective. Control ensures use of the correct muscles and augments strength development by utilizing gravity as resistance and by recruiting more muscle fibers. Instruct students to lift and lower, rather than throw and let fall, which lets momentum and gravity do the work.

Because calisthenics builds strength and increases the heart rate to the lower aerobic threshold, it, therefore, can be considered part of the aerobic workout if time is a factor, and all muscle groups can be developed. Do calisthenics before the aerobic workout to motivate and prepare students and include some in the cool-down.

When incorporating strengthening exercises, make sure to work muscle pairs, for example, both hamstrings and quads, though not necessarily one after the other. Also, work all muscle groups, if possible, for the best workout. If limited, concentrate on abdominals and when working abdominals, always work with hip flexed to neutralize the iliopsoas. Avoid activities that overtax weak abdominals and, therefore, by relying on the iliopsoas, may augment the lumbar curve (e.g., double leg lifts). Make sure all exercises are demonstrated and performed correctly. Finally, constantly remind students to use abdominals and extensors, when appropriate, in order to avoid stress to the lumbar spine and to maintain proper alignment.

The Aerobic Workout

There are primarily five training principles to apply to the aerobic workout. The first concerns *frequency*. Participation in aerobic activity must occur at least 3 to 5 days per week. The second principle is *duration*. Some authors claim that 12 to 15 minutes is enough. However, the majority recommend 20 to 30 minutes. The third factor is *intensity*. Aim for the Training or Target Heart Rate (THR), which is approximately 60 to 80% of the Maximum Heart Rate (MHR). The preferred formula for determining this is

$$[(220\text{-age}) - \text{RHR}] \times .60 + \text{RHR} = \text{lower end of range},$$
$$[(220\text{-age}) - \text{RHR}] \times .80 + \text{RHR} = \text{upper end of range},$$

where RHR equals Resting Heart Rate.

When taking the heart rate, use the 6-second count because the HR drops rapidly and because it's easier to multiply by 10; however, one study suggested that it may be inaccurate—up to 20 pulses off! Many instructors prefer the 10-second count. As to whether to take the carotid or radial pulse, one study indicated that in some individuals the carotid pulse can be artificially lowered by pressing hard enough to activate the carotid sinus reflex; however, this is not common and it is otherwise as accurate a measure (and for some of us is easier to find) as the radial pulse. In the beginning, take the pulse more frequently, that is, after each song in the aerobic phase. Later, reduce it to perhaps two times because students are better able to self-monitor. Also, in order to maintain continuity and the heart rate, use one tape for accompaniment, leaving only enough time to take the pulse between each song.

A fourth and equally important principle to consider is *progression*. Always start students at their lower threshold and increase the load gradually—the more out of shape, the more gradual. The final principle is that of *progressive overload*: In order to make improvements, you must continually tax the system. When 20 minutes are easy, or 10 push-ups are no problem, it's time to increase the workload.

Some additional teaching tips would include the following:

- Be a nag. Constantly remind students of alignment, correct turnout in plié, and proper use of abdominals.
- Alternate unilateral with oppositional movement.
- Work both sides equally—this applies for both stretch and strength work.
- Alternate muscle groups.
- Alternate high-impact movement (e.g., jumping) with low-impact movement (e.g., jazz square).
- To increase motivation, use music that your students like, and change the music about every 3 to 4 weeks (i.e., frequently enough that students don't get bored with it, but long enough that they can learn routines and look forward to familiar material). If you have a young crowd, use current/contemporary music.
- Choose movement that challenges yet provides a successful experience.
- Know your audience; for example, if they are athletes, you may want to initially limit the more complex dance steps.
- If you have the time and inclination, do fitness testing and measurements in the beginning and then periodically thereafter.
- Use the first class in a sequence to discuss concepts, technique (e.g., stretching), and safety precautions.

Choreographic style depends on the individual instructor. Freestyling and set choreography each have their place. For example, in the beginning quite a bit of freestyling may be done in order to introduce a broad variety of basic steps and locomotor patterns with high repetition, the amount of which depends on how quickly the majority of the class picks it up. As time goes on, however, the choreography becomes more structured and more complex. When introducing a routine, be prepared to keep things simple, and use high repetition until the students feel comfortable with the movement, then build on.

The Cool-Down

The final issue to be discussed is the cool-down. Cooling-down is necessary in order to (a) prevent pooling of blood in the extremities, (b) reduce the possibility of dizziness, (c) increase venous return, and (d) speed up the recovery process. To cool down use the first song to gradually reduce the movement intensity (repeat aerobic movements without jumping). This is a good time to work on technique, repeat warm-up type activity, and include more calisthenics. By the end of the first song, progress to the floor. The second song is used for stretching and for relaxation. If you do desire, take the Recovery Heart Rate (15 s × 4) to make sure students are under 100 beats/min, and, if consistent, as a determiner of increased fitness.

Safety Factors

An important aspect to consider when contemplating involvement in aerobic dance is safety. For example, medical assessment should be encouraged if not required. Although according to some research, not that many injuries or heart problems have been associated with aerobic dance, a check-up is nevertheless recommended and may, in fact, provide some legal protection. The Aerobic and Fitness Association of America recommends: If under age 30, a check-up only if the student has not had one in the last year; age 30-39, within 3 months of starting a class, including an EKG; at 40-59, same and a stress test; and at age 59 and over, immediately preceding the initiation of a program.

A preliminary questionnaire and/or fitness testing will help you determine the level of your students and spot "time bombs," (people with heart conditions, diabetes, epilepsy, a history of injuries, or who are obese). Keep an eye on the time bombs—the older, obese, or vulnerable students. When you take heart rates, question various students as to what their rates are and include the high-risk participants. Warn students of the potential risk inherent in aerobic dance and emphasize medical assessment. This will protect the student and may legally protect the instructor. If you can, get it in writing. Most importantly, know first aid and CPR, keep a first-aid kit handy, and know the local number of the paramedics.

Aerobics should be oriented toward the individual, so as a safety-conscious instructor you should emphasize that there should be no competition or comparison, constantly encourage students to monitor themselves and "listen" to their bodies, and remind them to control their initial enthusiasm. If possible, utilize demonstrators. (Ideally, the studio or school should have an additional demonstrator or two, or instructors could team teach.) Keep in mind, however, that the demonstrator needs to be trained correctly. Utilizing the better students as demonstrators is helpful. There are always a few students who catch on quickly and do the movements well. In that case, you can let them continue the routine or sequence while you go around making corrections and helping individuals.

Finally, when possible, offer various levels of instruction; this way gradual progression can be emphasized. Beginners will not feel they have to keep up, thereby limiting success and enjoyment and risking injury and ineffective training, and more fit or advanced people will get more out of it. Also, you can orient the class toward high-risk people, if need be. For these reasons, avoid drop-in type classes. Also, people tend to be less consistent when progression and continuity is not emphasized.

Injury Prevention

Closely allied with safety is injury prevention. Following are some actions to take. Do:

- Warm up and stretch.
- Constantly emphasize correct alignment.
- Wear correct shoes (especially if doing high impact work).
- Dance on appropriate floor surfaces.

To avoid shinsplints wear good shoes, dance on a good floor, warm up the ankles, utilize all muscles involved in jumping and landing (all muscles of foot and ankle, knee, and hip), work through the foot (from toe to heel), and wear leg warmers; they help to retain warmth in the lower leg and ankle muscles. One of the most important things to do is to strengthen abdominals. Many musculoskeletal problems can be avoided with strong, well-utilized abdominals.

Along with the do's are some don'ts. Do not:

- Hyperextend the lumbar or cervical vertebrae when not warmed up, when not necessary, and when not appropriate to the exercise.
- Overbend at the joints—you lose control of the action and risk stressing the tendons and ligaments.
- Do anything that is more likely to work the psoas than the abdominals when it is the abdominals you want to work.
- Hyperextend or "lock" the knees.
- Fling the extremities, especially prior to or during warm-up; this tends to use momentum which effects the ligaments and tendons rather than the muscles.

Conclusion

A fulfilling aerobic dance experience requires knowledge, training, and sensitivity on the part of the instructor. In short, enthusiasm is great but it is not enough. Ideally, instructors should be educated in anatomy, kinesiology, exercise physiology, dance/movement, nutrition and weight control, and CPR and first aid. As the instructor, take yourself and your students seriously. Though some people may like the Barbie doll cheerleader style, many, especially men, are turned away by it. You are a professional. Take the opportunity to educate your students. Give one or two lectures on the heart or the muscles or whatever you feel is important, and constantly use correct terminology and anatomical terms; or you might give handouts covering all the information that you cannot verbalize in class. But be careful to avoid guruism—You do not know everything. Send them to physical therapists if that is what they need.

Finally, consider certification and contribute to standardization. Let us work toward objectifying teacher training for the instructor's and the student's sake. Those of us who are qualified professionals have something to offer and it should not be taken lightly. Dancers, become involved. You have much to contribute and to gain. After all, lifelong fitness is the goal.

PART IV

The Use of Body Therapies and Motor Reeducation in Dance and Athletics

When an athlete is injured, the usual treatment may be biomechanical intervention to restore strength to the injured area; or, with serious injuries, invasive surgical techniques may be required to repair damage to the body part. Increasingly, both athletes and dancers have sought noninvasive rehabilitative and preventative techniques that would not only strengthen a dysfunctional body part but also repattern movements so that the injury-inducing actions are not repeated. Often the performer has attempted to "erase" an unsound movement pattern by learning a sound one to cosmetically superimpose over it. Needless to say, the results have usually been disappointing, for the performer merely gains another movement pattern to try to control.

A noninvasive alternative to the conscious repatterning of muscular movement is neuromuscular recoordination through a variety of integrative movement systems, or body therapies. They are based on perception and imaging, and the results are painstakingly gradual and subtle for athletes and dancers who are accustomed to gross movement experiences. In her article, Myers discusses the major body therapies and how they can alter neuromuscular repatterning, specifically postural alignment. Breathing and ideation are central to the practice of most integrative movement systems, and their integration into training and performing situations can ultimately lead to anatomically sound optimal performance. This was the basis of Kneeland's (1966) controversial approach to movement repatterning in ballet technique, although her resultant system is unlike the body therapies in that it is grounded in gross motor activity of the ballet class. In athletics, autogenics seems to most closely resemble the integrative movement systems used in dance.

Meglin illustrates the values of breathing and ideation in her article dealing with Sweigard's integrative movement system, ideokinesis. She adds credence to Sweigard's theories by offering documentation from current sports medicine literature that parallels some of Swiegard's reasoning. Although little substantive research in the literature supports the validity of body therapies (mainly because, as Myers points out, it is difficult to apply the traditional scientific method to the assessment of psychophysical processes), the findings of scientific disciplines have helped to move the body therapies out of the realm of mere conjecture into an arena adjacent to biofeedback mechanisms.

Reference

Kneeland, J.A. (1966, March-June). The dancer prepares, *Dance Magazine*.

17

Perceptual Awareness in Integrative Movement Behavior: The Role of Integrative Movement Systems (Body Therapies) in Motor Performance and Expressivity

Martha Myers
CONNECTICUT COLLEGE
NEW LONDON, CONNECTICUT, USA

"A foot cannot feel," said Moshe Feldenkrais (1972) quoting the Hebrew sages. "If a man does not feel he cannot sense differences and of course he will not be able to distinguish one action from another" (p. 58).

On the body level, differentiation is essential to learning. The human organism is designed to sense and respond; proprioceptive, kinesthetic, and somatic systems provide vital sensory feedback. The cerebella and hypothalmic circuits serve as comparators and adjusters. The central nervous system not only monitors a movement program once it is launched, but detects errors. "If there is a mismatch between the intended program (or model) and the actual movement, appropriate corrections can be made by the central nervous system, even without conscious decisions. The better the programs have been learned, the fewer the corrections that are needed" (Brooks, 1983, p. 667).

Whatever may be the many and multilayered factors leading to movement patho-mechanics, an essential part of clearing the way for establishing new motor programs depends upon sensing and moving, maintaining a constant

---

Martha Myers is also Dean of the American Dance Festival in Durham, North Carolina, USA.

dialogue between sensory and motor systems. We learn best by actively do-ing, exploring, discovering. Efficient motor programs are also dependent on visualizing clear, accurate images of the intended action, as well as "good sensory images of our bodies and their motor capabilities" (Brooks, 1983, p. 668). The body-therapy systems can be important resources in training proprioceptive awareness and more efficient motor programming.

Concepts and practices in all areas of human performance and rehabilita-tion are being effected by the explosion of scientific research in sports train-ing and medicine. This expanding interest in new approaches to motor learning and performance has brought renewed interest in the body-therapy systems. The value of their approach to neuromuscular repatterning is increasingly recog-nized as an important component in movement education and skilled perfor-mance training. The principles and interventions of the body therapies augment traditional injury-prevention resources and encourage more efficient motor programming. Body-therapy educators, analysts, and practitioners also address a neglected area of rehabilitation—namely, that space between the end of medical rehabilitation and the return to skilled performance.

These systems focus on motor control at the proprioceptive level to facili-tate reeducation and repatterning. They use noninvasive techniques to repair bodily dysfunction, to restore more efficient, fluent use in everyday life, and to perfect performance in skilled sports and arts activities. Their roots can be traced to the late 19th century, to medical gymnastics, physiological psy-chology, neurology, and the work of individual health or physical educators, and innovators in movement education such as Delsarte, Dalcroze, and Dio Lewis. They have also borrowed from Eastern martial arts and philosophy.

Progenitors of the major systems developed a body of theory and practice that allowed them to train practitioners who have further elaborated and in-tegrated the systems. The most familiar of these are the Alexander technique; Feldenkrais awareness through movement; Laban/Bartenieff movement anal-ysis and fundamentals; Rolfing, the integration of human structure; Selver's sensory awareness; Todd/Sweigard ideokinesis (ideokinetic facilitation); and Jacobson's progressive relaxation.[1]

I will focus here on how certain sensory and perceptual motor skills are developed through the body therapies to alter neuromuscular patterning, par-ticularly with regard to posture. As defined by Cratty (1968), "Perception is an ever continuing, as well as an immediate phenomenon. . . . The process involves organizing, feeling change, and selecting from among the complexi-ty of events to which humans are continually exposed, so that order may be attached to experience" (p. 23). The body therapies are especially concerned with proprioceptive awareness. The proprioceptive organs (Golgi tendon or-gans, Pacinian corpuscles, muscle spindle, labyrinthine receptors) provide cues regarding internal bodily changes that help keep the body in balance and motion, responsively adapting to the environment.

---

[1]There are a number of other systems, some more recently evolving—such as Trager Psychophysi-cal Integration, Aston patterning, Bioenergetics, and Bonnie Cohen's Mind/Body Centering—whose theory and practice are becoming more widely recognized.

As Higgins (1977) pointed out,

> In skilled movements perceptual processes, in large part, function to match not only environmental conditions but also organismic variables such as size, shape, age, sex, and experience. The interrelationship is functionally a match between information detection, information processing, motor response, and the form and structure of the organism. (p. 113).

Because a movement once learned is performed automatically, proprioceptive impulses only occasionally penetrate consciousness. Thus the first step in unravelling an undesirable muscular habit is to become aware of what it is, and how it feels.

The first perception essential to repatterning involves those proprioceptive responses that give the feeling of tension in the muscle (i.e., stretch, contraction) and the awareness of where limbs are in relation to each other and to space. All of the body therapies emphasize this tuning in—bringing to consciousness an awareness of habitual muscular actions, that is, lifted shoulders, dropped chest, forward head—common to the *random body*, as Ida Rolf describes the postural configuration of the average man.

Body therapies are additionally interested in where and how the pattern developed, in its psychogenic and cultural origin, and the body percept underlying it. The intricate connection between neuromuscular patterning in posture-gesture and locomotion, and emotion (affect) is recognized and addressed in the experiential process of this work. Alexander, Feldenkrais, Selver, Jacobson, and Sweigard have especially focused on ways to enhance the individual's awareness of muscular tension as a necessary condition for releasing it and discovering new and more effective patterns. Imposing new patterns on a distorted body system and body percept (new "rights" for old "wrongs"), which is an accepted approach in much postural and motor-skills learning (including dance), often creates equal distortions and problems (i.e., the elevated-abducted scapulae are now depressed and adducted). Without restoring basic anatomical balance and proper kinesiological use, the new patterns make further knots in the individual's psycho-physical behavior.

Movement patterns are not single units but complex sequences of action. For this reason, body therapists often speak of unravelling patterns of postural or related dysfunction rather than simply of substituting new patterns. Movement is seen as part of the total schema of personality and behavior. The goal of improved motion is fuller responsivity to the environment—enhanced affect as well as efficiency. Modifications occur through a multilevel process as well as through discrete interventions. This is not to say that direct biomechanical interventions are not also necessary, but rather that the systems under discussion offer important correlate learning resources. They can also help to integrate musculoskeletal training with performance quality and expressivity.

The body therapies use numerous interventions for enhancing proprioceptive awareness in neuromuscular learning. I will discuss here breathing and ideation as they modify postural alignment. Both of these are aids in isolating smaller motor units to sense their underlying structure, sequencing, and integration into larger motor patterns. As breathing becomes fuller, for example, the individual gradually becomes aware of the relationship of breath shape, phrasing, effort range, and flow to his preferred movement patterns, discovering among them some that are not only inefficient but uncomfortable. He or she may also recognize certain affects that connect to these as he or she refines his or her perceptions. Through trial and error, as in Feldenkrais, or through ideation, as in Sweigard, he or she learns to recognize and respond to increasingly microlevel proprioceptive feedback, gradually improving sensorimotor programming, unravelling and altering detrimental neuromuscular habits.

I use the term *sensorimotor response* to refer to those smallest of motions (subprograms) we can sense at the initiation of a movement and as we follow its sequential pathway and flow throughout the body. As Cratty (1968) described it,

> Skill acquisition rests upon the development, with practice, of the individual's ability to perceive and to act upon increasingly subtle cues. This increased attention to the more finite components of the task. . .enables more adequate error-minimizing techniques to be developed, while at the same time maximizing methods of attending to the positive components of the task. As movement behavior is reorganized, unwanted, abbreviated, and unnecessary components are omitted from the learning program. (pp. 254-255)

At an even deeper level, I am using micromovement to refer to that moment prior to making any motion at all—the moment, usually unconscious—preceding initiation of an action. Neurologically, it is postulated that a lag exists between the onset of brain activity preceding an action and the conscious intention to move (*Brain/Mind Bulletin*, 1984). Conscious control seems to rest in our ability to inhibit an action in those milliseconds between intention to move and the muscular response. The individual learns to recognize and respond to these smallest of kinesthetic cues and through feedback from the central nervous system to redirect action based on information they provide. As described by Sweigard (1974), feedback can be reinforced through "concentration, refinement of the concept of the ultimate goal, the help of visual aids or audio-devices, and through development of an awareness of the cues with which sensory receptors supply us" (p. 146). This concept of inhibiting initiatory action at the most minimal neural threshold (substituting new neuromuscular initiation for the action to be performed) is central to the Alexander technique, and to Sweigard also.[2]

Muscular action does not occur in isolation (as in movement of biceps or gluteii alone), but, as Bartenieff (1974) pointed out, involves "several muscles grouped around one joint or. . .kinetic chains that involve several joints of one limb or coordinate parts of the torso with the limb pattern (p. 13). This, as she sees it, accounts for the difficulty of *correcting*," that is, redirecting a movement once it is initiated. Thus she emphasizes the importance of finding the correct initiation of a movement to coordinate the desired chains of action.

An example can be seen in lifting an arm. If the movement is initiated by a marked elevation of the scapula, the arm is unable to reach fully into verti-

---

[2]Examples: Alexander directions for improving head-neck articulation by sensing (through touch biofeedback from the teacher) which initiations must be inhibited to allow the head to move "forward, up and out"; Sweigard direction to visualize the head as a balloon floating upward off the vertical column.

cal space, even if an attempt is made to correct the error as motion proceeds. The same is true if the scapula is first forcefully depressed or downwardly rotated as suggested by many dance teachers. If, on the other hand, movement is initiated by an outward and upward reach from the fingertips, the scapula will smoothly and automatically undergo the upward rotation necessary to allow for the full completion of the movement. As observed by Bartenieff, spatial direction is an essential facilitative cue in motor programming.

To heighten proprioceptive awareness of changes in initiation, consequent body part sequencing, and the effect of this on directions of motion through space, movement must be slowed down. I have not found it easy to motivate students accustomed to the satisfactions of gross motor activity (dancers especially) to work at the micro- or subprogram level. At first they find it frustrating to recognize or respond to elusive proprioceptive cues, to work slowly, and with small increments in order to facilitate this. One exercise sequence I have found useful for helping them appreciate the relevance of microlevel experience and analysis to their movement performance is the following:

From the Moslem-prayer position (kneeling, buttocks resting on heels, torso rounded forward), I use touch, breath, and imaged movement (ideation) to help students activate lower abdominals, deep pelvic muscles, and hip extensors to gain finer control of the lumbar spine. Most students, if asked to roll up to squat-sitting from this position, will initiate from the head, upper or midthorax, lifting the pelvis off the heels. Placing one hand on the anterior pelvis (ASIS) and another on the sacrum, I suggest that the pelvis is a sandbag, already heavy from sand falling through the torso downward to the sacrum. The image of sensing (or sending) breath into this area is also an effective aid.

I ask them to initiate the roll of the torso up to heel-sitting from this caudal point, inhibiting the impulse to move from a more cephalic point in the spine. Their first efforts most often end in failure—no motion in the lumbar but extreme motion in other sections of the spine. But gradually faint muscular action can be felt in the hip extensors as abdominals are engaged. As the movement continues, the erector spinae become activated to complete the trunk extensions. With practice, the pelvis lowers toward the heels, and related patterns and preferences can be pointed out (i.e., how this alters the relationship and integration of lumbar, thoracic, and cervical curves; the portion of the spine that is preferred for initiating movement; etc.). Sequential unfolding of the body into vertical sitting alignment also reveals their hidden coping mechanisms for dealing with a forward head, round shoulders, and restricted use of the ribs.

Sports-science researcher Dave Costill (cited in Jerome, 1980) noted that most Olympic gold medals "are won not by breakthroughs but by the tiniest margins, by inches and ounces and hundredths of seconds. Sports science contributes by vastly expanding the points of attack; pick up a sixteenth of an inch in 16 different places, and you've gained an inch. Science can help the athlete organize his efforts in order not to let any of these sixteenths slip away" (p. 100). In enhancing quality and expressivity in movement, sixteenths of an inch are important too. The body therapies offer additional tools for realizing the goals of sport and dance science by helping to speed and refine sensorimotor learning.

Ideokinesis

A number of experimenters and theorists in the 19th century such as William James and Herman Lutze were interested in the effect of imagined movement in physiological processes. Body therapists in the early 20th century—Alexander in England, Todd in the United States, and Elsa Gindler in Germany—may well have been aware of this work as they developed their individual approaches to movement behavior. Sweigard's work in ideokinesis has focused on the scientific theory and validation of ideation.

Sweigard (1974) used the term *ideokinesis* to describe the theory and practice of imaging an action in order to induce change in habitual neuromuscular patterning. "Experimental evidence shows that concentration on visualizing a movement without trying to perform it voluntarily results in statistically significant changes in body relationships" (p. 146). Sweigard insisted that it was not only useless but destructive to tell students which parts of the body to hold or release, which muscles to use. Rather, she pointed out, it is the concepts, the gestalt, of the movement that is essential to efficient motor learning; that is, "what is the movement to be performed, not how is it to be performed. The nervous system takes care of the 'how' of movement in accordance with a clear concept and mental picture of movement—the process is ideokinetic" (p. 169). As Irene Dowd (1983), a leading exponent of ideokinesis, explained, "When I visualize a particular movement pattern, I will be initiating impulses along certain neurological pathways to the various muscles, and inhibiting impulses to other muscles and training this into the system."

In visualizing the movement desired (whether to alter the relationship of normal spinal curves or to change the spatial tracing of a tennis swing), one is sending messages to the central nervous system that in turn directs the muscles to produce the desired action. Research using electromyography has shown that visualizing a motion such as a développé, high dive, or slalom run elicits minute neuroelectrical impulses at the subcortical level, as if actually performing these actions. To improve alignment, for instance, a student can be given images of lengthening the spine downward (as in Sweigard); of directing the neck, back, and head forward and up (as in the Alexander technique); of connecting one's movement to points in an icosahedron surrounding the body (as in Bartenieff)—all of which encourage release of musculature specific to a particular area (cervical, cranial, pelvic, etc.) or initiate new spatial pathways of the limbs.

The work of ideation is often done on the floor in a position of zero gravity, with the eyes closed, to enhance concentration and perception. Often the tactile guidance of a teacher or partner is helpful in isolating the difference between volitional movement (putting the head in the desired position) and allowing imagery to guide it there. Through touch biofeedback, the experienced teacher can help the student learn to inhibit gross volitional action—engaging more subtle kinetic chains, recruiting deeper muscles, and finding appropriate ones for the task—again not only for efficiency but for full postural responsiveness and expressivity. Sommerhoff in 1974 (quoted in Higgins, 1977) spoke of a kind of modulation or sculpturing of input from all levels of the central nervous system that ultimately can result in "precise matching of action to environment. This sculpturing may be effected either by selective excitation or selective inhibition. In this manner the higher centers achieve the required level of discrimination in the evaluation of the stimulus situation and of articulation in the execution of the motor responses'' (p. 71).

Breathing

Breathing, particularly as a method of tension reduction, was also of interest to 19th century physicians and physical educators. The value of breathing, however, is more than a means of relaxation as practiced in the body therapies; it is a major modality for enhancing kinesthetic awareness and musculoskeletal alignment from which repatterning work can begin. These repatterning systems emphasize concentration, reducing stimuli so finer sensorimotor feedback can be perceived. Reducing unnecessary muscular activity, whether through breathing, imagery, progressive relaxation, or other means is considered essential in this work, not only to refine sensory perceptions, but to recognize total body patterns and the intricacy of their interconnections. Improperly understood, however, this aspect of the work can lead to the "noodle syndrome"—not so much tuning in but tuning out, using insufficient muscular activity to support movement.

Observing an individual breathe provides an experienced analyst with information regarding basic psychomotor patterns. These affect not only body segments such as thorax or shoulder girdle but total body movement including that of vital organs. Posturally, breathing coordinates the behavior of the spinal curves, orchestrating the flow of movement from the head through the torso and limbs. It is a prime resource for sensing full three-dimensional motion throughout the body; it stimulates joint proprioception and muscular release, which leads to more balanced muscular action.

A pattern of breathing that emphasizes a single spatial plane (i.e., sagittal) pushes the anterior portion of the thorax forward. This is often the culprit in postural dysfunction such as protruding ribs. Laban/Bartenieff concepts of body shaping can be particularly helpful in addressing the interactive relationship between breathing and postural imbalance. Bartenieff (1974) pointed out how, in the technique of tai chi, breathing is adapted to the shape flow of movement toward and away from the body, thus regulating an "even exchange of in-out breathing. . . .In part, this is achieved by blending the phases of change in the direction of the movement with the start and finish of the breathing phases" (p. 13). The variety of spatial patterns in this technique she sees as important in assuring differential adaptations of breath and thus of body motions in relation to the kinesphere (the space surrounding the body). This full use of space, shaping, and adapting movement (body part and joint connection-articulation) to facilitate interaction with the environment supports human communication and motor programming. It is a neglected component in much dance and fitness training.

Laban's (1974) choreutics, and Bartenieff's (1980) movement analysis are especially helpful in work with breath patterns. I have been impressed with the results of directional imagery, especially involving Laban's spatial concepts in dealing with the problem of protruding ribs. By suggesting the image of energy moving on a diagonal line from the manubrium through the center of the thorax to the right and left posterior superior iliac spine, and in diagonal lines from the sacrum toward the acromial process, a breath pattern of fuller dimensionality is encouraged. Adding the thought that these lines are spiral, as in a revolving barber pole, rather than straight, adds dimension to the breathing action. A number of body therapy systems incorporate the use of obliquity and rotation in their movement practices. Often brief practice of this intervention will cause the ribs to fall back into a more integrated relationship with other body segments.

When the diaphragm participates more fully and evenly in breathing, motion in adjacent body parts (arms, shoulders, head) becomes capable of more varied shaping and dynamics. It is my experience that students with postural malalignments (disconnections between body segments, such as forward head or lumbar hyperextensions) respond more quickly and effectively to work that addresses these problems on a one-to-one level through breathing or ideation than they do with continued classroom practice alone. Certainly, there is not time, nor often interest and expertise, to use such means to unravel long-standing sensorimotor patterns in the teaching of specific skills in sports and dance classes.

Dealing with numerous students and the time limits of traditional classes, one is tempted to use verbal directions such as "pull in your ribs" or "anchor the ribs to the pelvis" as shortcuts for achieving desired changes. But these instructions are iatrogenic. Forceful images or muscular manipulations of the body can evoke contractions and holding patterns in response. Images and touch are central to motor learning, but they are a double-edged sword. As linguists point out, our manner of expressing concepts shapes our thought, and thought in turn conditions behavior.

The power of breathing patterns to modulate alignment and motion is not surprising when one considers the extent of the body cavity occupied by the lungs and diaphragm, amplified by layers of connective tissue and musculotendinous extensions. It is not only metaphorical to say that one breathes throughout the body. A student recently described the experience of this after a session in the lab. I had noted in watching her take class that she looked as if she were forcibly anchoring her head to her body, breathing shallowly, using far more muscular effort than necessary to perform movements at the barre. Every muscle in her neck was visible, with corresponding immobility of shoulder girdle and sternum. We worked on establishing a rhythmic interplay between the upper thoracic vertebrae and sternum, encouraging reciprocal energy through these parts to the cervical spine and head. Releasing tension through breathing and imaging, she was able to increase motion in small increments—16ths of an inch—of flexion-extension and rotation of the upper thoracic spine. Gradually she enlarged this extension and was able to restore more three-dimensional interplay in scapula-clavicular-humeral movement and head-neck alignment. At the end of two sessions she sighed, "I understand now what you meant when you said 'the body doesn't have to hold itself up.' But I've been *doing* that all my life!"

She later reported that she had experienced a remarkable difference also in her sleeping patterns. "I'm not approaching sleep as a preparation for battle, waking up with my body and teeth clenched." For her, learning had taken place, not by following an outside model or making disjunct corrections of body parts, but by discovering how her patterns could become more integrated through interventions that allowed malalignment habits to dissolve. Her own heightened proprioceptive awareness, supported with accurate understanding and visual images of the neuromuscular patterning desired, provided her with tools to use to continue modifying her movement, adapting specific skills to the needs of her own body.

Breathing is an important component of safer, more effective stretching and strengthening exercises in dance, fitness, and sports. Calling on a muscle to actively shorten (as in lifting a heavy object) from an already contracted state diminishes its power. By the same token, less stretch is obtainable from a contracted muscle. It is more painful and potentially dangerous. Coordinating the breath in both stretching and strengthening can facilitate these actions.

Finally, habits of holding the breath (commonly seen when approaching a difficult movement in dance or sports) disrupt flow, rhythmic interplay of body parts, and coordinative reflexes, causing a host of problems—from losing balance to spraining a joint. Held inhalation is part of the startle response in which we also freeze gaze. Look down the barre of a dance class and you will see numerous examples of students whose fixated gaze is interfering with motor performance and expression (integrative movement behavior).

Conclusion

I am aware that no research in regard to assumptions underlying this discussion has been cited. Little has been done! Assessment of psychophysical processes or evaluation of the quality of a movement performance has proven difficult within the parameters of the traditional scientific method. Partly for this reason, nonmedical practices such as the body therapies have not attracted funding for research. A change in socio-medical climate has created a broader interest in adjunctive health practices and a renewal of research in several of these systems. Implications for the validation of this work are important.

Collaborations between performers and scientists such as those of the American Dance Festival and Duke Medical Center are producing research on dancers' injuries, physical characteristics, and nutrition, it is hoped will extend in the future to body therapies. Research from a number of scientific disciplines, however, is contributing to an understanding of some of the mechanisms underlying these systems, such as the Alexander technique. More are in the planning stages. Among these are studies (reported by Geyer, n.d.) by Makaoto Igarashi of the Department of Otolaryngology at Baylor University, Texas, whose experiments revealed that the equilibrium of monkeys was severely impaired when desensitized and deprived of proprioceptive feedback from the top two cervical vertebrae. And the studies of T. Fukada, of Baylor University, have helped skilled athletes use posture of the head and cervical spine to improve their motor-coordination. Dr. Barry Wyke, of the Neurological Unit, Royal College of London, pointed out that 50% of the bodily total of such receptors are located in the upper spine. All of these lend support to Alexander's clinical findings of the dynamic interaction of head-neck in postural alignment.

Until further studies are done, one must evaluate results of body therapy theory and practice on anecdotal and clinical evidence. It seems justifiable, however, to suggest at this point that the body therapies can provide important adjunctive training, both one-on-one and in group, for the elite dancer-athlete or the ordinary person. They can also help each individual realize his unique performance potential whether that is winning a gold medal or being more vitally and expressively alive.

References

Bartenieff, I. (1974). *Notes from a course in correctives*. New York: Dance Notation Bureau.

Bartenieff, I., with Lewis, D. (1980). *Body movement: Coping with the environment*. New York: Gordon and Breach Science.

Brain/Mind Bulletin (1984, February 13), p. 2.

Brooks, V.B. (1983). Motor control: How posture and movement are governed. *Physical Therapy, 63*(5), 664-673.

Cratty, B.J. (1968). *Movement behavior and motor learning* (2nd ed.). Philadelphia: Lea and Febiger.

Dowd, I. (1983). Lecture-demonstration. Presented at the American Dance Festival Body Therapy Workshop.

Feldenkrais, M. (1972). *Awareness through movement*. New York: Harper and Row.

Geyer, J. Unpublished paper (producer, Nebraska Educational Television Network).

Higgins, J. (1977). *Human movement: An integrated approach*. St. Louis: Mosby.

Jerome, J. (1980, April). The last ounce of strength. *Quest*, p.101.

Laban, R. (1974). *The language of movement: A guidebook to choreutics* (Annot. & edited by Lisa Ullman). Boston: Plays.

Sweigard, L. (1974). *Human movement potential: Its ideokinetic facilitation* (pp. 167-169). New York: Dodd, Mead.

18

Ideokinesis as it Applies to Injury Prevention

Joellen Meglin
UNIVERSITY OF OREGON
EUGENE, OREGON, USA

We are in an age when information processing is so rapid that the amount of information conveyed is limited only by what an operator can respond to; an age when a rotation of the hand signals to a computer the simulated path that is a pilot's intention; an age when we cannot escape human engineering. In the field of dance, how is the dancer to respond to the increasing amount of research in physiology, motor learning, and dance medicine? How is this research to be applied sensibly?

Obviously teachers cannot spout dance science at every turn, between barre exercises. Moreover, there is a distinction between knowing a fact or concept and assimilating it at the body level. Any dancer knows to avoid pronation, but whether that same dancer is pronating in the heat of performance is a different matter. And whether that dancer can reverse pronation by a means that is not injurious in other ways through overcompensation or excessive muscle tension is still another. The problem lies in the limits of sensory processing or, more exactly, the mechanism of sensory processing.

The fallacy of inferring function from observations of structure has been pointed out by MacConaill and Basmajian (1969): "Observation alone [without experiment] tells us only the functional potentialities of this or that muscle, not its functional acts" (p. 5). Yet, improving a dancer's image of structure will improve her use of it. In an age of biofeedback, it should not seem unreasonable that the simple act of observation can create change in movement habits that are ingrained and relatively automatic; for example, in landing from a jump. In this context, change means consistent, involuntary differences in the performance of a movement. Obviously a dancer could voluntarily try to force supination of the foot on landing to protect the medial arch. Change, in ideokinesis, involves the subcortical reorganization of neuromuscular impulses. The idea of inducing change in the central nervous system at a subcortical level is put into proper context when we realize that it is possible to influence the output of the autonomic nervous system through meditation as evidenced by experiments by Benson (1975) and others.

Neuromuscular organization has been seen by some researchers as a constraint that limits the potential of the organism: Jacobsen, in the 1930s, conceived that the gestalt of muscle tensions was related to neurosis (cited in Benson, 1975); Todd (1937) believed it simply limited the efficient functioning of the human body; Sweigard (1975) elaborated Todd's work into the theory and practice of ideokinesis as a method of counteracting inefficient neuromuscular organization. Sweigard is something of a maverick in her concern with achieving balance and stability in stationary positions preliminary to movement. Posture is not a hot topic in the field of rehabilitation and physical medicine. The *Excerpta Medica* does not list a single abstract since 1977 under the subcategory of postural exercises. Yet it will be seen that Sweigard's concept of posture is infinitely subtle and dynamic.

Theory of Ideokinesis

The theory of ideokinesis as evolved by Sweigard postulates that improvement of the mechanical balance of the skeleton is possible through neuromuscular recoordination. This is effected by mental practice of imagery analogous to the desired effects. For example, imagining a line from the center of the knee to the center of the femoral joint will achieve a better alignment between these two structures. The imagery is aimed at aligning the skeletal framework more closely with the central axes of the body, thereby providing the bony framework with reduced resistance to gravity and giving the bony levers biomechanically advantaged starting points. By minimizing muscular effort in neutral posture, muscles are freed up for movement and can function from their resting lengths when movement is initiated.

The method of mental practice used is visualization of lines of movement: vectorial, planal, or rotational actions imagined in various locations throughout the body. These may be imagined in a purely spatial sense or with eidetic associations. "Visualize the buttocks as unbaked loaves of dough sliding downward to the back of the heels" is an image whose goal is to release tight lower back muscles via an imagined line of movement to lengthen the spine downward. Because voluntary interference may inhibit the formation of new neuromuscular habits by evoking old ones, passive visualization is essential.

Central to Sweigard's theory is the idea that "cognitive interference with muscle action by imposing voluntary control" is incorrect (Sweigard, 1975, p. 169). The emphasis by teachers and dancers alike on voluntarily tightening muscles to counteract technical faults or to attain technical goals actually impedes and restricts movement. "Making a correction" by forcing a visible result may actually pattern incorrect use of muscles. Of course it is possible to see that the shoulders are grossly out of line with the hips or that the head protrudes forward. Yet, how is it possible to determine exactly to what extent to use counterbalancing muscle groups to center the head delicately on top of the spine without distorting the finely balanced, natural curvatures of the spine? Or, to repeat concerns expressed by Teitz (1982), how does the dancer create a subtler balance, as in using the posterior tibialis, flexor hallucis longus, and peroneal muscles to maintain the strong ankle support in *demi-pointe* or on *pointe* that is crucial to the avoidance of inversion and eversion sprains? Micheli (quoted in "Medical Problems," 1982) found that even dancers who demonstrate well-trained, neutral backs revert to lordotic postures when they begin moving, confirming the futility of voluntarily trying to maintain the correct alignment in performance.

But if making a visible correction is wrong, what is right? According to Sweigard (1975), a goal- or image-oriented correction is best:

> Probably the most important ingredient in motor learning is goal orientation
> . . .*what* is the movement to be performed, not *how* it is to be performed. The
> nervous system takes care of the "how" of movement in accordance with a clear
> concept and mental picture of the movement. (p. 169)

Trying to intervene directly in muscular actions (as opposed to merely changing the movement's velocity or direction, for example) may only disturb protective, reflexive, synergistic reactions. Yet, exercises performed with perceptual intention—perceiving or imagining space, direction, position, locus of movement, or initiation with reference to the whole—are valuable to the dancer.

Advantages of Ideokinesis

Ideokinesis is preferable to voluntary patterns to maintain posture such as pelvis-tucking and spine-flattening for the following reasons: First, held muscles have not much in reserve because they have already used much of their contractile power (Dowd, 1981). They tend to become overdeveloped and bound (hypertonic), reducing their ability to lengthen when needed to allow stretch. Specifically, the resultant increased viscosity of bound muscle may bring the stretch reflex into play too soon, limiting movement range (Sweigard, 1975, pp. 144-145).

Second, voluntarily held postural patterns are often based on misconceptions of good alignment. A held pattern may isolate one body section to the detriment of the integrity of the whole, thereby actually placing more stress on the structure. For example, spine-flattening or attempting to reduce the forward curve of the lumbar spine may, over time, strain the vertebrae and discs. And, because the abdominal muscles coordinate with the muscles of the limbs best when activated from their resting lengths, a held contraction of the abdominals may interfere with this function (Sweigard, 1975, p. 292).

Rather than forcing an isolated action in a localized area, ideokinesis seeks to use images related to the whole to attain the correct action indirectly. Maintaining the concept of the whole allows the dancer to focus on those parts that function as stabilizers and equilibrators. Steindler (quoted in Sweigard, 1975, p. 146) has said that "the stabilizing and equilibrating efforts which do not manifest themselves in visible motion play the most important part in locomotor performance." Together with focusing only on the part moving, the dancer generally will focus on superficial anatomical changes. Obviously that is where we visually perceive the result of movement. But movement is much more efficient when conceived and initiated from the center of the joints. This principle is illustrated by laterally flexing the spinal column from the central axis of the trunk rather than from the surface of the back (Sweigard, 1975, p. 57). In sum, the goal is to develop the dancer's powers to imagine movement instead of to imitate movement.

The Mechanism of Recoordination

The question remains as to the mechanism of neuromuscular recoordination. If indeed balance is programmed largely at a subcortical level, how is change possible? Sweigard argues that conditioned reflexes are originally dependent on cortical reinforcement to become established. More particularly, muscle spindles, which demonstrate both afferent and efferent innervation, are part of a reflex arc that is subject to reinforcement (Sweigard, 1975, pp. 165-167). They provide the mechanism for the stretch reflex—a contractile response to stretch (Sweigard, 1975, pp. 144-145)—that is intimately related to our ability to balance as we are continually bombarded from without and within by forces that create deviations from balance. Hence we are talking about reinforcement of the proprioceptive senses as opposed to voluntary efforts to effect change. This reinforcement may take the form of visualization of imagery or mental practice (Sweigard, 1975, p. 167).

Ideokinetic Experiments

What experiments have been performed to test the theory of ideokinesis? As early as 1931, Sweigard designed an experiment wherein the treatment was essentially ideokinesis. Although the study lacked a control group, Sweigard did achieve significant results in terms of reliable differences in skeletal alignment as measured by the relationship between selected bony parts. For example:

> The mid-front of the pelvis moved forward and upward with concomitant backward and downward movement of the back of the pelvis at the most prominent part of the sacrum. (Sweigard, 1975, p. 191)

Subsequently, Sweigard based her further development of the theory on her clinical practice with dance students at Juilliard.

A more recent experiment was performed by Studd (1983) at the University of Oregon. Studd used ideokinetic imagery in a dance-technique class for her experimental treatment group, while using relaxation techniques in another class for her control group. She found significant differences in the performances of the two classes as measured by expert ratings of videotaped performances of technical phrases.

Ideokinetic Approach

Ideokinesis, as evolved by Sweigard, consists of a three-pronged approach: visualization in the constructive rest position, visualization accompanying basic voluntary movements, and improved conscious use of body mechanics. The constructive rest position is supine, with elbows draped across the chest, soles of the feet on the floor, and knees tied together with a sash to prevent their falling apart. The rationale for this position is that it is mechanically balanced; it may be maintained with minimal muscular effort; hence there is minimal interference from preexisting neuromuscular patterns with the formation of new ones.

Ideokinesis must be differentiated from relaxation techniques. Although release of muscular tension allows stretch, it does not create tonus (Sweigard, 1975, pp. 250-257). The nine basic lines of movement around which imagery is organized promote muscle tone where it is needed, as in the abdominals, the adductors of the medial thigh, and the muscles of the medial arch. The second phase of the process is the practice of basic voluntary movements. For example, the thigh is flexed from the constructive rest position using imagery to promote control of the thigh close to the pelvis (as opposed to peripheral control) and to promote stabilization of the movement from the abdominals (instead of bracing in the opposite hamstring). Additionally, the abdominals are contracted from their resting lengths, which are established by the constructive rest position (Sweigard, 1975, pp. 289-290).

In the third and final phase, good mechanics in daily movement help to transfer and generalize the positive effects of the first two phases. For example, moving from the femoral joints instead of bending the spine helps to alleviate the stress on smaller, weaker joints and to maintain the integrity of the spine.

Dance Mechanics

Unless the dancer transfers the neuromuscular patterns activated by the ideokinetic process to her particular genre of dance, new patterns probably will not supplant the old ones practiced for years in the classroom. Although Dowd has extended the application of imagery to more complex movements, systematic application of ideokinesis to standard dance vocabulary has not yet been attempted.

I would like to look at two movements from the standard ballet barre: *fondu* and *frappé*. *Fondu* is a bending motion of a single supporting limb; simultaneously the gesture leg folds in toward the standing leg. Applicable lines of movement would be (a) a vector from the spine downward, (b) a line from the center of the knee to the center of the femoral joint, and (c) a vector along the central axis of the body upward (Sweigard, 1975, pp. 237-249).

Organization of the movement around these images will prevent increased lordosis on the *demi-plié* like action of one leg; center the action in the femoral joint, which is designed to take the weight of the descending center of gravity;

initiate the action in the femoral joint so the natural flow and sequencing of the two-joint muscles are not disrupted; and maintain the vertical integrity of the trunk. I have heard the *fondu* described as follows in the class of an excellent teacher: "Bend the ankle, then the knee [hip flexion omitted]; now stretch the ankle and the knee." The problem with this description is that it works against the natural coordination of the two-joint muscles of the lower limb. The hip joint must be seen as an integral part of the action, and the action of either flexion or extension should be conceived to occur simultaneously in all joints or in sequence from the central joints to the peripheral joints. Clearly, the teacher's choice of images will direct either a correct action or an incorrect one.

Frappé involves a sharp motion that transiently slides the ball of the foot along the floor and then releases, triggering an arch through the metatarsal area, followed by a quick retraction of the foot with a folding action in its ankle. Although several lines of movement are applicable, focus should be on the one from the big toe to the heel during the folding action of the ankle. The stated effect of this line of movement is to reduce pronation and eversion (Sweigard, 1975, p. 243). In this case, it balances the action of the dorsiflexors of the foot by reinforcing the tibialis anterior to prevent excessive eversion.

How do faulty concepts of movement interfere with efficient neuromuscular patterning and predispose a dancer to injury? In answering this question, we will relate the specific category of injury of chondromalacia patellae to faulty concepts of movement. Ende and Wickstrom (1982) suggested that dance students with chondromalacia patellae overuse the quadriceps mechanism in an attempt to achieve recurvatum, that is, hyperextended knees. Sweigard (1975, p. 82) supported this idea with her contention that the emphasis of some teachers on "pulling up the knees" on rise, or *relevé*, contributes to retropatellar pain. In her view, an overdeveloped quadriceps mechanism does not necessarily improve neuromuscular coordination. Dowd (1981, p. 2) said that muscular imbalance in any direction predisposes to injury. Ende and Wickstrom (1982) indicated that the vastus medialis is not only intact but well-developed in dancers with chondromalacia patellae.

In such cases rehabilitative treatment that prescribes only the traditional quadriceps-strengthening exercises is questionable. Roy and Irvin (1983) stated that performing isometric or isotonic quadriceps sets may actually aggravate the condition. Although treatment today usually emphasizes strengthening all the muscles around the injured joint, ideokinesis may have something to offer as a measure preliminary to exercise. According to Roy and Irvin (1983, p. 37), chondromalacia patellae is associated with quadriceps mechanism malalignment, which in turn may be associated with soft-tissue imbalance around the femoral joint. In such cases the line of movement from the center of the knee joint to the center of the femoral joint seems particularly useful because its purposes are to balance muscle action around the femoral joint, to improve the relationship of the knee joint to the femoral joint, and to improve the mechanical balance of the knee.

Sweigard (1975, pp. 67-71, 78-83) described other faulty concepts or poor mechanics of movement that may put stress on the knees and become the long-term mechanisms of injury to the patella:

1. Wrongly initiating a movement pattern at the knee joints; for example, executing the *demi-plié* by bending the knees because that is the visible result. Sweigard contends that the synergy of movement should begin at the femoral joints; otherwise, subtle timing differences between actions in the knee and femoral joints can impede efficiency and good mechanics at the knee joints.
2. Restricted rotation in the femoral joints that forces the knees to rotate in order to compensate. Many authors cite the maneuver of "screwing the knees" at the barre, but the problem goes beyond the dancer's positioning. Unless the femoral joints are perceived to be the locus of locomotor movement, the knees will take the stress. For example, consider how taxing on the knee is the action of a low run with a pivot away from the limb performed with minimal rotation at the hip.
3. Fractionating the normal functioning of two-joint muscles, as in *grand battement en avant* or *attitude derriére*. Normally extension or flexion occurs simultaneously throughout the joints of the lower extremity. It is not suggested that we eliminate these movements from the vocabulary but merely that, in warming up, there be gradation or proper sequencing of exercises that practices the more natural movements first.
4. Walking in turn-out in daily movement. This resists the natural efficiency of the internal rotation of the tibia in relation to the femur and promotes inefficient use of the feet.

Clippinger (quoted in "Medical Problems," 1982) asserted that if motion and stability are controlled from the pelvis, stress on the knee can be diminished. She observed that where there is a lack of rotation at the hips, the dancer will use a locking back of the knees to try to balance and stabilize, and that an excessive grabbing of muscles that may result can cause overuse or malalignment syndromes. She further found that a shift of emphasis to the proper muscles (i.e., deep outward rotators, abdominals, and adductors) to control hip action can decrease patellar compressional forces aggravated by overuse of the quadriceps and gluteals. This approach, which examines proximal musculoskeletal function in relation to injury occurring distally, parallels Sweigard's clinical approach.

Other authors have stated the necessity for taking the entire postural pattern into consideration. Marr (1983) criticized the traditional focus: "The stressful areas of spine and knee will be treated by traditional medicine as separate entities rather than the total postural compensatory biomechanical picture" (p. 125). Later, in regard to chondromalacia patellae, Marr wrote that "attempts to treat this condition as a separate entity usually provide only temporary relief. The condition requires analysis of total body movement" (p. 127).

There is increasing evidence that researchers are willing to investigate the overall postural pattern in looking for factors predisposing to injury. Teitz (1982) found that, if abdominal or back strength is inadequate to keep the weight centered in the pelvis, the dancer may invert or evert the foot on *demi-pointe*. Several authors have noted the relationship between increased lumbar lordosis and faulty concepts of turn-out. In sum, when dealing with an injury, we must consider the entire postural complex. The solution lies within the correctness and eloquence of the dancer's whole neuromuscular gestalt.

Applying Ideokinesis

This notion leads us directly to the implications for the use of ideokinesis as a rehabilitative tool:

1. Ideokinesis improves mechanical balance, thereby reducing stress on musculoskeletal structures. This is important because of the principle that, if subjected to the same stresses (i.e., if the activity is not altered or the injured part not made stronger than before the injury), injury is likely to recur.
2. Visualization can be practiced in an immobile state before movement is advisable. In conditions that require absolute rest, such as Achilles tendinitis, it may reduce the initial trauma of return to movement after prolonged lack of use. It may also relieve the documented dancer's anxiety stemming from complete passivity in the face of the injury.
3. It focuses on rehabilitation of balanced use of muscles. There is a benefit to preceding traditional muscle-strengthening exercises with this. Exercises designed to compensate for specific weaknesses may overcompensate, again resulting in a pattern of imbalance and predisposing to injury. General exercises alone will tend to develop muscles according to already existing and possibly imbalanced patterns of strength and weakness.
4. Visualization may allow the dancer to avoid alienation of an injured part and to integrate it into patterns of movement earlier and more completely. Roy and Irvin (1983, p. 91) stressed the importance of practicing a normal gait motion with only as much weight as the limb will bear to allow proprioceptive contact to be retained "so that the sensory system does not 'switch off' the affected limb" (p. 91). Ideokinesis allows a similar but nonmoving practice of proprioceptive activity.
5. Its theoretical basis is analogous to that of proprioceptive neuromuscular facilitation. Naming PNF as a technique that is used to overcome neural inhibitions that hinder rehabilitation, Roy attributed its theoretical basis to "stimulating proprioceptors such as the muscle spindles, the Golgi tendon organs, the pacinian corpuscles, and the free nerve endings to promote a response" (Roy & Irvin, 1983, p. 119). Roy and Irvin (1983, p. 395) also mentioned the importance of doing exercises for the sake of proprioceptive feedback. For example, they advised balancing on one foot with eyes closed for ankle injuries. Ideokinesis, whose theoretical mechanism is stimulation of the proprioceptive senses and the afferent-efferent loop, would seem to accomplish similar purposes.

    Experimental evidence suggests the importance of such techniques. Glencross and Thorton (1981) designed a study to test the hypothesis that injury to the joint structures would damage joint mechanoreceptors, resulting in distortion of proprioception. Their positive results may indicate that either a degree of proprioception is permanently lost following injury or that it simply has never been restored. In conclusion, the quality of the neuromuscular response rather than simply the bulk or strength of muscle should be looked at in evaluating rehabilitative processes. This paper has explored the use of ideokinesis as a preventive and rehabilitative process with the underlying beliefs that a fundamental goal of dance medicine is the education of the dancer, and that ideokinesis provides a medium with which to achieve this purpose.

References

Benson, H. (1975). *The relaxation response.* New York: Avon Books.

Dowd, I. (1981). *Taking root to fly: Seven articles on functional anatomy.* New York: Contact Collaborations.

Ende, L.S., & Wickstrom, J. (1982). Ballet injuries. *The Physician and Sportsmedicine,* **10,** 113.

Glencross, D., & Thorton, E. (1981). Position sense following joint injury. *Journal of Sports Medicine,* **21,** 23-27.

MacConaill, M.A., & Basmajian, J.V. (1969). *Muscles and movements: A basis for human kinesiology.* Baltimore: Williams and Wilkins.

Marr, S.J. (1983). The ballet foot. *Journal of the American Podiatry Association,* **73**(3), 125-127.

Medical problems in ballet: A round table. (1982). *The Physician and Sportsmedicine,* **10,** 101, 103-104.

Roy, S., & Irvin, R. (1983). *Sports medicine: Prevention, evaluation, management, and rehabilitation.* Englewood Cliffs, NJ: Prentice-Hall.

Studd, K. (1983). *Ideokinesis, mental rehearsal and relaxation applied to dance technique.* Unpublished master's thesis, University of Oregon, Eugene.

Sweigard, L. (1975). *Human movement potential: Its ideokinetic facilitation.* New York: Dodd, Mead and Co.

Teitz, C.C. (1982). Sports medicine concerns in dance and gymnastics. *Pediatric Clinics of North America,* **29**(6), 1413-1417.

Todd, M.E. (1937). *The thinking body: A study of the balancing forces of dynamic man.* New York: Dance Horizons.

PART V

Emerging Research in Dance Science

One thing is painfully clear about dance science and medicine: Not enough research on dancers' injuries has been done to provide adequate information to help the dancer. Although a great deal of sports medicine research is applicable to dance, barriers between the disciplines of dance and athletics prevent a totally mutual exchange of information and its application. The barriers are primarily related to goals of the dancer and athlete, which are as different as qualitative and quantitative measures themselves. Consequently, it stands to reason that the goal-seekers' needs and characteristics may be different also. Skrinar's article bears this out, and she challenges dancers to question, examine, and perhaps relinquish traditional tenets about dance training. The premise of her challenge is a respectable one. A dancer's training must keep up with the demands of a constantly changing aesthetic; otherwise, the studio experience will contribute nothing to the art or to the well-being of the dancer.

Studies such as those presented herein by Clanin and Solomon signify the increased documentation of injuries requisite to the understanding of dancers' needs. Their findings enhance the sparse collection of data concerning types of injuries associated with a specific dance idiom. As this kind of information becomes substantiated by further corroborative research and activity-specific research, physicians may be able to evaluate, treat, and rehabilitate dancers' injuries with increased precision. Clanin's study generated data relative to ballet, modern dance, and jazz, whereas Solomon's study focused specifically on the modern dance idiom. Of similar intensity was Kravitz' research into only one idiom, classical ballet. He further delimited his investigation to only one malady associated with pointe technique, resulting in the strongest evidence to date that directly related pronation of the feet to bunion deformity around the great toe. The strength of his findings lies in the sophisticated equipment he used for collecting data from the dancers' feet. This suggests that the conscientious researcher should seek out the latest laboratory equipment for the most accurate findings. In Kravitz' case, the latest equipment at his disposal was the electrodynogram computer.

When sophisticated equipment is not available, standard tools of movement analysis can still provide useful information for the treatment of dancers' or athletes' injuries. In the final article, Martin applied Laban movement analysis, a traditional dance tool, to the study of a sport skill, the discus throw. Her study represents a unique procedure in the study of human performance. Whereas dance researchers usually apply procedures and tools that are associated with the sciences, Martin took a typical dance tool into the realm of sport. At last there is a true interchange taking place between sports medicine and dance science and medicine in spite of their inherent differences.

19

Motor Learning Research May Help the Dancer

Margaret Skrinar
DANCE KINESIOLOGIST
SHERBORN, MASSACHUSETTS, USA

Dance is not being well taught in this country because teachers in general do not have a clear understanding of how movement is learned. The neighborhood dance teachers who cover everything from tap, ballet, acrobatics, hula, fire baton, and toe-tap dancing with jump ropes are not the only offenders. Most conscientious, well-trained, sensitive, and creative teachers who care about and love dance simply are not doing the necessary job. Admittedly these are provocative charges; nevertheless, the following is provided to support my contentions.

Teaching Dance

Before considering a few of the ways teachers have failed to teach movement efficiently and effectively, an examination of why these circumstances may have arisen is necessary. First, most will agree that dance has been a macrocosmic population whose size has not yet been established. As many children have likely danced as have played Little League baseball. Yet, even with so many participants, dance as an art form has rarely been taken seriously by the general public. To the masses, dancers have either been little girls in tutus innocuously walking on tiptoe or sensuous women jiggling their bodies in time to rock music. Because dance is not taken seriously, the teaching of dance has been allowed to effectively go unchecked. No one has bothered to question it. In contrast, sports training has been deemed valuable in our society, valuable enough to the public and its consumers to have been questioned.

Second, because dance is rarely researched, dancers are frequently suspicious of questions. A mentality has surfaced that rejects dance research because it requires systematic quantification. True, quantification demeans art; but quantification of how the instrument of dance, the body, is trained is necessary and healthful. Further, it can be done without encroaching on aesthetic preferences. Dance teaching can be systematically examined without truncating the art.

Third, the constant change in aesthetics, a factor that sets dance training apart from sports training, makes it difficult for teachers to continually reexamine and redesign classes. Changes in aesthetics by choreographers or artistic directors should be reflected in the dancers' training, yet this is not happening on a broad scale. An example of how teachers are failing is represented by the widespread teaching of classes in one of the big-three modern techniques—Graham, Cunningham, or Nikolais. Those techniques may be appropriate for Martha's, Merce's, or Nik's dancers but not for others. Only when their choreography is duplicated is their training regime appropriate. Given that aesthetic perspectives in dance vary between and within individuals, it follows that choreography should differ. Curiously, dance is generally taught as it has been for decades, although choreographically major changes are occurring regularly. Dance training is not keeping pace with dance as an art form. For this to continue is comparable to training high jumpers to do the scissor kick but expecting them to execute the Fosbury Flop in competition.

In summary, the teaching of dance technique is not what it should be, in part because no one is extensively questioning why or what is being done and because training procedures are not keeping pace with ever-changing aesthetics. What can be done? Although not a panacea, the field of motor learning can provide some answers. The purpose of this paper is to (a) share what little we know about dance-specific motor-learning research, (b) speculate on what the research findings might mean, (c) raise questions for future research, and (d) suggest what can be done until more research is completed.

Jean Held in 1981 at the Second Annual Body Therapy Workshop at Duke University recommended motor learning research as a means of updating and increasing effectiveness and efficiency in dance training. A smattering of isolated research has supported this notion. Investigations completed to date have been sporadic and lacked continuity but have provided some insight. Most work has been generated as theses or dissertations; consequently, follow-up research to questions raised by the initial work has rarely occurred. In this article motor-learning dance research is classified into four areas of focus: perceptual skills, learning, instructional-cue use, and transfer. The results of these draw a sketchy picture of the psychomotor makeup of dancers and their training.

Perceptual Skills

Perceptually, two studies have indicated a self-selection process may have been working for those who have chosen to dance. In other words, teachers may not have been developing perceptual skills in dancers; students may have arrived in class with those skills. Gruen (1955) studied 60 professional dancers (30 females and 30 males) from major New York City companies in which ballet, modern, and Afro-American dance were represented. He administered four perceptual tests to the dancers as well as to 99 nondancer controls. Three tests were physical and one written. Gruen found that, with one exception, dance experience was not a factor regarding increased perceptual abilities. Balance was the only differentiating factor; dancers were better balancers than nondancers. Differences among dancers were not found. Coupling the latter finding with the fact that dancers with as little as one year of experience were included in the study, Gruen concluded that balance was likely developed within the first year of dance training.

Gruen's study implies that perceptual skills such as hand-eye coordination, rhythm, visual discrimination, and body control were not learned in dance class, but were either acquired elsewhere or genetically inherited. Yet it is likely that most teachers would list at least a half dozen or more perceptual skills that they believe are developed while studying dance. If Gruen's findings were accurate in that classes, rehearsals, and performance have not developed perceptual skills, then what has actually been learned in dance?

Bowman (1971) looked at how beginning dancers learned a 21-count movement phrase with regard to space. Using 14 untrained college freshmen, she found that the perceptual learning style of field dependence-independence was significantly related to how and what was learned. Field-independent subjects learned more quickly and thoroughly than the field-dependent students. At one end of a continuum, field-dependence indicated an inability to identify items when they are outside the expected setting. Conversely, field-independence measured one's skill for locating items outside the expected context. Common screening tests for this have been childrens' hidden picture games that have asked them to locate something like 10 parrots in a setting of vehicles.

Bowman's and Gruen's studies appear to contradict each other with regard to field-dependence. Gruen found no differences between his control group and the dancers. Bowman found her most successful beginners were field-independent. Because people tend to gravitate toward an activity when they are successful, her findings lead one to suspect that dancers ought to be more field-independent than nondancers. Although not significant, Barrell and Trippe (1975) found just the reverse to be true; controls were more field-independent than professional male ballet dancers. These contradictory findings in addition to Gruen's observations about dancers' perceptual abilities point out how little is known about either the natural skills students bring into the class or the teacher's influence on the perceptual makeup of dancers. Further research should investigate how teachers are affecting perceptual abilities and other performance variables.

Learning

Bowman's work also dealt with learning schemes. She found that most learning errors occurred with lateral locomotor movement as well as timing. Further, she observed that her subjects chose to use whole rather than part learning. These results indicate that, at least for beginners, significant time should be spent working side-to-side and on temporal problems rather than on the commonly emphasized forward and backward movement. Coupling Gruen's and Bowman's results, the question arises as to which is the more valuable approach to improved balance, timing, or plane changing abilities—general work or the conventional specific skills (pliés, tendus, leaps, turns, etc.). Clarkson,

Kennedy, and Flanagan's work (1984) on timing and reaction times of dancers suggests that consistency of movement patterns may be one critical general ability that dance training develops. In the future, critical dance skills need identification. Perhaps if those general skills were attended to in beginning classes, specific skills would be more easily learned during later training stages.

Continuing the theme of learning, it has appeared that men learn dance more efficiently than women. Four studies spanning professional and college dances over 30 years have established that males study 5 to 6 years less than their female counterparts (Gruen, 1955; Hellerman & Skrinar, 1984; Hellerman, Skrinar, & Dodds, 1984; Skrinar & Zelonka, 1978). It is not known whether motivation, movement history, sex biases, or some other factors have made the difference. Dancers must find out why this is so in order to prevent further waste of each female dancer's training time.

Instructional Cues

The learning of movement skills is influenced by the type of instructional cues provided. Cuing, or directions, occur visually, verbally, kinesthetically, or in any combination of these three. The literature indicates that teaching methods combining all types of cues are more effective than those using only one type (Cratty, 1973). Furthermore, for efficient skill acquisition each ability level has its own cuing needs (Cratty, 1973; Singer, 1980). Three studies indicate that regardless of level, idiom, or class purpose, verbal cues dominate instructional time. Visual-verbal cues are used considerably less, with virtually little or no kinesthetic, kinesthetic-visual, kinesthetic-verbal, or visual instructions occurring (Borrelli & Skrinar, 1982; Cheffers, Mancini, & Martinek, 1980, Lord, 1979).

Borrelli and Skrinar (1982) studied cuing patterns in 6 teachers who taught both beginning and advanced dance major technique classes in one of two idioms, ballet or modern. They found the use of verbal instruction was significantly ($p < .05$) greater than all other forms, while visual-verbal cues were used significantly ($p < .05$) more than the remaining type of cues (see Figure 1).

Lord (1979) and Cheffers (1980) found similar results between types of classes. Verbal instruction time dominated both technique and composition classes. Cheffers found that students spent 67.7% of technique class time listening to verbal teaching instructions and 52.1% during composition class. In classes where movement and observational instruction time (visual and kinesthetic cues) should prevail, it is disconcerting to learn how few opportunities there are. In a performing art, how can dancers efficiently or effectively learn to see or move if they do not spend significant amounts of time doing and watching? All teachers must become more aware of how much time they spend talking.

The literature on skill level suggests that, while a combination of all types of cues is important, learning is maximized when combinations for beginners emphasize kinesthetic and visual cues. Following that, progressively more verbal instruction should be provided with advancing skill (Cratty, 1973; Singer, 1980). The theory is that beginners with limited mental and physical dance vocabulary cannot profit from as much class talk; they need time doing and watching. The advanced student with an expanded dance vocabulary is able

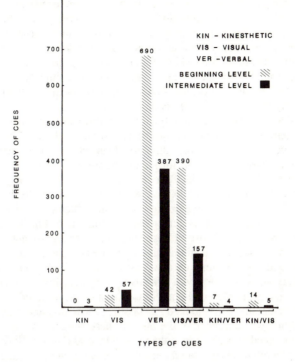

Figure 1. Cuing patterns of instruction

to listen and digest verbal instruction or corrections without the actual physical experience. Borrelli and Skrinar (1982) not only found all classes predominantly verbal but that beginning classes were significantly ($p < .05$) more verbal than the advanced.

It appears that teachers do not adjust their instructional methods to the level or type of class. Furthermore, it seems the beginning dancer may be jeopardized the most. Beyond that, all dancers likely spend too much time passively listening. Dance teachers need to systematically experiment with sweeping changes in their instructional approach to different types of classes at all levels.

Transfer of Movement

Cuing is not the only problem area. The use of transfer as an instructional tool is inefficiently utilized in dance classes. Transfer suggests that the learning of one task may positively or negatively influence the learning of other tasks. Negative or positive transfer is affected by the degree of similarity in the stimulus and response elements of each task. Negative transfer occurs when the stimulus elements for each task are identical but the response elements are dissimilar (Cratty, 1973). During technique class the stimulus elements are relatively constant; the setting, the teacher, the accompaniment, and so on, are unchanged. Yet the response elements between the warm-up and dancing phases of class can be quite different. For example, in a ballet warm-up students stand at a barre, often sideways to a mirror and alternately work one leg at a time in essentially a unidirectional facing. During the center dancing phase the students, using some skills from the warm-up, face toward the mirror, stand away from the barre, and execute movement that quickly and frequently changes directions and shifts legs. Practice of skills during the warm-up could be negatively transferring to the center work.

Gray and Skrinar (1984) indirectly looked at how use of the center of gravity likely transferred from warm-up to dancing phases of modern and ballet classes. Using all levels of class from beginning to advanced dance major classes, they determined the frequency of use for six different-sized bases of support (very narrow, narrow, medium, wide, grounded, and in the air). They found that warm-up for classes within an idiom varied significantly from the dancing phase ($p < .01$). That is, transfer regarding use of the center of gravity could well have resulted in decayed skills during the dancing phase. Further, they found that ballet's and modern's use of base supports were significantly dissimilar during warm-up, yet similar in the dancing phases of class. A disproportional use during warm-up of very narrow bases in ballet and grounded bases in modern dance was contrasted with a relatively even distribution of base-support use while dancing in either idiom. Similar results were found in an unpublished follow-up study that looked at classes, rehearsals, and performances. Each condition was unrelated to the other in base-support use, with class being more unrelated to performance than was rehearsal (Gray & Skrinar, 1982).

Future research needs to examine if there are other ways in which warm-up time may be more efficiently utilized. The result could mean, for example, that if their time were spent more efficiently, professional ballet dancers would not need to spend 8 to 10 hours per day, 6 days per week in classes, rehearsal, and performance.

Table 1. Identification of support base

Base of support	Area*	Positions
Very narrow	$\leqslant 0.2$	One foot demi-pointe
Narrow	$0.3 - 0.7$	One foot flat, two feet together in demi-pointe
Medium	$0.8 - 1.4$	Feet shoulder width apart
Wide	$\geqslant 1.5$	Feet beyond shoulders
Grounded	—	Weight-bearing body part on ground outside area of wide base
No base	0	Body in air

*Relative area in proportion to medium base, which is defined as 1.0.

Table 2. Mean percentage of base use in warm-up and dancing phases

Base sizes	Ballet Warm-up	Dancing	Δ's[1]	Modern Warm-up	Dancing	Δ's[1]
Very narrow	6	9	+3	0	5	+5
Narrow	34	23	−11*	13	21	+8
Medium	51	42	−9*	33	39	+6
Wide	8	13	+5	14	20	+6
Grounded	1	0	−1	40	6	−34*
No Base	0	13	+13*	0	9	+9*

[1]Increases or decreases of "dancing" over "warm-up".

Availability of Research

Unfortunately motor-learning research is not readily available to dancers. The little that exists paints a bleak picture. The accessible documentation suggests that dancers may not be provided with optimum opportunities for successful psychomotor skill development. The art form is demanding more movement expertise each year, yet the best ways to realize that expertise in dancers are not always being applied.

Clearly, dancers need to consult with motor-learning and motor-development personnel as well as teacher behaviorists. These professionals can assist in evaluation and redesign of classes. They can help define new models for teaching dance as well as develop testing tools that are sensitive enough for the needs of dance. Until further research is completed, it is essential that the dance community do some basic reading and study in motor learning, motor development, motor control, and teacher behavior. Few, if any, dance curricula recommend, let alone require, such course work of their students. Yet, as it appears, most dancers teach if they do nothing else with their training. After graduation from a conservatory or college department they could likely teach before they perform or choreograph. Unfortunately all of these dancers, who may be well trained as performers and choreographers, may be far less prepared to teach.

I have suspected that in the past many potential dancers have "washed out" of dance, possibly because of ineffective and inefficient teaching. After all, where have all those adults gone who as children filled every small-town dance studio? Perhaps their enthusiasm was subconsciously thwarted by repeated failure. This may have been a result of their teacher's ignorance about how movement was learned rather than their own inability. Without a foundation in motor learning this trend, if it is one, could continue.

Finally, even if all of the studies cited here are erroneous in their findings, they must be acknowledged for initiating questions about the teaching of dance. Large numbers of people spend considerable money and time studying dance. As consumers they deserve the best that dance can offer. Perhaps the best is the status quo, perhaps not. Motor learning research can provide dancers with some of the answers. If dancers begin to take the teaching of dance more seriously, perhaps the public will take dance more seriously. Then, like sport, dance may step into new realms of technical accomplishment and greater public participation.

References

Barrell, G., & Trippe, H. (1975). Field dependence and physical ability. *Perceptual and Motor Skills, 41*, 216-218.

Borrelli, G., & Skrinar, M. (1982). Instructional cue use in two dance idioms (abstract). *Kinesiology for Dance, 5*(1), 6.

Bowman, B.A. (1971). *Learning experiences in selected aspects of a dance movement sequence.* Unpublished doctoral dissertation, University of Michigan, Ann Arbor.

Cheffers, J.T.F., Mancini, V., & Martinek, T. (1980). *Interaction analysis: An application to nonverbal activity* (2nd ed.). St. Paul, MN: Paul S. Amedon and Associates.

Clarkson, P.M., Kennedy, T., & Flanagan, J. (1984). A study of three movements in classical ballet. *Research Quarterly for Exercise and Sport, 55*(2), 175-179.

Cratty, B. (1973). *Teaching motor skills* (pp. 60-64). Englewood Cliffs, NJ: Prentice-Hall.

Gray, M., & Skrinar, M. (1982). *Base support use in class rehearsal and performance.* Unpublished manuscript, Smith College, Department of Dance.

Gray, M., & Skrinar, M. (1984). Base support in two dance idioms. *Research Quarterly for Exercise and Sport, 55*(2), 184-187.

Gruen, A. (1955). The relation of dancing experience and personality to perception. *Psychological Monographs: General and Applied, 69*(14), 1-16.

Hellerman, A., & Skrinar, M. (1984). Relationship of technical skill rank to age, gender and number of years in dance training. *Research Quarterly for Exercise and Sport, 55*(2), 188-190.

Hellerman, A., Skrinar, M., & Dodds, P. (1984). *Gender differences in dancers' acquisition of novel movement pattern, physical education department.* Manuscript submitted for publication.

Lord, M.C. (1979). The teaching of dance: A characterization of dance teacher behaviors in technique and choreography classes at the university level. *Dissertation Abstracts International, 40a*, 5778.

Singer, R.N. (1980). *Motor learning and human performance* (3rd ed.). New York: MacMillan.

Skrinar, M., & Zelonka, N.H. (1978). A descriptive study of ballet and modern dancers at three levels of training. Unpublished study, University of Pittsburgh, School of Education.

20

Injury Patterns in University Dance Students

Diana R. Clanin
ILLINOIS STATE UNIVERSITY
NORMAL, ILLINOIS, USA

Dennis M. Davison and Janice G. Plastino
UNIVERSITY OF CALIFORNIA, IRVINE
IRVINE, CALIFORNIA, USA

Until recently, dancers have been regarded by themselves and by the medical profession solely as elite artists; beings whose constitutions have been defined by the ephemeral qualities of their art form, and thus often identified by themselves and their audiences with the illusionary nature of the roles they perform. Perhaps these images have contributed to the perpetuation of melodramatic, romantic, silently suffering dancers whose pain was evidence of their dedication to their art.

In fact, when hurt or injured, many dancers fail to receive appropriate medical attention and continue to suffer pain needlessly. Such underuse of appropriate medical care has even led to premature termination of many promising careers. The reasons for this are many: they begin with the denial of injury by the dancer out of fear of losing coveted roles or a place in a company. Further, few health professionals have been specifically and adequately trained regarding the unique psychological and physiological needs of dancers. With few notable exceptions, little has been published regarding the specific injuries of dancers (Rovere, Webb, Gristina, & Vogel, 1983; Washington, 1978).

To more precisely define the nature of dance injuries and the factors predisposing thereto, the incidence of dance injuries was studied during 2 consecutive years in a major university dance department.

Methods

The study population consisted of 268 students enrolled in the comprehensive curriculum of the Dance Department School of Fine Arts, University of California, Irvine. The students, ranging in age from 18 to 38 (mean, 26), performed at intermediate and advanced levels (e.g., pointe work for the women in ballet). Their intensive interdisciplinary course included daily classes in ballet, modern, jazz, or other dance forms in preparation for, or concurrent with, professional dance careers.

When an injury occurred, the student was screened and referred for initial evaluation by an athletic trainer (certified by the National Athletic Trainers Association) in the university's sports medicine and training room facility. When appropriate, dancers were treated at that facility alone; when indicated, they were referred to the University Student Health Service for consultation with a primary physician or an orthopedic surgeon, specializing in athletic injuries. Screening, initial evaluation, and definitive care information were recorded at the time, and then stored for later analysis using the Statistical Package for Social Sciences on the University DEC-10 computer.

Results

During the academic years 1981-82 and 1982-83, 335 injuries were documented in 159 dancers. Table 1 itemizes their locations and frequency. Of the 335 injuries, 38% occurred on the dancer's right side, 48% on the left, and 14% were bilateral. Table 2 details the treatment modalities utilized for the injuries. Twenty-three (7%) were treated by a primary physician, 19 (6%) by the orthopedic surgeon, and the remaining 293 (87%) by the athletic trainer alone.

Table 1. Location of injuries

Location	Frequency
Neck	5
Shoulder	9
Thorax	3
Upper extremities	6
Upper back	32
Lower back	33
Hip	26
Knee	50
Lower leg	61
Ankle	31
Foot	30
Toe	6
Other	9

Table 2. Treatment modalities

Treatment	Cases	Frequency (%)
Ice/ice massage	223	66.6
Modification of activity	85	25.5
Oral medication	76	22.8
Immobilization or support	53	15.9
Electrostimulation	50	15.0
Hydroculator	47	14.1
Therapeutic exercise	32	9.6
Total activity restriction	23	6.9
Massage	21	6.3
Ultrasound	18	5.4
Whirlpool	18	5.4
Contrast treatments	10	3.0
Technique correction	10	3.0
Surgery	4	1.2

Because most students were training in several dance forms concurrently, only 143 of the 335 injuries could be attributed to a specific dance form. Of these 143 occurrences, ballet accounted for a majority of injuries to the feet (14 of 20), knee (12 of 14), and ankle (8 of 13), and for all injuries to the hip (5) and upper back (3). Back injuries occurred predominately in modern dance (13 of 27), although a disproportionate number of lower back strains resulted from jazz dancing.

During the 2-year period, 79 of the 159 dancers had one additional injury, 35 had two, 22 had three, 12 had four, and 11 had five or more additional injuries. When restricting analysis of these episodes to those occurring at the same site as the original injury, 54 incidents were noted (see Table 3). Of these, most frequent were first degree hamstring strains (10), ankle sprains (7), Achilles tendinitis (7), and lower back muscle spasm (6).

The etiology of 190 of the 335 injuries could be determined, as given in Table 4. Of the 194, 107 could be attributed to one of the major dance forms in the curriculum. Particularly noteworthy are the large number attributable to overuse and performing movement beyond the dancer's current technical ability.

Discussion

Three earlier reports have examined injuries in dancers. Shaw (1977) retrospectively surveyed university dance students throughout the United States by mail questionnaire. Also using a questionnaire, Washington (1978) reported on the incidence of injuries in professional theatrical dancers. Rovere, Webb, Gristina, and Vogel (1983) described musculoskeletal injuries in theatrical dance students who were treated in their sports medicine unit.

Table 3. Types of recurrent injuries

Injury type	Frequency
First degree strain	11
First degree sprain	8
Second degree sprain	2
Tendinitis	7
Muscle spasm	6
Nerve impingement	3
Tibial stress syndrome	3
Herniated disc	2
Synovitis	2
Meniscal tear	2
Contusion	2
Bursitis	1
Stress fracture	1
Epicondylitis	1
Chondromalacia	1
Hallux valgus	1
Loose body	1

Differences among those three studies and the present investigation might be expected from the age of the subjects, the form(s) of dance activity in which they regularly participated, and their individual level of expertise in a particular dance genre. It should be noted that many university dance students exhibit higher body weights than their professional counterparts, a factor that

Table 4. Etiology of injuries

Cause	Number	Ballet	Modern	Jazz	Baroque
Overuse	79	15	8	3	1
Hazardous movement	27	13	4	6	
Predisposing anatomy	20	4	2	1	1
Incorrect technique	14	7	2		
Fall	10	7	2	1	
Improper stretching	9	3	3		
Pointe work/shoes	9	9			
Pas de deux work	7	7			
Slippery substrate	7	3	1		
Overweight	4	1			
Fatigue	3	2	1		
Insufficient warm-up	1	1			

might predispose a dancer to lower extremity or back injuries. Finally, variation in study design (retrospective questionnaire versus diagnosis by a health care professional) may explain some of the differences.

These findings are consistent with the other studies in noting a relatively high frequency of relatively low-grade injuries that were varied in location. Washington (1978) found the knee to be the most frequently injured site in his study of theatrical dancers, as did Shaw (1977) in university dancers. This study, in agreement with Rovere et al. (1983), found the lower leg and the ankle to be the locations most susceptible to injury.

These differences may reflect the respective schedules of the professional dancer, who spends the entire day in class, rehearsing, or in performance, and of the university dancer, whose daily dance training is interspersed with other academic classes and activities. The university dancers in this study began their training at a later time in life than do dancers who successfully achieve professional status. Psychological stresses too are probably of a different nature for professional than for university dancers, although both appear to underreport injuries and disregard the need for prompt, definitive treatment.

References

Rovere, G.D., Webb, L.X., Gristina, A.G., & Vogel, J.M. (1983). Musculoskeletal injuries in theatrical dance students. *American Journal of Sports Medicine, 11*, 195-198.

Shaw, J.L.H. (1977). *The nature, frequency and patterns of dance injuries: A survey of college dance students.* Unpublished master's thesis, University of Utah.

Washington, E.L. (1978). Musculoskeletal injuries in theatrical dancers: Site, frequency, and severity. *American Journal of Sports Medicine, 6*, 75-98.

21

Concepts in the Prevention of Dance Injuries: A Survey and Analysis

Ruth Solomon
UNIVERSITY OF CALIFORNIA
SANTA CRUZ, CALIFORNIA, USA

Lyle Micheli
CHILDREN'S HOSPITAL
BOSTON, MASSACHUSETTS, USA

During the spring and early summer of 1983 I visited every major modern dance company and class in the greater Boston area. After observing the work being done, I asked everyone present who had experienced a debilitating injury in the previous 5 years to fill out an extensive questionnaire that I had devised in collaboration with Lyle Micheli, director of the Sports Medicine Division of Children's Hospital. The sampling gathered in this way was augmented by questionnaires that I had distributed to students in four university dance programs—two on the West Coast, one in Ohio, and one in New York—taught by instructors whose work I know well. Ultimately, from a total population of 358 dancers contacted there were 164 responses, representing 229 injuries (see Table 1). The basic composition of the sampling is described in Table 2.

My purpose in conducting this survey was to provide a data base for studying injuries in a significant sampling of the modern dance community. For the present paper I have chosen to explore the ramifications of three interrelated sets of data having to do primarily with the prevention of injuries. This choice is conditioned by my own predilections as a trainer of young dancers: by my sense that those of us who teach, choreograph, and direct share a responsibility to protect those with whom we work, and that we really can make a difference in preventing injuries if we know what to look for and how to interpret what we see.

Table 1. Injuries reported from survey

Total population approached	35
Total number of respondents	164 (46%)
Total number of injuries	229
Those with one injury	164
Those with two injuries	47
Those with three injuries	13
Those with four injuries	5

Table 2. Description of sample (n = 164) by age, sex, and primary technique used

Mean age	Sex	Primary technique	
M = 25.5 years	F = 77%	Ballet	22%
	M = 23%	Modern	74%
		Jazz	4%

Eclectic Sampling

The first finding is that today's modern dancer, as reflected in my sampling, is so eclectic as to rule out any direct equation of specific techniques with particular types of injuries. One factor is the involvement of today's modern dancer with ballet. For the time being I am more concerned, however, with the aspect of eclecticism that manifests itself in a tendency to train and perform in a variety of modern styles. My questionnaire provided space for each subject to record as many as four different teachers with whom he or she had studied, along with the styles being taught in each case. Virtually every subject utilized all four spaces. Only 4 listed just one teacher, or teachers representing only one style; 11 listed only ballet. Hence, again, my sampling lacks the purity to equate injuries with techniques or styles.

Nonetheless, in Table 3, I have broken down the injuries sustained by those subjects who mentioned having trained in each of the five largest modern techniques plus ballet) by site of injury. Table 4 provides a baseline for evaluating these data by listing the frequency of injuries by site for the sampling as a whole. The knee and ankle are injured with almost exactly the same frequency, accounting accumulatively for almost 40% of the total injuries. The low back is the third most vulnerable site, and, taken as a single entity, the back produces 23% of the total, while the hip adds 11.4%. No other site is statistically very significant.

Due to the eclecticism of the sampling, very few data in Table 3 appear to be particularly aberrant. Simply to give an example of how this game can be played, however, it might be instructive to focus for a moment in a comparative way on the columns for Graham and Horton techniques. These share a common "rap" in the folklore of the field for being hard on the knees and lower back. In my sampling this reputation might be said to hold up for the

Table 3. Styles of injury site

Site	Ballet	Limón	Cunningham	Graham	Horton	Humphrey/ Weidman
Neck	7	2	5	3	2	0
Upper back	11	9	2	4	5	3
Low back	28	16	9	10	8	2
Shoulder	4	3	2	1	0	0
Ribs	1	1	0	0	0	1
Hip	17	10	8	;6	3	1
Knee	39	22	15	15	4	5
Lower leg	8	6	4	5	3	3
Ankle	34	22	11	9	5	13
Foot	11	9	5	2	4	4
Hamstring	7	4	2	5	3	1
Total injuries	**167**	**104**	**63**	**60**	**37**	**33**
Respondents who studied technique	118	76	49	47	27	24
% of sample	7.20	46.3	29.9	28.7	16.5	14.6

Graham knee, but it definitely is not true of the knee in Horton; conversely, the low back (and the back as a whole) is particularly vulnerable in Horton, but not in Graham. (I calculate these trends as follows: Table 4 shows 46 knee injuries out of a total of 229 for the general sampling, or 20.1%. The Graham figures are 15 knee injuries out of 60, or 25%, but Horton shows only 4 of 37, or 10.8%. For the low back, the general percentage is 15.3%; Graham's low back percentage is 16.7%, Horton's, 21.6%.) Figure 1a provides a complete listing of these percentages, while Figure 1b-e break out each site and introduce some design interest to an otherwise drab picture.

Table 4. Injuries by site

Site	Count	Percent of responses
Neck	10	4.4
Upper back	18	7.9
Low back	35	15.3
Shoulder	5	2.2
Ribs	1	0.2
Hip	26	11.4
Knee	46	20.1
Lower leg	16	7.0
Ankle	45	19.7
Foot	16	7.0
Hamstring	11	4.8
Total responses	**229**	**100.0**

0 Missing cases   164 Valid Cases

To return now to the contrast between Graham and Horton techniques: How does one explain these data, and what might one conclude from them? I would suggest that the body mechanics at work in these two techniques really are quite different, and it is therefore natural that they should have different effects. One basic mechanism in Horton is the "hinge"; thus one often "hinges" one's body weight down to the floor. In Graham, one much more often brings the body weight up off the floor and onto the knee. The difference is that the lowering process involved in the Horton technique engages the quadriceps muscles in such a way as to stretch and strengthen them, and, as our friends in sports medicine have proven, there is no better way to avoid knee injuries than by strengthening the quads. The Graham movements, however, require weight-bearing by the knee, and dancers who are not proficient in using the pelvis to reduce this weight can easily run into trouble.

Turning to the back, the constant use of contraction-release in Graham technique stretches and strengthens the pelvis muscles on the front of the spine, which serve as a key controlling factor in preventing low-back injury. By contrast, the Horton hinge in this physiological area, if done incorrectly, simply

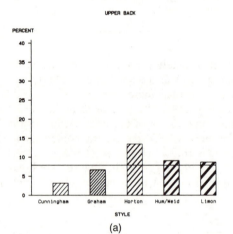

(a)

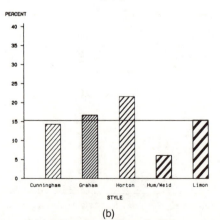

(b)

Figure 1. Percentage of injuries by style and site

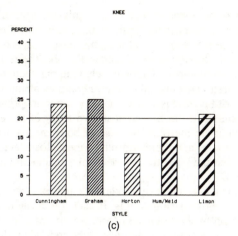

(c)

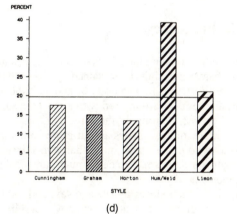

(d)

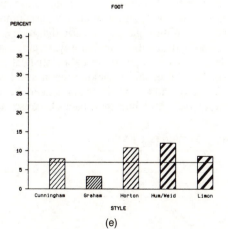

(e)

Figure 1. cont.

drops weight into the lower back. I believe this same principle accounts for the low incidence of injury in the Graham ankle and foot. The medical profession has found that many ankle and foot injuries are caused by an imbalance in strength between dorsiflexors and plantar flexors. The tremendous preponderance of flexed-footwork in Graham technique may help to create a proper balance in this area and thus aid in the prevention of injury.

To reiterate what I believe is a valid and very important principle that emerges somewhat tangentially from this comparative study of the effects of various techniques on injuries: the repetitive use of body mechanics that strengthen compensatory muscles and thereby produce musculoskeletal balance tends to reduce injuries, but the repetition of mechanics that create muscle imbalance encourages them.

Beyond this principle, however, I cannot emphasize strongly enough how conjectural this line of investigation is. In fact, I indicate that injuries among today's dancers probably result less from prolonged exposure to particular movement styles than from peculiarites of the individual dancer's anatomy.

Differences in Frequency

A second major finding of the study is that some significant differences of frequency do exist between the injuries sustained by male and by female modern dancers. These are illustrated in Tables 5, 6, and 7. Table 5 shows that, on the whole, males and females are injured with almost the same frequency (57 injuries compared to 172, or roughly the same 1:3.5 ratio as the sampling), but in terms of multiple injuries, males are far more vulnerable. Indeed, fully half of the subjects who experienced more than two injuries were men, and although these figures are too small to be of much statistical significance, one has to wonder about them.

Table 6 breaks down the injuries by site and sex, and Table 7 focuses more closely on specific diagnoses. For all areas above the hip, men have a disproportionately high number of injuries, knee injuries are split in accordance with the 1:3.5 male-female ratio, and women have predominate heavy injuries to the ankle and foot. With regard to specific diagnoses, men are particularly prone to upper body dislocations and muscle strains; spondylolysthesis, with its 0:5 female dominance, appears to be a statistical anomaly. Women predominate in patella injuries and in ankle tendon and ligament damage.

The findings in Table 6 tend to confirm what dancers have always thought and said about themselves: "Men hurt their backs because they partner," and

Table 5. Frequency of injuries by sex

Number of injuries	Females	Males
One injury	127	37
Two injuries	36	11
Three injuries	7	6
Four injuries	2	3

Table 6. Injury site by sex

Injury site	Male	Female	Row total
Neck	3	7	10 4.4
Upper back	9	9	18 7.9
Low back	10	25	35 15.3
Shoulder	2	3	5 2.2
Ribs	0	1	1 .4
Hip	7	19	26 11.4
Knee	10	36	46 20.1
Lower leg	4	12	16 7.0
Ankle	8	37	45 19.7
Foot	2	14	16 7.0
Hamstring	2	9	11 4.8
Column **Total**	**57** **24.9**	**172** **75.1**	**229** **100.0**

"women are susceptible to foot and ankle injuries because they dance on toe." These arguments are, of course, carried over from ballet, and their applicability to a sampling of modern dancers may be limited. I would suggest, for example, that the demands made on the male and female foot and ankle in modern dance are too similar to explain the discrepancy with which we are dealing here. With regard to partnering as a cause of male injuries, my findings specifically do not implicate it. Table 8 shows that only four male injuries were directly attributed to lift-partnering, and although this figure is disproportionately high in relation to female lift-partnering injuries, it falls well below four other causes of injuries in males.

Causative Effects

Although I believe that the anecdotal explanations of what causes dance injuries are too simple, several of my findings do seem to support their emphasis on the causative effect of the art form. Spondylolysthesis is a case in point. That extreme and repetitive arching of the back is a primary cause of this con-

Table 7. Diagnosis of injuries by sex

	Male	Female	Row total	%
Muscle strain, neck	1	2	3	1.5
Vertebral dislocations, neck	2	1	3	1.5
Spasms, neck/upper back/low back/shoulder	1	3	4	2.0
Pinched nerve, neck/upper back	1	2	3	1.5
Muscle strain, upper back	2	3	5	2.6
Vertebral dislocations, upper/low back	2	2	4	2.0
Dislocations, shoulder	2	0	2	1.0
Torn/pulled intercostal muscles	0	1	1	.5
Muscle strain, low back	4	6	10	5.1
Ligament sprain, sacroiliac	0	3	3	1.5
Herniated disc, low back	1	2	3	1.5
Spondylolisthesis	0	5	5	2.6
Nerve injuries, hip/low back	1	3	4	2.0
Bone bruise, low back	1	0	1	.5
Ligamentous injuries, hip	1	4	5	2.6
Muscle strain, hip	1	5	6	3.1
Dislocations, hip	0	3	3	1.5
Tendinitis, hip	0	2	2	1.0
Bonespur, hipsocket	0	1	1	.5
Strained groin muscle	0	1	1	.5
Strained tensor fascia lata	1	0	1	.5
Torn sartorius	1	0	1	.5
Pulled/torn hamstring	2	7	9	4.6
Adductor pull	0	1	1	.5
Meniscal tears	1	1	2	1.0
Meniscal tears, medial	0	4	4	2.0
Ligamentous injuries, knee	2	6	8	4.1
Medial collateral (tear 2, sprain 3)	1	4	5	2.6
Lateral collateral, sprain	0	1	1	.5
Anterior/posterior cruciate (tear 1, sprain 1)	1	1	2	1.0
Stretched patellar ligament	0	1	1	.5
Patellar tendinitis	2	2	4	2.0
Chondromalacia	2	10	12	6.1
Dislocations of kneecap	0	4	4	2.0
Infection (floor burn)	1	0	1	.5
Calf strain	1	0	1	.5
Tendon plantaris, tear	0	1	1	.5
Stress fractures, tibia, fibular	0	4	4	2.0
Shin splints	2	8	10	5.1
Ligamentous injuries, ankle	3	16	19	9.7
Muscle tear, ankle	1	0	1	.5
Sprained ankle	0	3	3	1.5
Peroneal tendon, strain	0	1	1	.5
Achilles tendinitis	1	15	16	8.2
Strained hallucis longus	0	1	1	.5
Bonespur, on talus bone	0	2	2	1.0
Tendinitis, foot	0	1	1	.5

Table 7 (cont.)

Stress fracture to instep	0	1	1	.5
Fractures, toes, phalanges	1	5	6	3.1
Mortons neuroma	0	1	1	.5
Osteoarthritis	0	1	1	.5
Total	**43**	**153**	**196**	**100.0**

dition in dancers is a widely accepted medical fact. Male dancers certainly will be required to arch their backs in any modern technique, but these movements are a far larger part of the female dance vocabulary; hence, the female is more susceptible to this injury, as reflected in the data. Similarly, we are beginning to recognize that the kind of turnout that dancers persistently practice can cause the patella to become vulnerable, leading to dislocations or chondromalacia—two of the major injuries more commonly seen in females. Male modern dancers are also asked to turn out, but perhaps because they tend to start training later—often not until they are in college—less is usually expected of them in this area, and therefore fewer demands are made. For this reason, one could argue, they have fewer patella injuries.

Conversely, I know of nothing in the modern dance idiom that should account medically for the male-female discrepancy in ankle and foot injuries—unless it is a further result of the rotated alignment caused by turning out. I suspect what we are seeing here is a physiologic predisposition to injury;

Table 8. Cause of injury by sex

Cause	Male	Female	Total	Responses (%)
Overuse/stress/repetition	4	27	31	12.6
Faulty technique/incorrect alignment	9	20	29	11.8
Use of particular style of movement	7	22	29	11.8
Gradual deterioration	8	19	27	11.0
Leap/jump	6	17	23	9.3
Over-stretch	3	16	19	7.7
Recurrence of earlier injury	3	13	16	6.5
Fall	3	9	12	4.9
Insufficient warm-up	2	8	10	4.1
Twisted ankle	1	8	9	3.7
Tension	1	8	9	3.7
Hard surface	2	6	8	3.3
Lift/partnering	4	2	6	2.4
Someone else	1	4	5	2.0
Unknown	1	3	4	1.6
Roll	1	2	3	1.2
Spasm	0	2	2	0.8
Fatigue	0	1	1	0.4
Weakness	1	0	1	0.4

simply put, the female foot and ankle may become injuried more often because they are anatomically more vulnerable than their male counterparts. By the same token, my experience indicates that the low-back area tends to be tighter in males, which might produce a higher inclination toward back injuries. Whether we are in fact dealing with injuries that result primarily from meeting the demands of an art form or from anatomical weaknesses, the message of these findings should be clear to those who train dancers: they should be especially watchful of upper and low backs in males and feet and ankles in females, and build components into their techniques (such as lateral and medial ankle strengthening, dorsi-plantar flexion, and pelvic-strengthening exercises) to help avoid injuries in these areas.

Microtraumas Versus Macrotraumas

The data from Table 8 is reorganized in Table 9 to focus on what I belive is the pivotal finding of my entire study. This table divides the self-reported explanations of how my subjects' injuries occurred into microtraumatic causes on the one hand, and macrotraumatic causes on the other. The distinction is that those injuries on the left side of the table—fully two thirds of the total— are seen to have developed over a sustained period of time as a result of gradual physiological deterioration; those on the right side happened suddenly—that is, they can be attributed to specific events. The mechanism at work in microtrauma can be illustrated by one dramatic example: each time a dancer lands from a jump his or her body weight is magnified 2 or 3 times upon impact. The effect of this added weight travels through the body like a sound wave, applying pressure to the entire musculoskeletal structure. Given the number of times this phenomenon occurs in the course of a dancer's day, it is clear

Table 9. How injury occurred

Microtraumatic causes (overuse/gradual deterioration)		Macrotraumatic causes (sudden impact)	
Overuse/stress/repetition	31	Leap/jump	23
Faulty technique/incorrect alignment	29	Overstretch	19
Use of particular style or movement	29	Fall	12
Gradual deterioration	27	Twisted ankle	9
Recurrence of earlier injury	16	Lift/partnering	6
Insufficient warm-up	10	Someone else	5
Tension	9	Roll	3
Hard surface	8		**77**
Spasm	2		(32%)
Fatigue	1		
Weakness	1		
Unknown	4		
	167		
	(68%)		

that the body not properly prepared or anatomically aligned for optimal joint loading can be damaged. I would emphasize that these results are self-reported and therefore cannot be objectively substantiated, yet the discrepancy—68% to 32%—is significant enough to lead me to conclude that the overwhelming majority of modern dance injuries are the result of microtraumas.

Conclusion

We have isolated two factors in connection with dance injuries—namely, the unique anatomical characteristics of the individual dancer's body, and the demands of the art form to which that body is subjected—and have suggested that dance injuries occur at the point where these factors meet. Now, with the concept of microtrauma, we are prepared to describe what is happening at that point. Basically, the art form is requiring repeated use of the body in a specific way over time—repetition is the *sine qua non* of all dance technique—and the body is deteriorating at its weakest point. Or, as the cause-effect dichotomy is always complex, the body is performing a repetitive task—learning a technique—in ways that create tension or imbalance and thereby bring about its own destruction. At any rate, repetition, or what is often called the overuse syndrome, is the culprit.

In a sense, we are simply confirming the common wisdom: If you dance hard for a long time, you will get injured. That is indeed what my study indicates. The question is, though, whether it is necessarily so. I believe it is only if you work *incorrectly*, and I would conjecture that dancers could dance injury free if, from the earliest training on, their unique anatomical characteristics and working patterns were carefully adjusted to the demands of the technique by which they chose to be trained. By way of arguing this point, it is useful to look more closely at the two main factors in dance injuries—anatomical peculiarities and the demands of the art form. Some characteristics of anatomy—scoliosis, for example—are congenital. These are seldom immutable but, if not considered in early training, they definitely will exert a potentially damaging effect on the body. Other characteristics are not anatomical in this sense at all; they result from how the body is used. Thus, for example, many dancers develop an early habit of holding the pelvis out of line. This causes muscle imbalance, an apparent malalignment, and a good deal of stress in the lower back. The point is that dancers may move the way they do because they are malaligned, or they may be malaligned because of the way they move. Either way they are vulnerable to injury for reasons that could almost surely be corrected.

On the other side of the ledger, the demands of the art form raise the same cause-effect type of issues. Dance technique can be presented in such a way as to have a beneficial, even therapeutic effect on the body; elements can be built into any technique class, or recommended for use outside of class, to help dancers deal with their individual problems. Their repetition then becomes and ally. If, however, the technique is presented without an awareness of how it suits each individual's body, then the repetition it necessarily entails can have an injurious effect. Some dancers, especially the more experienced ones, will recognize their potential vulnerability in this situation and make their own adjustments. As I have suggested throughout this paper, though, the main responsibility for fitting demands to bodies rests with those who supervise the training.

What is at stake is more than the prevention of injuries—although that is a noble goal in itself. Modern dance is an art form in which performers can continue to grow well into their mature years. Youthful dexterity is only one ingredient in the making of a modern dancer—indeed, a relatively minor one compared to the expansion of both craft and performance skill that often comes to those who have had time to get beyond the mere learning of steps. It is important, therefore, to prolong careers, and one important way to do this is to balance anatomy, technique, and the way the body is being used to accomplish that technique. The health of the art form depends in large measure on this kind of complex, time-consuming, and altogether necessary process.

22

Bunion Deformity and the Forces Generated Around the Great Toe: A Biomechanical Approach to Analysis of Pointe Dance, Classical Ballet

Steven R. Kravitz, Carla J. Murgia, Stephen Huber,
Karen Fink, Mark Shaffer, and Lorraine Varela
PENNSYLVANIA COLLEGE OF PODIATRIC MEDICINE
PHILADELPHIA, PENNSYLVANIA, USA

A high correlation exists between the development of static forefoot deformity and dance activity (Sammarco & Miller, 1982; Schneider et al., 1974). Although forefoot deformity is prevalent among many dance forms, it is characteristically evident in the feet of classical ballet dancers. Inclusive of hallux-abducto-valgus and bunion formation, splayfoot and lesser digit hammer and mallet toes, these forefoot deformities are primarily related to the unusual stresses and strains applied to the foot while performing the disciplined movements required in classical ballet pointe work. Dancing en pointe requires good coordination and adequate muscle strength for body control to withstand the weight-bearing stresses in order to maintain position. Attempts at pointe dancing before sufficient balance, strength, and coordination are achieved result in compensatory changes that may lead to forefoot deformities.

Some of the compensatory changes can result in hallux valgus or bunion formation. If early training does not include development of intrinsic and extrinsic foot muscles in order to raise the arch, muscle imbalance can develop (Hicks, 1954). This intrinsic muscle imbalance has been recognized as a predisposing factor in hallux valgus formation (Sammarco & Miller, 1982; Inman, 1974; Mann & Coughlin, 1981; Shaw, 1974). Hiss hypothesized that a relationship existed between muscle imbalance and hallux valgus (Hiss, 1931). Without this muscular control, the long-standing strain caused by classical ballet training tends to stretch the medial foot ligaments. Such chronic strain can result in hallux valgus. In addition, conditions of ligamentous laxity have been a consistent finding in dancers and other athletes (Grahame & Jenkins, 1972). McNerney and Johnston (1979) contended that generalized ligamentous laxity may predispose the individual to pronation and lead to hallux valgus formation. When the ligaments are flaccid, the foot may begin to roll in at the ankle, as the dancer tries to increase his or her turnout. This motion involves pronation of the subtalar joint, eversion of the heel (calcaneus), and unlocking of the midtarsal joint with resulting hypermobility (Root, Orien, & Weed, 1977). Patients with hypermobile joints often present with hallux valgus (Mygind, 1953). Another important cause of bunion formation is shoegear (Barnett, 1962; Lam & Hodgson, 1958). Some types of shoegear can exert an indirect pronatory force on the foot causing a direct deforming force on the great toe (Halebian & Gaines, 1983). The static deforming force within the pointe shoe forces the metatarsal heads together and forces the great toe into abduction. Also, "the deforming forces of weightbearing plus the force of constraining shape of the pointe shoe contribute to the development of hallux valgus" (Sammarco, 1982).

Increased symptomatology secondary to bunion and other forefoot deformities resulting from dance activity may be responsible for shortening the career of the professional ballet dancer (Sammarco & Miller, 1982). The more knowledge gathered about the biomechanical forces affecting the foot of the classical ballet dancer, the better our understanding of the destructive forces applied to the forefoot in dance and the greater the probability of controlling these forces. This paper presents a biomechanical approach to the understanding of the development of hallux valgus and bunion formation in classical ballet pointe stance, using electrodynographic analyses and biomechanical evaluations of classical ballet dancers. This baseline study suggests that control of biomechanically induced forces may decrease the rate of bunion development, theoretically lengthening the career of the classical ballet dancer.

Review of the Literature

The biomechanical factors involved in hallux-abducto-valgus deformity cause a progressive subluxation of the first metatarsal-phalangeal joint. Root et al. (1977) have stated that "hypermobility of the first ray. . .influences the rate of the development and extent of the final deformity" (p. 378). Pronation of the subtalar joint causes many changes to occur within the foot, resulting in an eventual hypermobile first ray. These changes primarily involve altered muscle function, which allows abnormal forces to produce joint subluxations and the development of hallux-abducto-valgus deformity.

Calcaneal eversion increases ground reactive forces against the first metatarsal head causing the first ray to dorsiflex and invert relative to the hallux. This motion occurs during propulsion, when the hallux is being stabilized by its plantar flexors against the supporting surface and is thus not able to follow the first metatarsal as it becomes hypermobile. Therefore, as the unstable first metatarsal is moving in the sagittal and frontal planes, the weight-bearing hallux is then able to follow, and the first metatarsal-phalangeal joint subluxes. Midtarsal-joint breakdown, medial-column instability, and hypermobility of the first ray associated with calcaneal eversion (subtalar joint pronation) cause abnormalities in muscular origin and insertion attitudes relative to the joint axes. These changes produce abnormal forces leading to development of hallux-abducto-valgus deformity.

Adductor and abductor hallucis muscles, components of the sesamoid apparatus, are of primary importance in stabilizing the relationship of the hallux to the first metatarsal. Their effectiveness is hampered by first metatarsal dorsiflexion and erosion of the crista located on the plantar surface of that bone. The crista's prominence is eroded through abductory forces exerted by the tibial sesamoid that develop secondarily to the muscular imbalance produced through the dorsiflexed and inverted metatarsal (Root et al., 1977). Apparent lateral migration of sesamoids becomes evident as the first metatarsal adducts and the hallux abducts. Associated with the loss of transverse plane stability, this leads to a cyclic phenomenon as the plantar intrinsic musculature produces a predominately abductory force upon the hallux as the muscles attempt to stabilize this toe against the supporting surface during propulsion (Shaw, 1974). During this mechanism, the abductor hallucis muscle loses most of its ability to stabilize the hallux in a direction toward the midline of the body, and the adductor bowstrings and becomes a very impressive abductor of the hallux (Root et al., 1977), leading to the ultimate abduction position of the great toe.

These changes cause the clinically apparent hallux-abducto-valgus deformity, often with concurrent development of adventitious bursa overlying the dorso-medial prominence of the first metatarsal head, known as a bunion. It is the authors' intention to present (a) a biomechanical model for the development of this deformity as related to a dancer's performance of turnout in any of the five classical dance positions and (b) a commentary on pointe stance.

To attain a technically correct and aesthetically pleasing foot position of turnout, it is often necessary for dancers to ''cheat'' in their performance because of limited external rotational range of motion at the hip joint. Thus, in an attempt to approximate a 180° position, the dancer will apply an external torque at the leg with respect to the thigh. Similar force is applied to the foot, causing it to abduct relative to the leg, and thus pronate. The resultant pedal motion has been called rolling in at the ankle, although it is not obtained at the ankle joint, but rather through pronation of the subtalar joint and subsequent calcaneal (heel) eversion. There is simultaneous unlocking and breakdown of the midtarsal joint, resulting in the collapse of the entire medial column of the foot with associated hypermobility of the first ray and subluxation at the first metatarsophalangeal joint as discussed previously. Pedal pronation is thus a result of forced turnout.

The component of external rotation of leg relative to thigh has been measured in a flexed knee position by the authors to be approximately 10°. As the dancer straightens the knee from a flexed position of plié to an extended straight knee, the external rotational relationship of tibia to femur is no longer allowed to exist, causing a reactionary internal rotation of the tibia relative to the thigh. While this occurs, the foot (planted firmly on the ground in one of the five dance positions) is forced to abduct relative to the internally rotating leg segment. This transfer of a transverse plane load from knee to foot causes the subtalar joint to pronate as the foot abducts to the internally rotating talus, which is locked into the ankle mortise. Calcaneal (rear foot) eversion and subtalar joint pronation develop. Eversion of the foot causes an increase in the ground reactive force against the first metatarsal head, which reacts by attaining a dorsiflexed and inverted position (Root et al., 1977).

It has been stated that abnormal subtalar joint pronation of the foot associated with first metatarsal-phalangeal joint malfunction is the primary cause of most bunion (hallux-abducto-valgus) deformities, and the cause of many hallux-abducto-valgus deformities is mechanical malfunction at the first metatarsophalangeal joint (Jordan & Brodsky, 1951; Rogers & Joplin, 1947; Root et al., 1977; Silver, 1923). Eversion of the foot during propulsion causes the first ray to move into a dorsiflexed position in response to the vertical ground reactive forces exerted against the first metatarsal head. The elevated first ray position restricts the range of hallux dorsiflexion, inducing subluxation of the first metatarsophalangeal joint during propulsion. "This saggittal plane subluxation increases the instability of the first metatarsophalangeal joint and hastens the development of the hallux-abducto-valgus deformity (Root et al., 1977, p. 384).

En pointe dancing requires heel lift and the ability to supinate the foot through propulsion to perform sur les pointes. After supination, the foot abducts to attain a comfortable stance position. Therefore, the dancer is actually supinating to get up en pointe and then to some extent abducts (pronates). This is particularly evident in passé because of the adduction of the lower extremity toward the midline of the body. Foot abduction also occurs in relevé (see Figures 2, 3, and 6). Thus, our research indicates that there exists a pronatory component of supinated en pointe position. We theorize that this pronatory component induces mechanisms with inherent pathology based on pedal biomechanical laws.

Methods

A platform was built to simulate dance-floor conditions in the classroom and performance situations. The platform was constructed of laminated pine with a surface area of 3 by 4 ft placed on a horizontal wood support frame constructed of 2- by 4-in. studies. A barre was included to supply minimum dancer support for the exercises.

The forces produced on the foot during relevé and passé were analyzed using an electrodynogram computer system (a portable microcomputer and data collection system). Small sensors, applied to the foot at the positions shown in Figure 1, fed electrical signals into a recorder pack strapped around the subjects' waists. A specific uniform count was given during which the dancer rose from flat to pointe position. The same count was used for passé and relevé. After the task was performed the recorder pack was removed and plugged into the computer console. The printer then produced a graphic representation of each sensor site as a percentage of the subject's body weight as a func-

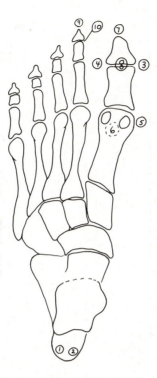

Figure 1. Sites of sensor attachments

tion of time. The amount of shock and force was analyzed for each site independently. This offered a sophisticated method of comparing one weight-bearing site to the next.

The electrodynogram has been accepted as a tool for grait analysis, allowing the physician to pinpoint abnormalities of the walking cycle for the purpose of diagnostic and therapeutic considerations. The authors, through the support of the Langer Group,* were able to develop a computer program useful in researching pointe dance.

Protocol for Data Collection

The transducers were placed on the foot in the following positions:

1. Lateral tubercle of the calcaneus
2. Medial tubercle of the calcaneus

---

*Langer Biomechanical Group, Inc., Deer Park, NY.

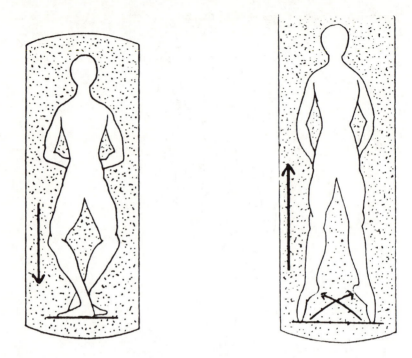

Figure 2. Fifth position to demi-plié to second position Echappé relevé en pointe

3. Medial aspect of the first interphalangeal joint
4. Lateral aspect of the first interphalangeal joint
5. Medial aspect of the first metatarsal head
6. Plantar aspect of the first metatarsal head
7. Distal tip of the great toe
8. Dorsal aspect of the hallux interphalangeal joint
9. Distal aspect of the second digit
10. Dorsal aspect of the second digit at the interphalangeal joint

The purpose of dorsal placement was to detect "knuckling over," which is plantar flexion of the interphalangeal joints. In addition, placement of the sensors was directed toward the distal aspect of digits to analyze pressure generated at these sites.

Sixteen dancers participated in the study. Each dancer performed two sequences of dance movements:

1. Fifth position to demi-plié to second position échappé relevé en pointe (see Figure 2)
2. Fifth position to demi-plié to passé relevé en point with the right foot in passé position (see Figure 3)

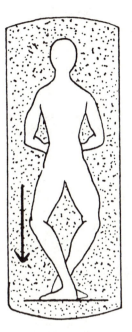
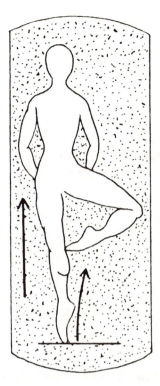

Figure 3. Fifth position to demi-plié to passé relevé en pointe

The movement from fifth position to each of the final positions was performed in a time interval characteristic of allegro ballet movement with the final position held approximately 3 s. The count protocol (1 count, 1 s) was as follows:

Count 1 - extended knee flat stance in fifth position
Count 2 - demi-plié
Count 3 - final position (either échappé relevé or passé)
Count 4 onward - hold final position

The movement was recorded on the sensor pack and fed into the microprocessor, which analyzed the data to report pressure as a percentage of body weight.

We sectioned computer printouts of recorded data in order to visualize the force measurements as a function of time (see Figures 4 and 5). The greatest percentages of peak force and peak shock occurred during the transitional period from fifth position to the final position as indicated by the encircled curves in the graphs. We also tested the sequential order of pressures produced by segmental addition. We then ranked the sites by the amount of pressure gener-

Figure 4. An illustration of the Electrodynagram printout for the passe. Note the steep curve in section 2. (The printout has been reduced four times.)

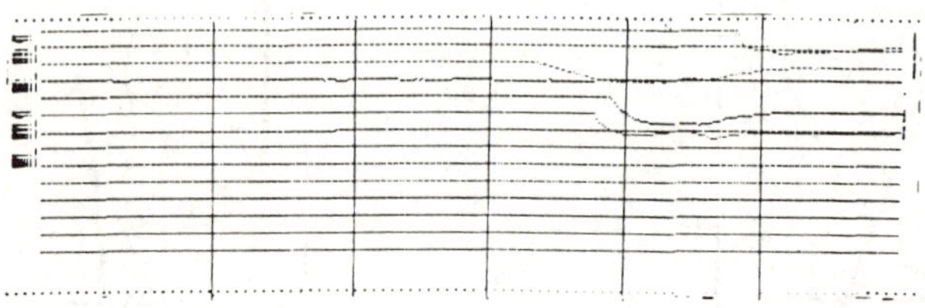

Figure 5. An illustration of the Electrodynagram printout for the releve. Note the less steep curve in sections 2 and 3, as compared to section 2 in figure 4. This would suggest the amount of additional force generated at the medial aspect in the one point stance passe.

ated from highest to lowest by assigning point values ranging from 5 to 1. Assigning numerical values aided in the observation of primary and secondary forces. Placement or transducer sites reporting the greatest amount of pressure were assigned a value of 5. The results are given in Tables 1 and 2.

The means and standard deviations for the same transducer sites are shown in Table 3. Because of the small sample size and the number of outliers, it was decided not to proceed with statistical tests. However, upon review of the biomechanical principles of stabilization and the descriptive statistics generated in this pilot study, we believe that further investigation is merited. For the passé and the relevé exercises, forces were generated through the medial aspect of the forefoot when the dancer was in the process of reaching the final position and when settled in position. In addition, there was a difference in the amount of force generated between the relevé and the passé in magnitude and distribution. Our study revealed many individual differences that indicated some variation in structure and technical style. However, there is commonality with respect to medial forces. As one might expect, plantar aspects generated impressive force when in transition. Indeed, the greatest force and shock generally occurred during transition. Surprisingly, distal aspects reported only moderate forces.

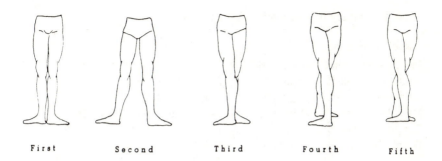

First   Second   Third   Fourth   Fifth

Figure 6. Classical ballet positions

We plan to expand this study, adhering to the following:

1. Enlarge the sample size, including more trials per dancer.
2. Vary the position of the transducers in order to detect the amount of forces transferred through the forefoot.
3. If transitions produce more forces and shock, include other types of dancers.
4. Examine the relationship between the length of the second digit and peak force readings.

Table 1. Primary and secondary forces in the relevé

Transition to relevé

Plantar—1st metatarsal head $4_1 + 4_2 + 4_3 + 4_4 = 20 + 16 + 9 + 8 = 53$
Medial—1st interphalangeal $4_1 + 3_2 + 1_3 + 1_4 = 20 + 12 + 3 + 2 = 37$
Lateral—1st interphalangeal $2_1 + 6_2 + 1_4 = 10 + 24 + 2 = 36$
Medial—1st metatarsal head $2_1 + 3_2 + 2_3 + 2_4 = 10 + 12 + 6 + 4 = 32$
Distal—2nd digit $1_1 + 2_2 + 2_3 = 19$
Dorsal—2nd digit interphalangeal $1_1 + 2_2 = 13$

Settled in relevé

Distal hallux—$1_1 + 2_2 + 1_3 + 1_4 + 3_5 = 5 + 8 + 3 + 2 + 3 = 21$
Dorsal—1st interphalangeal $2_1 = 10$
Lateral tubercle—$1_1 + 1_3 = 8$
Lateral—1st interphalangeal $2_2 = 8$
Medial—1st interphalangeal $1_2 + 1_3 = 4 + 3 = 7$
Medial—1st metatarsal head $1_2 + 1_3 = 4 + 3 = 7$

Ranked sites by pressure generated from highest to lowest.
Code—4_5 denotes 4 incidences of greatest pressure = 20 points
    4_4 denotes 4 incidences of 2nd greatest pressure = 16 points
    4_3 denotes 4 incidences of 3rd greatest pressure = 12
    4_2 denotes 4 incidences of 4th greatest pressure = 8
    4_1 denotes 4 incidences of 5th greatest pressure = 4 points

Table 2. Primary and secondary forces in the passé

Transition to passé

Plantar—1st metatarsal head $6_1 + 4_2 + 2_3 + 1_4 = 30 + 16 + 6 + 2 = 54$
Medial—1st interphalangeal $4_1 + 5_2 + 1_4 + 1_5 = 20 + 20 + 2 + 1 = 43$
Lateral—1st interphalangeal $4_1 + 3_2 + 1_3 + 3_4 = 20 + 12 + 3 + 6 = 41$
Medial—1st metatarsal head $1_1 + 7_3 + 2_4 = 5 + 21 + 8 = 34$
Dorsal—1st interphalangeal $1_1 + 1_2 + 2_3 + 1_4 = 5 + 4 + 6 + 2 = 17$
Distal—hallux $1_1 + 2_2 + 1_3 + 1_5 = 5 + 8 + 3 + 1 = 17$

Settled in passé

Distal—hallux $5_1 + 4_2 + 1_3 + 1_4 = 25 + 16 + 3 + 2 = 46$
Medial—1st metatarsal head $3_1 + 2_2 + 2_3 + 1_4 + 1_5 = 15 + 8 + 6 + 2 + 1 = 32$
Dorsal—1st interphalangeal $2_1 + 2_2 = 10 + 8 = 18$
Distal—2nd digit $1_1 + 1_2 + 1_3 + 1_4 + 1_5 = 5 + 4 + 3 + 2 + 1 = 15$
Lateral—1st interphalangeal $1_2 + 2_3 + 1_4 + 1_5 = 4 + 6 + 2 + 1 = 13$
Medial—1st interphalangeal $1_1 + 1_4 + 3_5 = 5 + 4 + 3 = 12$

Ranked sites by pressure generated from highest to lowest.
Code—4_5 denotes 4 incidences of greatest pressure = 20 points
4_4 denotes 4 incidences of 2nd greatest pressure = 16 points
4_3 denotes 4 incidences of 3rd greatest pressure = 12
4_2 denotes 4 incidences of 4th greatest pressure = 8
4_1 denotes 4 incidences of 5th greatest pressure = 4 points

Discussion

At the onset it was felt that the dancer abducts the foot en pointe. This became apparent during an analysis of multiple photographs of the world's most respected dancers. The feet of 40 dancers were studied, both in relevé and passé. Samples of passé show more foot abduction because the extremity was adducted toward the body's midline. Because abduction of the foot occurs as the foot pronates, the foot not only pronates when flat as a reaction to forced turnout but also pronates en pointe. It is our contention, after discussion with many dancers (at the School of Pennsylvania Ballet and the Philadelphia College of the Performing Arts) that this is done following supination and the rise to en pointe position, to allow the dancer to find a more comfortable and stable toe stance. In the passé, foot abduction is a necessary result of the lower extremity's adduction.

Electrodynogram analysis showing high pressure values on the medial aspect of the foot would be consistent with this observation. As shown in our data, consistently high values were present for the medial aspect of the first metatarsal head and medial hallux interphalangeal joint. The lateral hallux interphalangeal joint also demonstrated large values due to the tendency to develop bunion and hallux abductus deformity and the necessity for buttressing against the second toe.

Table 3. Mean and standard deviations for transducer sites

	M[a]	SD
Relevé		
Lateral tubercle	1.82%	2.43
Medial—interphalangeal of the great toe	.95%	1.42
Plantar—metatarsal head of the great toe	.86%	1.14
Lateral—interphalangeal of the great toe	.58%	.68
Medial—metatarsal head of the great toe	.51%	.9
Distal—hallux	.47%	.59
Dorsal—interphalangeal of the great toe	.46%	.62
Passé		
Medial—interphalangeal of the great toe	2.24%	4.37[b]
Plantar—metatarsal head of the great toe	1.27%	1.65
Distal—hallux	1.17%	1.72
Lateral—interphalangeal of the great toe	.85%	.99
Medial—metatarsal head of the great toe	.67%	.87
Dorsal—hallux	.54%	.13
Distal—2nd digit	.2 %	.47

[a]M indicates the mean of the percentage of body weight generated as force through the indicated transducer sites.

[b]The standard deviation is large here due to two outliers recording excessive pressure at this placement.

Summary

A review of pedal biomechanics with respect to pronation of the subtalar joint, subsequent unlocking of the midtarsal joint with the production of the first ray hypermobility, and bunion hallux-abducto-valgus development has been presented. Dancers who utilize the five classical ballet positions without achieving full turnout at the hip joint often force the turnout by applying external torque to the leg relative to the thigh. A flexed knee, as in plié, will allow for some external rotation of the leg relative to thigh to exist. As the knee extends, this relationship is reduced, causing the leg to internally rotate relative to the thigh and the foot, which is planted firmly on the supporting surface. Abduction of the foot leads to pronatory reaction and the subsequent pathological changes described with first metatarsal phalangeal joint deformity.

Pointe stance often involves foot abduction, as was shown through photographic interpretation and observation at the testing trials. The authors also have observed similar reactions in class and stage work. Abduction is greatest in passé due to the adduction of the extremity toward the body's midline. Foot abduction is a pronatory component. The authors contend that the supinated pointe stance has a pronatory component, allowing the dancer to achieve a more comfortable and stable position once up on her toe.

Electrodynogram computer analysis was performed on a simulated dance surface. The data indicated consistently high values for percentage of body weight on the medial aspect of the first metatarsal head and medial aspect of the hallux interphalangeal joint. The lateral aspect of the hallux interphalangeal joint also showed high values through the computer printout because of the tendency to abduct the great toe and the necessity of the second pedal digit to buttress against this motion.

Pronatory forces produced by forced turnout and abduction of the foot in the non-pointe stance (in one of the five classical positions), once identified, may be controlled. Theoretically, limiting excessive pronatory forces can decrease the tendency of developing first metatarsal phalangeal joint deformity associated with the stresses produced from these pronatory motions. It is the authors' hypothesis that controlling these destructive movements can positively augment pedal reaction to forced turnout, decreasing the rate of deformity development, and, in individuals potentially negatively affected by such deformity, may increase the length of the dance career.

References

Barnett, C.H. (1962). The normal orientation of the human hallux and the effect of the footwear. *J. Anat. Lond., 96,* 489-494.

Grahame, R., & Jenkins, J.M. (1972). Joint hypermobility—Asset or liability. A study of joint mobility in ballet dancers. *Annals of the Rheumatic Diseases, 31,* 109.

Halebian, J.D., & Gaines, S.S. (1983). Juvenile hallux valgus. *Journal of Foot Surgery, 22,* 292.

Hicks, J.H. (1954). Mechanics of the Foot. II: The plantar aponeurosis and the arch. *Journal of Anatomy, 88,* 25.

Hiss, J.M. (1931). Hallux valgus: Its cause and simplified treatment. *American Journal of Surgery, 11,* 51.

Inman, V.T. (1974). Hallux valgus: A review of etiologic factors. *Orthopedic Clinics of North America, 5*(1), 59.

Jordan, H.H., & Brodsky, A.E. (1951). Keller operation for hallux valgus and hallux rigidus. *A.M.A. Arch. Surg., 62,* 586-596.

Lam, S.-F., & Hodgson, A.R. (1958). A comparison of foot forms among the non-shoe and shoe-wearing Chinese population. *Journal of Bone and Joint Surgery, 40A,* 1058.

Mann, R.A., & Coughlin, M.D. (1981). Hallux valgus—Etiology, anatomy, treatment and surgical considerations. *Clinical Orthopaedics and Related Research, 157,* 31-41.

McNerney, J.E., & Johnston, W.B. (1979). Generalized ligamentous laxity, hallux abductovalgus and the first metatarsocuneiform joint. *Journal of the American Psychological Association, 69*(1), 80.

Mygind, H.B. (1953). Some views on the treatment of hallux valgus. *Acta Orthopaedica Scandinavica, 23,* 152.

Rogers, W.A., & Joplin, R.J. (1947). Hallux valgus, weakfoot and the Keller operation: An end result study. *Surgical Clinics of North America, 27,* 1295-1302.

Root, M.L., Orien, W.P., & Weed, J.H. (1977). *Normal and abnormal functions of the foot* (pp. 349-379, 384, 395). Los Angeles, CA: Clinical Biomechanical Corp.

Sammarco, G.J. (1982). The foot and ankle in classical ballet and modern dance. In M. Jahss (Ed.), *Disorders of the foot* (chap. 59, p. 1633). Philadelphia: W.B. Saunders.

Sammarco, G.J., & Miller, E.M. (1982). Forefoot conditions in dancers. Part II. *Foot and Ankle, 3*(2), 86, 93-98.

Schneider, H.J., et al. (1974). Stress injuries and developmental change of lower extremities in ballet dancers. *Radiology, 113*, 627-632.

Shaw, A.H. (1974). The biomechanics of hallux valgus in pronated feet. *Journal of the American Psychological Association, 64*(4), 193-201.

Silver, D. (1923). The operative treatment of hallux valgus. *Journal of Bone and Joint Surgery, 5*, 225-238.

23

The Use of Laban Movement Analysis as a Tool for Observing Movement Style in Analyzing the Discus Throw

Julie L. Martin
S.B. LEWIS & CO.
NEW YORK, NEW YORK, USA

Laban Movement Analysis (LMA) is a movement methodology that was originated by Rudolf von Laban and developed by him, and his colleagues, from the 1930's through the present day. It has been used as a base from which to view, experience, and teach human movement. Such fields of application are; dance, sports, dance therapy, anthropology, and non-verbal communication research.

The methodology is taught in three areas of concentration: first, what is known as "effort." This is know as, "the reflections of inner attitudes coming forth in movement." It is the qualitative changes that take place, not how fast or far someone moves but *how* they move with qualities of quickness, lightness, strength, sustainment, and so on. Second, the area of "space harmony" which deals with how the body moves through space and its relationship with the environment. Third, the "body level" or "fundamentals-work," developed by Irmgard Bartenieff, are exercises to help correct and connect the body's movements for more fluidity and efficiency. All three areas are interconnected and never seen as separate entities, but rather, areas that support each other.

This study was designed to view different throwers on film and, using five different parameters, chart each one. Based on the chart and my knowledge of the event, I will discuss technique (mechanics) and style (moving quality) in Laban terms. Carrying the study one step further, live observations of a thrower's skill will be made and followed up with recommendations. This step will integrate the fundamental body correctives. Although several throwers were actually filmed and observed during the study, Al Oerter has been selected as the thrower for the purpose of this paper. I do not intend to extrapolate the perfect throwing style, but rather, to investigate the different possibilities, their strengths and weaknesses.

This study is based on the hypothesis that a well-trained coach should have a clear and organized framework when observing movement. He must see the whole as well as the parts in viewing a particular skill. This will enable him to detect the interactions of different body parts that are occurring and not base his thinking on isolated facts. I believe Laban Movement Analysis helps the observer develop the ability to recognize the constant process of change in human movement, and how the body part interrelationships affect each other during this change.

History of the Discus

This particular track and field event was one of the original during the first Greek Olympic games. It has since evolved into a very precise science and study for the athlete to master. Still, the purpose remains the same: the person with the longest toss is the winner. As are all athletic events, it is functional movement with a goal orientation as opposed to purely expressive movement like dance. But even functional movement takes on an aesthetic appeal when all units involved are in tune with the purpose of the movement.

If one were to see the event for the first time, some general moving impressions might be: a spiraling explosion, a winding up to unwind, or a whirlwind of manifested strength. Taking a closer look, the athlete finds himself in the confines of a circle approximately 8 feet in diameter. He or she is holding a circular platter and moves along the diameter of the circle revolving 1 1/2 turns. While turning, the torque or twist in the body must be maintained until the right moment of release. Power from the legs and the sequencing through the body aid in transferring the energy into the disc as it is whipped from the body at the last moment of the "action phase."

One of the prime reasons this event is so difficult is because man finds moving more comfortable in a one dimensional direction of purely foreward and back, side to side, or up and down. Within 2 seconds, the thrower continually combines three spatial directions. He interchanges pure diagonal patterning, which includes three elements of global joint function, most visible in the hips and shoulders. Thus, the event lends itself to maximal facilitation of movement, resulting in "high spatial intensity."[1] To demonstrate this, at the point of explosion, or drive, the hips are thrust with three spatial pulls, forward, up, and across. Nowhere in the throw does the athlete use only one spatial pull. The thrower is confronted with counterbalancing these spatial pulls and inner-spatial tensions.

---

[1]Irmgard Bartenieff, "Laban Space Harmony in Relation to Anatomical and Neurophysiological Concepts," *Four Adaptations of Effort Theory in Research and Teaching*, (New York: Dance Notation Burea, Inc., 1970), p. 50.

Along with the spatial elements, the coach must consider the athletes physical strength, connectedness, the speed and momentum produced, his body weight distribution and its connection to the center of weight. Psychologically, it is necessary to take into consideration the athlete's mental temperament, feelings, and natural effort affinities[2] toward movement dynamics. All these variables contribute to the difficulty and inconsistency in mastering this skill and must be considered when training for the event.

In organizing the material, the first task was in deciding what parameters to use. Because the film was taken at a slightly slower speed, the effort phrasing is distorted. By starting with the other shape levels of observation and connecting the relationship of shape to effort, it is the author's intent to determine what efforts come through despite this handicap. The charts are organized in the following six categories.[3]

1. Sequence of Action—the description of the movement phase.
2. Body and Space Level—looking for peripheral, transverse and central movement as well as posture/gesture.
3. Shape—the body shaping in terms of one dimension spoke-like, two dimension arc-like, and three dimension carving, signified with the body parts that are producing the action.
4. Form
   Ball—refers to the body forming a ball or condensed shape.
   Twisted—refers to a twisting of the upper body against the lower body.
   Pin—refers to being one dimensional or vertical.
   Wall—refers to flattening out the shape of the body.
5. Crystalline Forms—related to the spatial trace form and tension that can be seen in relation to a polyhedron or spatial harmonic form.
6. Body Stress—aids in seeing body shape using convex or concave.

Today, with a greater understanding of the Laban material and sports biomechanics, the author would have chosen different parameters. These points will be discussed in the summary. A film sequence of Al Oerter has been included as a sample of what is seen on film (see Figure 1).

Film Observations

While throwing, Al Oerter does not give the sense of having a large kinesphere, that is, how far his gestures extend into space. Most of the arm and limb articulations are in his middle reach space.

Beginning with the first turn, he leads with the upper left side of the torso into a carving of the space with his left arm (see photos A-D). This results in a ball-shape condensing of the torso and a feeling that the torso is turning in the horizontal plane. Along with this, during the first turn, his right leg gathers

---

[2]See Glossary for further definition.

[3]See Glossary for further definition.

(A)

(B)

(C)

(D)

(E)

(F)

Figure 1. A film sequence of Al Oerter

(G)

(H)

(I)

(J)

(K)

(L)

Figure 1. cont.

the space with a three-dimensional hovering gesture (see photos E-G). This has a tendency to raise the hips too far off the ground, thus he loses a sense of being grounded with his pelvis under him and a direct line between his sit bones and heels. This throws him slightly off balance.

In the body level category, the chart shows the movement going from central, in the beginning, to transverse at the power position. At this point, the hips pull through with the predominate directions of forward and up, losing a little across directional pull (see photos J-L). Al remains postural throughout the throw, which means that he uses total body involvement. Al, though he uses simultaneous body part interaction in the first part of the throw, he leads the throw with his left shoulder. He then uses more successive sequencing once he transverses out of the power position.

The efforts are seen slightly distorted due to the slower speed of the film. All the same, there was clearly no use of space effort or an attitude of being aware of the space around him. Passion Drive[4] seems to describe Al best; he uses efforts of strength and quickness and the flow goes from free to bound fluctuating from throw to throw.

The relationship of efforts to his center of weight is evident. The center of weight was carried high in the torso and produced a feeling of strength manifesting in the upper torso. This ties into the idea of losing the groundedness through the first turn. The center of weight is not clearly channeled until the power position. (Using more space effort would help here.) Overall, there is no fluctuating or extreme use in the effort phrasing. This gives a monotone or even rhythm to the throw.

The finer points in his throw will be discussed under the live observation, along with the fundamentals that apply to the specific parts of the throwing sequence. In conclusion, Al's most outstanding feature is carving and adapting to space.

Live Observation and Practical Application

The thrower I chose to observe live, and apply the Laban material to, is Al Oerter, four times gold medal winner of the 1956, 1960, 1964, and 1968 Olympics. He is 46 years old and came out of retirement to make a bid for the 1980 United States Olympic Team. As for statistical information, Al is 6'4'' and approximately 270 lbs. He has no current physical impairment.

Evaluation of Throwing Session, Friday, May 19, 1978

I was armed with charts from the coding sheet. I planned to watch for flow, efforts, central, transverse, peripheral movement, etc. This was difficult because the throws were now live, and twice as fast as the films I had been watching. Therefore, I concentrated on body attitude and what was most apparent.

During his preparation ritual, which occurs each time he throws, Al stands behind the ring. While looking at it, he begins to pace back and forth, build-

---

[4]See Appendix for further information.

ing the energy and tension with a sense of anticipation and moments of quickness. Then, stepping inside the ring, he goes to the front. While standing with his left side to the throwing field, he looks out to the horizon, tosses the disc into the air, and catches it. At this point, Al reinforces the habit of closing off his hips and allowing the left leg to be diagonally in front of him instead of the left foot being diagonally behind him. This is similar to the desired position to land in, during the throw, called the power position. Then he goes to the back of the ring, takes one wind-up with the same sense of quickness, and throws.

The two main things Al seemed to be concerned with were: (1) The idea that, for the first turn, swinging his right leading leg around in a horizontal arc would help slow down the beginning of his spin, in order to maintain a slow-to-fast pace during the throw; and (2) during the explosive opening-out of the throw, pulling his left arm to the side and down, to open up his chest in order to feel the tremendous pull across.

Overall, Al has not changed very much in spatial patterning from the films I have of him taken in 1968. He is doing far too much work in his upper torso. A great deal of strength manifests itself there, possibly bound flow, or holding in, of his energy. He still loses his groundedness through the first turn and allows the center of weight to rise along with his hips. He folds his body in half, or convexes at the waist, and turns with a sense of turning in the horizontal plane with his upper torso. He has trouble hitting his mark after the second turn with this left planted foot. In fact, he never once hit it. This leads me to suggest that more emphasis should be put on the lower, in reeducating the ability to initiate movement (weight shift) and power through the hips. He never gets his hips around far enough, fast enough, or his left planting leg down to fully use the sequencing of the movement through the power position. He is, consequently, not using the entire thrust and power in the legs and hips because he does not establish a sound base to push from, and the upper takes over too soon, thus losing the sequencing.

I feel Al uses a great deal of strength and quickness throughout the throw, although there seems to be more predominance of it in his upper body. If he were to change his effort phrasing to quick, direct and strong, then quick and strong, he would have the rhythm of slow to fast without thinking about the arbitrary leg gesture in the first turn. Also, the idea of pulling through at the end would come much more naturally once has has the sequencing and a strong foundation from which to push.

Recommendations: I would like to work with smaller amounts of movement instead of the entire throw. I would first start on a fundamental level of feeling the center of weight, pelvic initiation, and staying aware of where the pelvis is in relation to the upper and lower body.

Evaluation of Session, Friday, May 27, 1978

We began by going over last week's evaluation and recommendations. Al agreed with them and was ready to go from there with my suggestions.

I had him lying on his back to relax and do the heel rock exercise. I talked him through the concept of allowing the weight of his body to sink into the ground in order to lose the sense of his body weight. By rocking his head back and forth, I tried to help him find the center of weight in his head. We carried this idea on to the rest of the body, first by sensing the center of weight while on his knees, then on his hands and knees. Finally, while standing and shifting weight, Al told me his center of weight was somewhere near his waist line instead of near the pelvic floor. This could be the basis of a lot of his problems in throwing because he allows the center of weight to rise and never really gets into that grounded feeling of lowering the center of weight which is necessary in the first turn of the throw in order to get more power from the legs.

The reason Al may not be using enough lower pelvic initiation may be because he concentrates on developing the superficial leg muscles, hamstrings, and quadriceps groups, and does not place enough emphasis on being aware of subtle weight changes. There is also a tremendous building up of Al's upper torso. This is an example of how athletes tend to weight train. They develop isolated muscle groups and there is no sense of the connection throughout the body and, in fact, might result in overdevelopment in unneeded areas.

Next, we went to the ring and I broke the throwing phrase down so that he could utilize efforts to modify his form. By using the effort configuration of strong and direct, and by leading with the left knee, his center of weight would lower and narrow his hips. Also, allowing a pure lateral shift before turning keeps the weight over the support leg and will better enable him to channel his weight after the turn. Another idea to get Al out into space is to have him spot the horizon while driving to the center of the ring.[5]

The sense of lowering his center of weight is very important for him throughout the throw in order to fully use strength effort and a sense that the lower body leads the movement. Also, the directness begins to channel his power. When he used spotting, his torso remained more vertical. This way, his pelvis stayed underneath him. He also began to hit the power position marks.

I don't feel Al connected or understood my use of efforts but, rather, connected with the exact spatial patterning and body part articulation. This may have been my fault for not working first with the center of weight in relation to efforts and locomotion.

The next drill we did was from the back of the ring driving across, adding the quickness to the strong and direct efforts. Al did this for a while and became absorbed with working things out, so I left him alone and observed him.

After a while, he picked up the disc and began to throw. In the beginning, his timing was a little off, which is to be expected when change occurs. The two best throws came somewhere in the beginning. It was very exciting because I saw for the first time a real sense of the direct effort, as though he channeled his energy. Even so, there still was not enough strength coming through in the lower body. This was the most progressive point of the day. He wasn't aware of it in the same way I was but he, of course, knew it was a good throw.

---

[5]Ernie Bullard, *The Linear Approach to the Discus*, (San Jose: L.K. Publications, 1975), p. 17.

The idea of getting direct effort in the second half of the throw is going to be difficult. The nature of the movement is transverse, and I believe it is easier for Al to get direct with more linear movement.

After about one-half hour of throwing, he began getting tired and resorted to some of the old habits. That is when I discovered that he loses his active attitude towards his weight, and flow and time efforts take over. The center of weight is no longer clearly controlled, so he must fight the momentum of the throw by binding his flow. This gives that heavy quality, and the bound/quickness produces jerky spurts of action. When he has active attention towards the weight effort, the pelvis stays under him and he is able to keep the momentum and all factors in control. Then the free flow comes through and makes the throw take on a smoother quality.

After a while, I asked him what he was thinking about. He said, "my feet coming down sooner," and a couple of other things about body-part articulation. This showed me that he was more comfortable working on body level corrections. This is usually the case in athletes when they are working for technique. I must watch that he doesn't become too gestural about his legs coming down quickly, but concentrate on his hips which might keep him postural; also, convince him of the idea that his center of weight motivates most of the throw.

After the workout, he mentioned that his muscles were sore right around his hip sockets. This shows that he was doing a lot of rotating in that area. At the end of the session, I wrote down some descriptive words in connection with the moving sense of the throw. I wrote down words like solid, resolute, purposeful, and channeled, for the first half of the throw. I added urgency for the second half. This was in hopes of bringing, for Al, more meaning and logic to the way in which we use efforts. Al is a very wise man and I feel very lucky to work with such a sensitive and experienced mover.

Eventually, we will be able to get away from thinking about positions and concentrate more on the process. I feel that if one were to clarify the special intent through effort phrasing, the throwing would become more efficient and consistent.

Summary

The movement and purpose for all the throwers was the same, yet individual style was obvious. The throwing phrase was short; so, in viewing it, I had to look for minute differences. One method that was helpful was seeing the exact body part initiation and trace forms by looking at the film on a moviola. This is a machine where one can slow down a film, stop, speed-up, or view it backwards. Gross observation was helpful only in getting at the body attitude (used here to mean overall impression). The smaller details helped substantiate this impression.

Another problem was finding an athlete to work with in applying the material. Special thanks go to Al Oerter. It was only when I started working with Al that I began to see the true interrelationships in the operability of Laban Movement Analysis. I took a total viewing approach when observing him. I looked for personality characteristics: the way he walked, the way he prepared for the throw, and, of course, the action and recovery phase.

I discovered very little complete use of the body, shape/space, effort triangle, in any of the throwers. When total use occurs, it is similar to the idea of synergy. The sum total will add up to be greater than the combined parts. This is one reason a linear way of thinking (mass × velocity = power) is limiting, or at least only a part of the story. Discus throwers, in general, are so concerned with building bulk and physical strength that they never fully reach their technical potential.

The observation tools that Laban Movement Analysis can give to coaches will help them see movement completely and from a different perspective. To consider only the science, or quantitative assessment, of movement discounts the human element or individual characteristic style the athlete incorporates in throwing. This natural organization towards movement is an integral part to consider when teaching or re-educating the athlete's skills. In other words, Laban Movement Analysis develops the eye in seeing the qualitative process of movement and the individual behind the movement.

Let me recapitulate a few concepts that may help others in the field make correlations between the art and science of movement. First, develop an eye for seeing the center of weight and how it moves over the base of support. This helps the athlete to stay balanced through the process of movement. Second, look carefully for the initiation of movement and how it sequences through the body. In other words, do all forces contribute and add to the throw? Third, what are the spatial configurations of the body parts and how does the body connect into space? Do all parts of the body support the movement, or are there superflous movements decreasing its efficiency? Is the entire body alive and aware of its surroundings and clearly defining its space? Fourth, look at the shape of the body, that is, condensing, expanding, or one, two, three dimensional movements; does it lend itself to the task or is it inappropriate to the movement? And, finally, look for the moving qualities in a person— are they reflected in the way he or she accomplishes the task? Are the movements quick when they should be more sustained or too bound when a free and loose quality would be better?

These points have been stated in general terms but they can be applied to athletes as well as dancers in determining whether they are moving efficiently and effectively. They also allow the viewer to see that there is a human difference in each athlete and that Laban Movement Analysis helps identify what those moving qualities are without being subjective.

References

Bartenieff, I., Davis, M., & Paulay, F. (1970). *Four adaptations of effort theory in research and teaching*. New York: Dance Notation Bureau, Inc.

Bullard, E. (1975). *The Linear approach to the discus*. San Jose: L.K. Publications.

Dell, C. (1970). *A primer for movement description*. New York: Dance Notation Bureau, Inc.

Author, N. (1972). *Space harmony basic terms*. New York: Dance Notation Bureau, Inc.

Appendix: Glossary of Terms

Central Movement—Movement that starts in the center of the body and moves outward.

Peripheral Movement—This is seen when there is a tension between the torso and the limbs as though the limbs are moving independently of the torso.

Transverse Movement—Movement that starts in the center of the body and moves to the periphery of the kinesphere with a sweeping motion.

Effort Elements—The description of movement quality or dynamics seen in the factors of flow, space, weight and time.

Posture—Total body alignment and used in a moving sense to mean how much the total body is involved in the action.

Gesture—A gesture is an isolated movement of one part of the body and more than one gesture can happen at the same time.

Body Attitude—Used, in this paper, to mean overall impression. Sometimes used to describe, metaphorically, the body's posture. Example: his arms are cutting through space.

Kinesphere—The space around oneself and how one relates to this space with small, medium, or far-reaching movements.